Why on Earth Homeschool?

The Case for Australian Christian Homeschooling

Storey St Publishing

By Rebbecca Devitt

Why on Earth Homeschool

© 2015 Rebbecca M. Devitt

All rights reserved. This book or part thereof may not be reproduced or used in any way without the express written permission of the publisher except for the use of brief quotations in a book review.

Ordering Information:
Orders online from our website at www.whyonearthhomeschool.com.
Please contact Storey Street Publishers: Tel: +614 4848 3948
Email: rebbeccadevitt@gmail.com. Postal address below. Online through usual sources.

Illustrated by Esther Hesford and Jessica Robertson.
Cover Design by Bryan Gehrke: bryan@mycoverdesigner.com.

First Printing, 2017

ISBN 13: 978-0-9942046-0-8
ISBN 10: 0-9942046-0-4

Postal Address:
Storey Street Publishing
Attn: Rebbecca Devitt
321 Old Coowong Farm Rd
Canyonleigh, NSW, 2577

To my parents, Bill and Antoinette Hesford, who made the brave decision to homeschool, to my wonderful husband, Tristan, for his loving support, to Lauren Demol, my inspiration for this book, and most of all to you, dear reader, as you consider serving God through homeschooling.

Acknowledgements

Kerry Robbins, the Fraser family, Jessica Robertson, Mathew Parr, Neville and Esther Hesford, Dr. Brian Ray, Kelly Reilly, Emma Deacon, Katherine Roberts and Michael, Melissa and Margaret Lepke.

Considerations

In some cases, where Australian studies are not available, the author has referred to relevant American studies.

Unless otherwise noted, Bible quotes are from the English Standard Version (ESV).

About Rebbecca Devitt

Rebbecca Devitt is an Australian Christian homeschooling writer and blogger at www.WhyonEarthHomeschool.com. She is a homeschool graduate who enjoys fellowship, Bible study and talking to others about Christian homeschooling.

Rebbecca was homeschooled in a Christian family after attending a Christian school for three years. She attended a church group made up largely of homeschoolers. Rebbecca feels overwhelmingly blessed by her parents, who pulled her out of school to homeschool. She hopes to share the joys of good, Christian education with others.

The author enjoys advocating for homeschooling in Australia and lobbies state and federal governments on this topic. Rebbecca is married to Tristan and has a high-octane puppy called Molly who loves teasing Chester, Rebbecca's cranky, old rabbit.

When it comes to writing, Rebbecca likes to write about issues affecting public, private and Christian schools as well as other subjects of importance to Christians today.

In time, Rebbecca hopes her book will inspire many Christian parents and influence them to choose one of the best pathways of Christian education available today; loving Christian homeschooling.

Contents

Introduction i

PART 1: WHAT IS WRONG WITH SCHOOLS 1

   1. Are Schools That Great? 3

   2. Peer Pressure 19

   3. Classrooms 33

   4. Schools Have Time Issues 45

   5. Bullying and Sexual Pressures 53

   6. Worldview Assumptions in School 67

   7. Preschools and Sacrificing Mums 87

   8. What About Christian Schools? 93

PART 2: WHAT IS RIGHT WITH HOMESCHOOLING 97

   9. About Homeschooling 105

   10. Homeschooling and Christianity 121

   11. Can I Afford to Homeschool? 135

   12. What About Socialisation of Homeschoolers? 143

   13. Better Academic Performance and Mental Health 157

   14. Critical Thinking and Broadened Creativity 167

   15. Close Family Ties 175

   16. Arguments Against Homeschooling Refuted 181

   17. Gifted, Disabled and Special Needs Students 205

   18. What About Secondary and Tertiary Education? 221

   Conclusion 235

From the Author 239

Appendix 1: Legal Requirements and Registration 241

Endnotes 245

'The Bible is authoritative on everything it speaks about, moreover it speaks about everything.'

Dr. Cornelius Van Til

Introduction

YOU MAY BE THINKING, 'I HAVE SOME IDEA about the benefits of homeschooling, but I want to discover just how effective homeschooling will be for our family.' 'My interest in homeschooling is based on my disenchantment with schools' ability to teach Christian values.' 'I want a book specifically for Christian homeschoolers in Australia.'

If any of these statements echo your thoughts, this book is for you. These chapters seek to clarify and expand ideas around homeschooling, showing why homeschooling is a great idea for Christian families in Australia. Drawing from extensive data and case studies, this book is one of the first Australian Christian homeschooling books.

While homeschooling is not for every Christian parent, homeschooling can be a great educational way of life for committed Christian families. At the very least, every Christian family should consider homeschooling. I hope this book will give those opposed to homeschooling an understanding of why some families choose Christian homeschooling and perhaps even change some minds along the way.

This book includes an extensive review of homeschooling research around the world, with a focus on Australian homeschooling.[i] Hundreds of

---

[i] **Note on Sampling Bias in Studies:** Within this book, you will find a myriad of studies on homeschooling, public school and Christian school students. Some of these studies suffer from (perhaps unintended) sampling bias as homeschooling populations have not always been randomly chosen. Often this is due to the closed

research articles have been reviewed and condensed to find agreement on homeschooling research. I have also conducted my own surveys and interviews with around 20 homeschooling parents and their children (many of which feature in this book). The studies, surveys and interviews complement my own knowledge of homeschooling and homeschooling groups which I have been familiar with since infancy.

The first half of this book will focus on some of the reasons many parents choose homeschooling, by outlining some of the shortcomings of school, from both a religious and academic standpoint.

Chapter 1 looks at assumptions underlying teaching theory and discipline in schools. Knowledge of these assumptions is vital to gain a good understanding of why schools do things and why Christians should have little to do with them.

---

nature of many home schools. Homeschooling parents often don't wish their children to be tested (that's the reason many leave the formal schooling system).

For example, the BOSTES study of Australian homeschoolers' NAPLAN performance, suffers from unintended sampling bias as NAPLAN testing is optional for homeschoolers. In this study, we see only 10% of homeschoolers represented, compared to a much larger representative population of school students. These homeschoolers have parents who:

(1) are interested in academic achievement as defined by the public system (i.e. somewhat value public education curricula)
(2) want to know where their children sit compared to school students
(3) care enough to educate their children academically
(4) are not wary of the school system.

Given this bias, some studies may have overly positive outcomes in favour of homeschooling. Despite the bias in many of these studies, I consider the weight of evidence in favour of loving, Christian homeschooling overwhelming.

Chapter 2 looks at the problems with the classroom setting, a design and social situation that fails to accommodate even some of the most suitable students in many ways. While schools may do a good job in some instances, Christian home schools will do a much better job. It will become clear that today's political correctness often masquerades as tolerance. This tolerance is often the foremost moral characteristic that is valued in schools; but, it fails to tolerate Christian students and fails to recognise Jesus as King. In short, school is not a normal environment and so it doesn't prepare children well for life outside school.

Chapter 3 addresses the massive problem of peer pressure in schools – especially for Christian children. In secular environments such as public schools, peer pressure can make the practice of Christianity difficult for Christian students. This is seen when we consider the sexualisation of schoolgirls and the pressure on schoolboys to join the sexual revolution.

Chapter 4 looks at the unnatural set up of schools and the amount of wasted time at school. I'll argue that the time children could have spent building up impressive portfolios is wasted by misbehaviour and classroom stalling while teachers scramble for control or seek to keep faster students occupied by giving them filler work – much of which spills over into unneeded and excessive homework that burns children out.

Bullying and sexual assault in schools are looked at in **Chapter 5**. We'll go through the problems with sex education, the fluidity of sexual morals in many schools, and also look at another possible source of bullying – teachers themselves.

Chapter 6 expands on worldview assumptions in schools. Specifically, we'll look at the damaging theories of Darwinism, Eugenics, Humanism and Self-Actualisation all of which cannot peaceably coexist with a strong Christian worldview.

We'll briefly address issues surrounding mothers who give up their careers for their children to homeschool in **Chapter 7**. We should also look at the best time to start formal schooling, and will discuss the cons of preschool, specifically starting your children's formal learning too early.

What about Christian schools? From a religious perspective, **Chapter 8** looks at why Christian schools are sometimes little better than secular schools. This chapter compares homeschooling and Christian school graduate outcomes and shows why Christian home schools are better places to bring up Christian children.

The second part of the book will concentrate on the benefits of homeschooling. **Chapter 9** will look at the Christian basis of homeschooling and compare the effectiveness of Christian schools versus Christian home schools for the transferring of the parents' Christian values. We'll look at why Christian home schools produce students with stronger Christian values compared to Christian school students, and why homeschoolers tend to stay with the faith their parents teach them.

Chapter 10 is about homeschooling in general. We look into many topics including the demographics of homeschooling, issues surrounding government control of homeschooling and the reasons people homeschool by grade level.

Chapter 11 demonstrates that homeschooling is at least as affordable as public schools and probably much more affordable than private schools. We'll roughly compare the cost of public, private and home schools and look into ways to make homeschooling more affordable.

The biggest issue of homeschooling is socialisation and we address this in **Chapter 12**. Using case studies and research on homeschooling from around the world, I will argue socialisation in the homeschool environment is much better than socialisation in the context of school.

Chapter 13 looks at research from different countries and compares the mental health and academic performance of homeschoolers and school attendees. We'll demonstrate the reasons why homeschoolers perform better in these areas, including the better sleep and more relaxed environment homeschoolers enjoy.

Chapter 14 shows how homeschoolers think more critically and are more creative, thanks to the social and educational environment they enjoy. You'll see how homeschooling can make children more employable and entrepreneurial compared to school students. We also look at why studies show homeschoolers make better leaders.

Family bonding and closer family relationships make for great families, as we'll see in **Chapter 15**. We'll see this is partly due to increased compliance and less argumentation on the part of the homeschooler, allowing children to be more teachable by their parents.

Chapter 16 deals with common arguments against homeschooling which may not have been addressed in previous sections.

Chapter 17 covers gifted, disabled and other special needs children. We'll discuss how suitable homeschooling is for families with children that fall out of the regular model school caters for. Using research and case studies, we'll tackle five special needs difficulties faced by schools and how they can be solved by homeschooling.

Because many parents are concerned about the next step after homeschooling, we'll look at further education opportunities in **Chapter 18**: Open Training and Education Network (OTEN), Technical and Further Education (TAFE) and Open Universities. These secondary education pathways make tertiary education more accessible. Tertiary channels we'll look at include college, TAFE and university.

By the end of this book, it will be clear just how many reasons there are to homeschool and even more so for Christian households. Equipped with this knowledge, you should be able to challenge homeschooling skeptics on the effectiveness of school in so many areas, especially the area of Christian values transmission. You will be able to confidently answer anyone who asks, 'Why on earth would you homeschool?'

Rebbecca Devitt

www.whyonearthhomeschool.com

PART 1: WHAT IS WRONG WITH SCHOOLS

1. Are Schools That Great?

WHY ARE YOU READING THIS BOOK? If you were to think about it, you would soon conclude pleasure or fear primarily drives your choice. These feelings drive many of our decisions in life, including our decision to send our child to school or educate them at home.

Many parents are motivated to homeschool because of the pleasure of spending more time with their children, whose company they enjoy. Other parents pray for school holidays to end. Some may prefer the comforts of a second income, while others are busy with running the household or choose 'me' time while their children are at school.

Pleasure is powerful, but not as powerful as fear. Fear can also drive the decision to school or homeschool. Some choose to homeschool because they fear their child may be bullied. Others have experienced pain themselves while going through the education system or have watched their children come home bullied or discouraged by staff or students at school. And then there are those who see the declining moral influences on children in schools and fear their own children would be affected. On the other hand, there are mothers[i] who actively choose school because they fear a loss of their independence and career identity through being 'just a Mum'. They may also fear homeschooling, thinking it may breed illiterate, bubble-wrapped children.

---

[i] Although I realise fathers sometimes have the primary role of education in homeschools, because mothers do the clear majority of homeschooling, this book will sometimes refer to mothers as being the primary homeschooler.

While fear is not generally considered to be a successful motivator, it can be a good thing if it alerts us to danger. It can also help us recognise the foolishness of one action and choose the wisdom of another. When fear is blinding, our emotions can lead us into bad decisions, but if we examine our fear in light of scripture, godly advice and prayer, it can have a positive effect and lead us to wise decisions.

Of course, fear may not come into it at all for some parents because they may have enjoyed their school experience and simply realised that school barely, if ever, taught them scripturally. They recognised school was plenty of fun, yet a great distraction from Christianity. Fitting in with the crowd meant a loss of personal identity and a gain of group identity – an identity tied to the central beliefs of the group.

But, this loss of personal identity stems from a loss of national identity in Christ. As we've thrown God out, we've thrown out a lot of Christian education, which benefits our school students personally. Although schools weren't originally designed to facilitate ungodliness, schools became effective tools for spreading ungodliness.

This spread came as universities stopped preaching the Bible and gradually became enraptured with humanistic ideals and offended by biblical ideals. In this chapter, we will be going back to the basics, examining what teachers now learn regarding school. We will see how the big thinkers and shakers of education have shaped our institutions to reflect ungodly ideals and practices. This book will show why masses of Christian parents are leaving schools in favour of homeschooling.

The Origins of Modern Education

Although this book is about Australian Christian education, Australia's educational theories originated from other countries, notably Greece, France and England. Some theories, like Plato's theories, are extremely ancient and originate from non-Christian roots. Due to these influences, Christian Australia has slowly become secularised and removed Christian thinking from its schooling. Therefore, many Christian homeschooling parents have turned from schools because schools have, in many cases, turned from God.

As the culture has changed, teachers turned from accepted biblical mandates to unstable, man-made theories. Australians gradually dropped Christian education and simultaneously accepted global influences that shaped – and continue to shape – modern, secular education ideals.

Perhaps, the denigration of modern Christian education started with a renewed interest in Plato's ancient book, *Republic*. *Republic* is considered the most influential book on education ever written. Socrates was Plato's teacher and the book, *Republic*, is Plato's account of Socrates' words as he questioned and answered his pupils on the definition of justice and the order and character of the city-state and the just man. Yes! It's complicated stuff. But, one big thing the book proposes is that **if we control children through education, we control future leaders and, therefore, the country**. Without controlling children through education, the city cannot control future leaders.[1]

However, Socrates admitted he knew nothing, saying, 'I am the wisest man alive, for I know one thing, and that is that I know nothing.' Without God, Socrates admitted he knew nothing, yet he still believed he could, and should, make up the rules.

Socrates proposed men should be just and search for wisdom, courage and temperance. So far so good. But, because Socrates decided what was 'good' for himself, he went astray. He began saying the state should regulate human reproduction among leaders, and children should be ignorant of their biological parents. Furthermore, sexual reproduction was good only when the fittest and strongest males united with females. Once a baby was born, it was to be taken from its mother and nursed by wet-nurses.

Socrates also believed wives and children should be shared with the state, encouraging ungodly sexual relations and the naked display of the body as nothing to be ashamed of. His beliefs led to the formation of the Etruscans, considered immoral by many, even pagan Romans. Their actions are, perhaps, too perverse to mention here because they adopted many of Socrates' recommendations.

How Modern Education Developed

From *Republic*, other influential books arose including Jean-Jacque Rousseau's book, *Emile*. *Emile* is thought to be the second most influential book on education after *Republic*. Rousseau furthered many of Socrates' views on education and inspired other educational writers like John Dewey. John Dewey's books have also been responsible for the gross increase in humanistic thinking in schools.

As philosophy turned more towards humanism, and further from Christianity, many important books on education marked the change. According to Grant Wiggins, president of Authentic Education, the following list of books are arguably the most influential books on education in all of history.[2]

- Adler, Mortimer — *Paideia Proposal*
- Apple, Michael — *Ideology and Curriculum*
- Bloom, Benjamin — *Taxonomy of Educational Objectives Vol 1*
- Boyer, Ernest — *High School*
- Bruner, Jerome — *The Process of Education*
- Callahan, Raymond — *The Cult of Efficiency*
- Dewey, John — *The Child and the Curriculum*
- Dewey, John — *Democracy & Education*
- Freire, Paulo — *Pedagogy of the Oppressed*
- Gardner, Howard — *Frames of Mind*
- Goodlad, John — *A Place Called School*
- Hirsch, E. D. — *Cultural Literacy*
- Kozol, Jonathon — *Death At An Early Age*
- Kuhn, Thomas — *The Structure of Scientific Revolutions*
- Lortie, Dan — *School Teacher*
- Montessori, Maria — *The Montessori Method*
- Neill, A. S. — *Summerhill*
- Piaget, Jean — *The Language & Thought of the Child*
- Plato — *Meno*
- Plato — *Allegory of the Cave from The Republic*
- Polya, Georg — *How To Solve It*
- Postman, N & Weingartner, C — *Teaching As A Subversive Activity*
- Rosenblatt, Louise — *The Poem, the Text, the Reader*

- Rousseau, Jean-Jacques — *Emile*
- Silberman, Charles — *Crisis in the Classroom*
- Simon, S & Howe, L — *Values Clarification*
- Sizer, Ted — *Horace's Compromise*
- Taba, Hilda — *Curriculum: Theory and Practice*
- Tyler, Ralph — *The Basic Principles of Curriculum and Instruction*
- Vygotsky, Lev — *Thought and Language*
- Whitehead, A. N. — *The Aims of Education & Other Essays*[3]

The list is fascinating. Not a few books criticise the school system. Some even advocate a looser model that allows freedoms like those seen in homeschooling. Other authors, like Ralph Tyler, criticise the school culture of bullying and impassiveness in teaching. Postman and Weingartner suggest good teaching has to be subversive to be good, as the school structure doesn't allow good teaching on its own whilst kids are forced to sit down and shut up. Instead, they propose teaching should be via student inquiry.

While some authors in the list are Christians, most are not believers in God. Many have Humanist sympathies. Therefore, many influential educators have not examined God's word on important educational methods. Instead, they have deemed themselves the end of ultimate knowledge, leading to error (Prov 14:12). For instance, *Values Clarification* is a book that analyses values without teaching a specific moral viewpoint – such as Christianity.

These secular educators hand down their theories to later teachers, transmitting material that, over the last century, has meant more and more educational methods are contradicting scriptural instructions. Contradictory material revolves around the faulty assumption that children are innocent at birth. Where this assumption is made, theories about teaching and discipline are in error.

Because so many influential educators are humanists, so much of our teaching theory is in error. If only a quarter of our revered educators are Christians (a conservative estimate), three-quarters of our education theory is coming from humanist philosophy.

If men think men can decide truth for themselves (this is humanism), they advocate for things like justice, not knowing how to define justice. They advocate for 'social responsibility', not knowing how to determine responsibility. Furthermore, things that are (scripturally) good, such as physical, loving discipline, are evil according to secular authorities.[4]

According to Dr. Ken Campbell, Associate Professor of Biblical Studies at Belhaven College, Mississippi, some Christian psychologists are furthering the humanist agenda by adopting their teachings, 'Although many [books] have been written by Christian psychologists, some may be misleading because of a tendency in Christian counselling to adopt non-Christian, even anti-biblical ideals. Few have succeeded in integrating scientific learning about human behaviour without also blending the *humanist framework* of thought with the Biblical paradigm'.[5] Perhaps this is unsurprising when we consider Paul's words in 2 Corinthians 6:14, 'For what partnership has righteousness with lawlessness? Or what fellowship has light with darkness?'

If we have those in 'darkness' educating our teachers and our children, it's not unusual that much sinful behaviour passes as normal, such as sexting and disrespectful behaviour. Furthermore, many teachers forget godly discipline of children in favour of no/ineffective discipline. Law constrains other teachers and forbids physical discipline or the teaching of biblical principles.

Lack of control, as many parents will realise, is detrimental as children need boundaries to mature. Without boundaries, children will suffer the consequences of their unruly and undisciplined behaviour in the future. They may then bring disgrace and embarrassment to the family as seen in Prov 29:15, '… a child left to himself brings shame to his mother'.

'Expert' Thoughts on Modern Education

Following old philosophers and psychologists, new teaching experts such as Dr. Berry Brazelton and Kristin Reinsberg hold a shared view on children's nature. They believe children react poorly because their needs are not met. According to these experts, if teachers (and parents) meet children's needs, children will automatically become good, because good is their set point.[6]

But, teaching children they need more things to be satisfied leads to selfishness. As children seek after their own welfare continually, they avoid seeking God and man's good. Instead, they make up their own truth, a truth that is defined as subjectively man-centered – humanism.[7] Although largely subjective, humanists agree they must all deny the Christian God.[8] So their beliefs and books, many in moral and educational fields, all show contempt for biblical concepts, especially important concepts like punishment. This is seen in the following list of modern educational academics. Their methods, all from prominent and influential teachers of education students, contradict many Bible principles:

How the Experts Say We Should Discipline Children			
Educational Academic	Theory	Punishment	Contradicting Bible Verses
Redyl & Wattenberge	Taught techniques to influence children so they gain self-control.	No. Situational help used in place of punishment.	**Loving physical discipline:*** Prov 13:24, 20:30, 22:15, 23:13-14, 29:15, Heb 12: 7-11. **Other discipline**: Prov 12:1, 13:18, 13:1, 15:5, 22:6, 29:17, 30:17, Eph 6:4, 19:18, Heb 12:5-6. **Godly training also needed**: Prov 6:23, 2 Tim 3:16, Eph 6:4, Mark 10:14, 2 Cor 5:20, Deut 6:7.
B. F. Skinner	Behavioural modification. Teachers use reinforcement techniques.	Withdrawing reinforcement.	
William Glasser	Highlight present reality to bring the child out of past problems, excuses or blaming.	No.	
Jacob Kounin	Teacher has *withitness* (coined word meaning the ability to focus on multiple things in the classroom), so the child doesn't become bored and create behavioural issues.	Yes, but verbal reprimand only.	
Haim Ginott	The child needs much personal attention. They are individuals so shouldn't be treated like clones. The child	No. Punishment only produces rancor and vengefulness.	

	should be addressed under the situation they've created, rather than looking at their behaviour.		
Rudolf Dreikurs	Democratic classrooms in which the child decides on issues as a social equal with the teacher. Should promote belonging and self-discipline. The pursuit of mistaken goals involves misbehaviour. Realigning goals reduces misbehaviour. Use friendly non-threatening discussions about their faulty goals and logic. Children should realise non-alignment with social interest/cause and stop the behaviour. Teacher attention is child's reward.	No. Reinforcement and praise not necessary either.	
Barbara Coloroso	Show the child what they've done wrong and so encourage student's ownership of their behavioural problem. Ownership encourages responsibility and inner discipline. Teacher suggests ways a child can solve the offensive problem.	No. Teachers shouldn't badger students or warn them how to behave.	
Alfie Kohn	Suggests a radically different classroom structure: learning too	No.	

	much material for exams leads to forgetfulness of material. Teacher should know what child needs and enjoys. Thought 30:1 child to teacher ratio is too high.		
Ronald Morrish	Teach 'right', 'wrong' and respect for 'legitimate authority'. Tell child the right thing to do, show them the right thing to do and act out the right thing to do. Insist child does task right and nags them until task done. Tell parents ways child might improve.	No.	

* I'm not suggesting schools should reinstate physical discipline, but lack of agreement with the Bible's standards is cause for Christians to rethink schools' model of discipline.

As you can see, few of these modern academics follow biblical mandates. Instead, many base their disciplinary methods on John Locke's theory of the *tabula rasa* or 'the blank slate' or mind, that says people are born good.[9][ii] The 'born good' theory denies our sinful natures and leads to insufficient

---

[ii] The tabula rasa is traced back to Aristotle's writings *On the Soul*, where the idea of the 'unscribed tablet' came into being.

correction and instruction in biblical matters. (This theory is prevalent among child psychologists today.)[10] [iii]

Philosopher Jean-Jacques Rousseau added to the *tabula rasa*, saying children were born good but became corrupt by society's evils. Rousseau thought public education painted a child's innocent mind with good and moral writing. ('Good' and 'moral' were, of course, defined by Rousseau!) Rousseau believed the state should be the one to do this brain painting in socialist, patriarchal schools. Schools were appropriate places because, in schools, parents were unable to interfere and contradict the socialist, man-centered teachers.[iv]

Rousseau argued children's education should belong to the State because 'education is of still greater importance to the State than to fathers [because] families dissolve, but the State remains.'[11] Here Rousseau shows his low view of the family.

[iii] Locke shows his man-centred preference when he says, 'I have always thought the actions of men the best interpreters of their thoughts.'
[iv] The theme of removing children from parents, originated from Socrates' theory, recurs here as Rousseau advocates the removal of parents in their children's education.

Education's Heroes Who Propagated the Theory of Human Goodness

Jean-Jacques Rousseau and John Locke

John Locke and Jean-Jacques Rousseau were philosophers living in the 17th and 18th centuries. These men continue to exert significant influence on today's teachers worldwide as their theories presuppose the innocence and goodness of man and thereby excuse men from original sin. Their theories discount God's words in Romans 3:10, 'None is righteous, no, not one.'

John Locke, a 17th century English philosopher, believed God gave all people natural rights, namely life, liberty, and property. He believed man had an empty mind or *tabula rasa*. Locke thought 90% of a person's morality and usefulness was a result of their education. He said, 'I think I may say of all the men we meet with, nine parts of ten are what they are, good or evil, useful or not, by their education.'

John Locke heavily influenced **Jean-Jacques Rousseau** who was an 18th century Genevan philosopher. Rousseau was loved by everyone who read his works and hated by everyone who knew him. His ideas were crucial in bringing about the bloody French Revolution, as he argued for anarchy on the basis that sovereignty should be in the hands of society, not individuals like kings. He also argued the State should teach children instead of fathers.

Rousseau believed humans were inherently good, although society corrupted them. At the time, Rousseau's theory was radical because the theory was in direct conflict with prevailing Christian thoughts of the day on original sin. Rousseau felt modern (Christian) civilisation, with its constraints, prevented people from being truly free. He believed society created an artificial system that constrained people unequally. Only 'savage man' was good, compassionate and free.

Along with John Locke, Rousseau's writings inspired many documents such as the American *Declaration of Independence* that changed Locke's original writings to 'life, liberty and the pursuit of happiness'.

While Rousseau claimed to be a Calvinist (he lived in the same city as John Calvin and was of Huguenot descent), Rousseau felt true followers of Jesus would not make good citizens because they had an allegiance to Christ, not the State. Rousseau believed men should be their own masters, not servants to anyone, including Christ.

Rousseau and Education

Rousseau's famous book, *Émile* (or *On Education*), was a discourse on the nature of man and the nature of education. Rousseau believed society 'must choose between making a man or a citizen'. They must reject the Bible's way of making a man (see Proverbs), and make a generic, uniform person, a unit of the State. Rousseau argued the best way to do this was to 'denature man' using social institutions like schools. These schools were supposed to take the 'absolute existence from [man] in order to give him a relative one and transport the I into the common unity'.

Although Rousseau qualified as one of the most irresponsible parents in history, he gave general parenting advice in *Émile*. Rousseau said he didn't feel he was able to educate children himself. Rousseau forced his partner to give up their five children for adoption as soon as his babies were born. He left his newborns on the steps of an orphanage because, he claimed, he couldn't afford to give them a good education. However, Rousseau would have known his children's education in the orphanage would have been much worse. Ten years later, Rousseau made inquiries about one of his sons, but no record was found (an unsurprising finding considering many orphans died).

Sadly, both Locke's and Rousseau's writings serve as favourite reading on social and political thought today. They still detrimentally affect school teaching, particularly in public schools as they contradict godly teaching about the innate sinfulness of humans. Their theories excuse teachers from godly rebuke, discipline, and instruction and encourage schools to make men of the State, rather than people of God.

Rousseau's pro-state, anti-family views are evident in his utopian worldview, delivered in the following sentence:

> *Public education…is one of the fundamental rules of popular or legitimate government. If children are brought up in common, in the bosom of equality, if they are imbued with the laws of the state and the precepts of the general will, if they are taught to respect these above all things, if they are surrounded by examples and objects which constantly remind them of a tender mother who nourishes them, of the love she bears them, of the inestimable benefits they receive from her, and of the return they owe her, we cannot doubt they will learn to cherish one another mutually as brothers…*[12]

But, after centuries of public schools, the idea that public school peers will cherish one another (because of their thankfulness to the State) is laughable. We laugh because we know peer pressure is what typifies school relationships.[v] Unfortunately, expecting children to respect one another has adversely affected students as it has set up false expectations as to the graciousness of a child's character, thereby leading to the failure of schools to institute disciplinary measures in line with the real and sinful nature of children.

The assumption that children are good is still propagated by many educators today, especially in teaching universities. Non-Christian teachers still offer their theories on the good nature of humans, the existence of sin and the solution to behavioural problems. But these man-made ideas are far from biblical. *Instead of saying children were born into sin because of Adam's sinful actions, secular sources deny sin and say children are born innocent and become corrupted by society.* They say the way to happiness is through satisfying our 'needs'. However, they propose to satisfy children by distracting them through material and secular pleasures. Therefore, humanist experts say we find fulfilment when we satisfy ourselves – not when we are satisfied in Christ.

---

[v] See Chapter 2.

Brainwashing Agendas

To control children is to control the nation. Many great tyrants throughout history have recognised this fact and tried to use schools and youth groups for their own political ends. Hitler, Mussolini and Lenin are three dictators who have used vulnerable children for their own diabolical purposes. They planned to, in some cases, take over the world by brainwashing school children. Sometimes children were even turned against their parents.

'The Hitler Youth' was the German youth organisation of the Nazi Party. German children were indoctrinated into thinking they were a superior race of people, which had the effect of propagating racism in the country. The aim of the Hitler Youth was to produce faithful Aryan soldiers, indoctrinated into fighting enthusiastically for the Third Reich. Hitler Youth activities included breaking up church meetings, spying on Bible studies and interfering with church attendance. Worse, the youth were taught to spy on everyone, including their parents. If anyone, including their parents, uttered anything against the Party, the children betrayed them to the authorities.

In the Hitler Youth, there was a heavy emphasis on military training. Teachers encouraged older boys in their cruelty towards younger boys so 'resilience' was learned. Teachers also thought cruelty would weed out the 'unfit' from the Youths' ranks. This cruelty fell in line with German thinking which came straight from Darwin's *Origin of the Species*, one of Hitler's favourite books.

Mussolini, the Italian Fascist leader during World War II, was a great admirer of Hitler and decided to create something similar to the Hitler Youth after he allied himself with Germany in the War. Mussolini took a keen interest in Italian youth education. He trained boys in physical fitness and expected the girls to mature into mothers who would produce a litany of good Fascist soldiers for Mussolini's reign. A famous saying of the day was, 'War is to the male what childbearing is to the female'. Just like the youth in Germany were expected to refer to Hitler affectionately by the name 'Führer' (leader or guide), Mussolini had children call him 'Il Duce' (leader). Boys were expected to attend age-specific youth movements after school called the Balilla. Members of the Balilla youth movement (for 8 to 14-year-olds) had to recite the following: *I believe in Rome, the Eternal, the mother of my country......I believe in the genius of Mussolini...and in the resurrection of the Empire.*

Lenin also had a youth organisation, called the *Vladimir Lenin All-Union Pioneer Organisation* whose mother party was the Russian Communist Party. The Organisation for children between 10-15 years ran from 1922 to 1991. Membership was optional, but almost all Russians joined ranks as the Organisation was a 'natural' part of growing up. Every member was required to set up an atheist's corner in their home with anti-religious pictures, sayings and poems. This practice was to oppose 'icon corners', small worship spaces Catholics set up with statues of Jesus and Mary.

Although the examples here are some of the worst kinds of youth indoctrination in recent history, indoctrination like that seen in Germany, Italy and Russia during WWII is happening today. For example, John Dewey, whose views are highly popular today, believed schools should be tools used for *political and social indoctrination*. Therefore, Christian parents should be aware of what groups have control of their children's thinking.

IS THIS INDOCTRINATION HAPPENING TODAY?

Hamas

Child soldiers in the Hamas camp of Gaza, Palestine, are being brainwashed with pro-Hamas doctrines today. These children belong to the 'Children's Army of Hamas'. In the training camps, children as young as ten are taught to fire rockets and use combat rifles, and anti-aircraft equipment at the same time as praising their Hamas leaders. Hamas also stresses the importance of teaching child soldiers to be anti-Semitic, as evidenced in their 1988 *Covenant of Hamas*. Hamas has preyed on, recruited and trained 17,000 teenagers from refugee camps run by the United Nations.

ISIS and Assad

In June 2015, ISIS kidnapped 500 children to become child soldiers or child suicide bombers. ISIS is notorious for using child soldiers and bombers, dubbing them 'caliphate cubs'. They indoctrinate these children by forcing them to behead dolls and carry the severed heads of victims around until they are desensitised to death. The government dictator fighting ISIS in Syria, President Assad, is also recruiting child soldiers from schools and sending them to the front of the battlefield.

More on child soldiers

Today, child soldiers come from many countries around the world including Afghanistan, Colombia, India, Iraq, Israel, Libya, Mali, Pakistan, Thailand, Sudan, Syria, and Yemen. They can be used for many purposes such as spies, cooks, fighters, messengers, suicide bombers, and human shields. Because girls make up 10-30% of these soldiers, many are used and abused sexually. Because children are so gullible, they can be easily lured or kidnapped into serving the army by promises of wealth, respect, and position.

Shrewd and cunning leaders know children can be brainwashed easily for the leader's political ends. Therefore, we must pay careful attention to our leader's agenda. What agenda do our leaders have?

WHAT ABOUT IN AUSTRALIA?

According to the *Daily Telegraph*, children in a Year 3 Wollongong public school are being brainwashed into becoming left-wing political activists.

After 9-year-old students launched a petition against child refugees in detention, the story of schoolyard propaganda came to light. The Liberal MP, David Leyonhjelm, received a petition from Year 3 students in the Helensburgh school. The petition struck the Senator as being disturbing political propaganda.

The petition which was written on the school's letterhead outlined how distressed the 9-year-old students felt over children refugees in detention. The petition came with drawings from the students with pictures of hearts breaking and children crying.

The school principal, Chris Connor, a former Labor deputy mayor and current councillor at Wollongong council, is being investigated by the NSW Department of Education for possible staff involvement.[13]

While there is no problem with children having compassion for refugees (indeed it is admirable), the alleged political agenda of the teacher is objectionable here.

2. Peer Pressure

PEERS EXERT A MASSIVE INFLUENCE OVER SCHOOL children and are stronger than any other influence in school, including teachers. Peers have the power to make each other supremely happy or utterly miserable. The latter is generally avoidable if children conform to the popular image at school.

If you've been to school, especially a Christian school, some of your peers were probably godly children from Christian families, who taught you how to live according to Biblical principles. Perhaps you're still friends with these great gems like I am.

However, if you went to school you probably saw more children that influenced you to go after the popular culture and popular kids (more than your parents would have encouraged you in these pursuits). Other kids you liked were charismatic and made you laugh. You stuck with them at every opportunity and loved listening to them. You probably thought many were naughty – but not evil. Many even came from 'good and moral families', although they weren't Christians.

The problem with non-Christian friends (and even some so-called 'Christian' children with ungodly attitudes) is often in their omission and inability to teach Christian children consistently useful lessons.

When children could have been taught with vigour and enthusiasm in a devoted and loving Christian family, they were left to make their own friends and hopefully remain pure, sometimes given little guidance. How much did your peers at school lead you to worship God?

While many exceptions exist, generally Christian parents are far more efficient at transmitting their Christian values to their children than peers are at spreading their Christian values to their peers. While parents can give bad tutelage, in general, it's usually the peers who are passing around the bong – not parents.

And because so many views between peers and parents collide, peers are sometimes found denigrating a child's parents ('They don't let you date till you're 18…gee, your parents suck!') Did your peers encourage the relationship you have with your parents to further your relationship with God? Healthy peer relationships that build family units are rare in schools, even Christian schools.

Peer relationships characterise themselves more in pressure to try sex, drugs and alcohol. Even though sex, drugs and alcohol are prevalent in schools, we are so desensitised to the effects of peer pressure (having experienced it ourselves), we consciously expect our children to immerse themselves in poor school culture and emerge unscathed. Researchers Maté and Neufeld, explain how desensitised many of us are to the issues of peer pressure and bad school culture:

> *Today's adults or parents think it is normal for children to be peer-oriented and often antagonistic toward their parents. They explain, however, that this is not natural, historical or good for children. 'Peer orientation masquerades as natural or goes undetected because we [adults] have become divorced from our intuitions and because we have unwittingly become peer-oriented ourselves.' For millennia, always until recently, culture was handed down vertically from generation to generation. Now, however, children are generating their own culture and transmitting it … horizontally within the younger generation.*[14]

Because many of us were raised in school institutions, we think peer influence is normal and safe (think of 'resilience training'). It's not. Our warped views only have the effect of worsening and increasing bad school culture because we don't address the problem – and that is that horizontal values transmission is often devoid of Christian doctrine.

Bully Factories

'Peer orientation breeds bullies and their victims. We have been dangerously naïve in thinking that by putting children together we would foster egalitarian values and [relations]. Instead we have paved the way for the formation of new and damaging attachment hierarchies... Because of the powerful attachment reorganisation that takes place in the wake of peer orientation, schools have also become bully factories...'[15]

Gordon Neufeld and Gabor Maté

Children learn from whatever environment they are placed in – that's the nature of children. They learn from parents, siblings, social milieu, television and movies. These inputs contribute to the whole person and determine a person's character when older.

In earlier societies where children worked alongside parents, they learned what their parents did, good or bad. Like apprentices, they learned everything from those they followed. And homeschoolers still learn like this. In the homeschooling environment, parents seek to limit the negative input a child receives and maximise the good.

But, learning culture from peers is sometimes detrimental to a child's relationship with God because peers are either non-Christians or immature Christians based on their youth.[16] Instead of getting strong godly influence from older, more mature parents, school students commonly receive little Scriptural training. Instead, they get plenty of damaging advice. And, because being a devoted Christian in school will rarely give you peer points, children often sacrifice their relationship with God (and their parents) to receive peer acceptance.

How Peer Pressure Affects Children

Peer pressure affects children's attitudes and behaviours profoundly. And, where toddlers attend preschool or daycare, peer dependency forms early. Peer dependency quickly develops at these facilities as toddlers are forced to form new social alliances, having lost much of their parent's protection. The peer group can replace a parent's protection thanks to its sheer size. But, the group often expects a sacrifice for the protection they offer. The sacrifice to peers often means the loss of individuality and conformity to the group for peer approval.

Unless Parents Stop All Peer Associations, Peers Are as Influential as Teachers and Parents

A 2010 study on peer groups and their influence on teenage substance use has discovered a teenager's peer group provides a greater influence on adolescent smoking compared to parents. In the study, published in the *Journal of Primary Prevention*, researchers propose social influences are crucial and predictive of teens behaviors around dieting, medication taking, sexual intercourse and substance use.

The article questioned whether parents could counter the negative effects of peer influence. Researchers concluded the only way parents could buffer this effect was to strengthen family ties and discourage teenagers from associating with peers who provide a bad example and engage in bad behaviors. They said a parent's influence over their schoolchild's choice to not smoke occurred when they prevented their children from forming friendships with other children who smoked.[17]

Peer approval drives school children to change their habits around drugs, music, clothing, smoking and alcohol. Peers also affect a child's attitudes about academic performance and decisions about who they will or won't date. In some cases, peers help and encourage other students in their walk with God. In many cases, however, children respond negatively to peer pressure. One homeschool father, Bill, recalled how his children dramatically responded to peer pressure in school:

As school progressed, I noticed my oldest child began to harden more. He wasn't listening to me anywhere near as much as he used to and I was having less influence. We guessed peers were the ones replacing our influence. It was definitely not the teachers' influence – because the kids were coming home with things the teachers wouldn't do, such as being naughty.

But, peer influence only gets stronger as time progresses. Dr. Urie Bronfenbrenner's studies found older children become more peer-dependant when they spend more of their elective time with peers. Bronfenbrenner said that as a child's trust in school peers increases, they simultaneously lose optimism, self-worth and respect for their parents.

The Peer Group Disease

The loss of respect for parents and older people is more noticeable when a child's manners and behaviour cement at age 11 to 12. Dr. Bronfenbrenner calls the replacement of parental values with peer values the 'social contagion' as children catch the unhealthy social habits of their peers.[18]

The contagion forces conformity among individuals as they start forming cliques or gangs. These groups rely on each other for their moral and intellectual values. This dependence can lead to devastating consequences such as too much dependence on other youth (see 1 Kings 12).

A Peer's Influence on Family Bonds

Peer pressure can weaken a parent's influence on their children. A child's peers comment on the family relationship, sometimes jeering at many disciplinary actions and encouraging rebellion. Peer groups often encourage less family intimacy and mock the child that makes the mistake of hugging their parent on the schoolyard. Siblings and parents are rarely a schoolchild's best friends. Rather, classmates hold the privilege family should hold. So, peer camaraderie excludes family and destroys a family's peace and accord.

Academics, Maté and Neufeld, address the peer group mentality, saying, 'We have been dangerously naïve in thinking that by putting children together we would foster egalitarian values and relating.' In other words, the idea children will develop good and fair values by looking at their peers is simplistic and dangerous.[19]

This dangerous idea ignores scripture verses such as Romans 3:23 and Isaiah 64:6. The latter denies man's goodness, saying, 'We are all infected and impure with sin. When we display our righteous deeds, they are nothing but filthy rags. Like autumn leaves, we wither and fall, and our sins sweep us away like the wind.' Someone infected with sin can easily infect someone else with that sin unless we are taught to hate sin and love God's ways.

> "I would always have to fight for social acceptance at school – and I would do just about anything to get it. When I was homeschooled my insecurities were overcome by parental love."
>
> *Joshua Hesford, Architect & Homeschool Graduate.*
> *(Questionnaire, June 2014.)*

Drinking and Illicit Drugs

Peers exert immense pressure on students when it comes to drug and alcohol use. Though drinking is illegal for youth under age 18, most 16-year-olds have already begun drinking. [20] Thanks to peer influence, alcohol is used by about 85% of teenagers over 14 years of age.[21] [vi] Underage binge drinking and drug taking are more popular among school students, even Christian school students, with many proudly exhibiting their ability to get drunk during weekends with their friends.[22] [vii] Some become severely intoxicated every

[vi] The Australian Institute of Health and Welfare says alcohol is the most widely used 'drug' in Australia.

[vii] In this study, Christian and homeschooled students in grades 7-12 were asked if they had ever drunk enough alcohol to be legally drunk. 12% of Christian students answered yes, while only 2% of homeschoolers answered yes.

weekend which can lead to hospitalization, chronic liver failure and sometimes, incidents of sexual abuse or unwanted pregnancies.

Despite the consequences of substance abuse and the money pouring into anti-drug and alcohol campaigns, the problem of alcoholism among our youth fails to improve.[23] [viii] Many Australians continue to drink alcohol at dangerously high levels, which are more noticeable in the under 25 age bracket.

This culture is instituted for a number of reasons, chief among which is peer pressure in schools. After being taught to turn to drink following hard circumstances, some rely on alcohol as an escape plan. Teens and older individuals who are not taught self-restraint, may drink themselves unconscious to avoid abusive or past abusive situations. Others who lose their identity as a unique individual in the sight of God sometimes have no reason to be self-restrained. These cases often harken back to detached or absent parents.

However, drugs cause as many deaths as alcohol. In 2005, 702 Australians aged 15-24 died from drug overdoses.[24] This statistic is unsurprising given 41% of Australians over 14-years-old have used illicit drugs in their lifetime.[25] Drugs, although abused less than alcohol, cause as many deaths as alcohol due to higher toxicity levels. Their addictive properties and unsafe manufacturing standards also make overdosing easier.[26] [ix]

During one study on illegal drugs, researchers found that taking marijuana *just once* was associated with a 40% increase in the risk of schizophrenia.[27] Considering over a quarter of Australian secondary school students reported taking marijuana, many school children are putting their health in jeopardy.[28]

[viii] Australia has spent $87 million on research into alcohol and alcoholism from 2000 to 2015. Men in their late 20s were most likely to drink at risky levels [2std drinks per day over a 12mo period] (32%), while for women it was younger adults aged 18-24 (15%).

[ix] In this study, Christian and homeschooled students in grades 7-12 were asked if they had ever used an illegal, non-prescriptive drug. 10% of Christian students answered yes, while only 2% of homeschoolers answered yes.

'Good' Students Are Also Taking Drugs

Delinquent students are not the only students at school taking drugs. High achieving students in prestigious Sydney schools are buying ADHD drugs to help them focus in exams. Around 7% of Year 12 students pay just $5 a Ritalin pill to energise themselves while they cram during late night sessions. Because Ritalin is a legal drug, many users wrongly consider it to be an acceptable drug.[29]

Pop Culture Promoting Drugs

The rise in drug use is far from surprising when our popular culture and their associated role models have been pushing substance use for a few decades with songs like:

- *Bad* – U2, 1984
- *Beautiful* – Eminem, 2007
- *Mr Brownstone* – Guns N' Roses, 1987
- *I Took A Pill In Ibiza* – Mike Posner, 2016
- *Beauty and the Beast* – David Bowie, 1978
- *Band on the Run* – John McCartney & Wings, 1973

With almost every child hooked up to their very own indoctrination machine in the form of a smartphone, we shouldn't be surprised when children follow their sparsely-dressed, drug-taking role models.

Sexualisation of Schoolgirls Due to Peer Pressure

Brittany Spears teen pop song *Baby One More Time* was America's best-selling song of 1999. The song also boasted another great accomplishment for the secular world. *Baby One More Time* is greatly responsible for the gross sexualisation of school girls around the globe.

The song is about a school girl's feelings after breaking up with her boyfriend. Pouting at the camera, Spears talks about her broken relationship while wearing a belt-skirt, midriff and a short tie shirt with bra showing. To pretend she's still a schoolgirl, Spears wears pink pompoms in her pigtails.

Behind her, a posse of similarly clad schoolgirls dance, copying Spears' seductive moves.

With over 10 million copies sold, *Baby One More Time* was voted the third most influential video in the history of pop music in a poll run by *Jam!*[30] The song has influenced schoolgirls, by the millions, to sexualise their wardrobes.

Now teenage shops like *Supre*, *Cotton On* and *Forever New* stock hordes of raunchy clothing like those worn by most music idols. Teens flock to copy these stars and make their dress imitate favourites like Beyoncé, Miley Cyrus, and our most recent good girl turned bad girl, Taylor Swift.

The Great Unspoken Problem: 'Domestic Violence' From 14-Year-Olds

Domestic Violence at Home

Domestic violence among teenagers and their families is on the rise in Australia. Over the last ten years, the *NSW Bureau of Crime Statistics and Research* shows an annual increase of 5.5% in young people dealt with by police for violent assaults at home among family. This number could be much worse, as half the cases of abuse are thought to be unreported.

According to Karen Willis, the executive officer of *Rape and Domestic Violence Services Australia*, domestic violence between children and their parents is the 'great unspoken problem'. Willis says that it's hard enough to discuss domestic violence with your spouse, let alone reporting a child to police that you've raised and loved.

Domestic Violence in Teen Relationships

Dating teens can get into a lot of trouble, according to Australian research. Astoundingly, 72% of teens embark on a romantic relationship by the age of 14. Even 20% of 11 to 14-year-olds are in relationships, despite just graduating from keeping their beds dry.

Early relationships are mostly secret as kids fear their parents' reaction to the relationship. Therefore, when violence enters the relationship, help may be hard to find as teens don't want to tell their parents because 'they might get mad'. Support is important for victims of violent teenage relationships as violence may be up to four times higher among 14 to 19-year-olds compared to among older people.[31]

Those that don't copy the stars by hitching up their skirts are bullied and accused of being too prim. On the other hand, stories about girls sexualising themselves to fit in and then consequently getting bullied for sleeping around (when the class was pushing them into the act) are common and tell a far sadder story of isolation and continual regret.[32]

Many children feel pressured to enter a relationship earlier than they would have without pressure from peers. Some girls are pressured into having sex by boyfriends. Others who resist the pressure to sleep around risk continual bullying for their choices.

Some schoolgirls are abused and forced to have sex or perform 'lighter' sexual acts, such as sexting much earlier than they would have without peer pressure.[x] Physical abuse among romantically involved teenagers is also common.[33] [xi] Adolescents who suffer dating abuse are also likely to form behavioural problems like alcoholism, promiscuity, violent behaviours, eating disorders and suicidal thoughts.[34]

Furthermore, the unintended publication of sexual acts online and through phones have meant these embarrassing events are never forgotten, especially by the person portrayed in the video. These publications, called 'revenge porn', can have horrific consequences. Take the Brazilian 17-year-old, Rebecca, who hung herself after a sex tape of her and two other minors was posted online. The Brazilian media said Rebecca's story was not unusual.

Or take Jessica Logan, an American 18-year-old, who committed suicide after nude photos were circulated on the internet after she broke up with her boyfriend.[35] 'Revenge porn' has become so common in Australia that some of our governments have enacted specific laws to tackle the issue.

These laws, however, can only do damage control. Perhaps the big issue at heart is about the morality our children are being taught and the influences telling teens this sort of pornographic posting is acceptable.

Boys Also Victims of Sexualisation

Throughout history, the measure of a man has often been determined by his libido. Those who can sleep with the most girls are given most glory by their peers, as evidenced by many modern teenage movies today.[36] There is rarely a movie in which a schoolboy says no to a schoolgirl (however, there are plenty of movies where girls say no to sex-crazed boys).

But, according to research by the University of Missouri, four out of ten high school boys and young college men say they were coerced into sex or sexual

---

[x] See Chapter 5.
[xi] Teenagers between the ages of 10-17 were studied.

behaviour by women.[37] Just like men, women can be perpetrators of sex and sexual abuse – in school or out of school.

Girls are much more responsible for aggressive behaviour towards boys than portrayed in the media. In fact, 31% of boys said they were verbally coerced into sex, while 26% said they were coerced by unwanted sexual behaviours.[38]

One writer suggests the numbers in this study are probably higher than reported because boys don't want to admit that they've had unwanted sexual attention because society tells them they should want sex all the time.[39]

Boys, like girls, must be protected from unwanted sexual advances. They must be protected from peer pressure that threatens to coerce them into unwanted sexual behaviour as much as girls. Failure by parents to protect boys from these acts may cause consequences such as:

- broken hearts,
- bad reputations,
- emotional instability,
- self-destructive behaviour,
- sexually transmitted diseases,
- insecurity and a loss of trust in women,
- the risk of becoming a premature parent with the financial burden of supporting children they may not see,
- future relationships suffer as the student becomes more desensitised to opening his heart up, having suffered heartbreak or break-ups and
- becoming the object of gossiping and rumours that can lead to bullying for both children/adolescents.

On the other hand, the advantages of purity involve:

- no risk of STDs,
- a clear conscience with God,
- no emotional baggage on entry into marriage,

- a sense of security inside a stable relationship and
- no sexual reference in marriage so husbands don't compare their wives to former partners and vice versa.

Sexual purity is sometimes harder to maintain in a school setting due to the high levels of peer pressure. Peer pressure can damage almost every facet of a child's life and lead to ongoing effects on the vulnerable. The worst thing about peer pressure is its tendency to make fools of those who follow bad children in school. As Proverbs 13:20 says, 'Whoever walks with the wise becomes wise, but the companion of fools will suffer harm'.

3. Classrooms

I'm afraid the schools will prove the very gates of hell

Unless they diligently labour in explaining the Holy Scriptures

And engraving them in the heart of the youth.

Martin Luther

SOME PEOPLE GENUINELY BELIEVE HOMESCHOOLING is a bad idea. They think kids will miss out on beneficial activities in school, creating a bad place to learn. Sylvia Bui, a schoolteacher, wrote an article called *Homeschooling is a bad idea*. She thinks homeschoolers suffer as they are deprived of classrooms which are 'good places'.

Bui sees classrooms as places where 'students are challenged and encouraged by other students' curiosity, and they sometimes benefit from an array of school staff. Schools provide structure and teaching beyond book-learning, such as behaviours and following orders, procedures, instructions, as well as participatory activities such as [sports, band practice and so on].'[40]

Could this statement be too positively biased towards classrooms? Let's have a closer look at Bui's statement:

1. *'challenged and encouraged by other students' curiosity.'* Curiosity is inherently neutral and can be used for good or evil. The statement above suggests curiosity aroused by other students is always a good thing. But, while curiosity can extend to learning how to use the Bunsen burner in science class for microbial analysis, curiosity can also propel students to learn how to sniff marijuana - using the

same Bunsen burner. And sometimes students are even more curious if the activity is prohibited.

2. *'they sometimes benefit from an array of school staff.'* Compared to homeschooling, the ratios of students to staff are almost always too high to get adequate social attention for each child (indeed, smarter children sometimes receive less attention because they need less academic help). [i] But, do we need all these highly-trained professionals to look after a child? Can't a loving parent be as good as many busy teachers, secretaries and gardeners? A plethora of research on this topic suggests parents are more than capable.[41] Homeschooling parents do the role of parent, coach, secretary, gardener, first aid officer, science, english, history and mathematics teacher – simultaneously. No moving around from classroom to classroom or from teacher to teacher needed.[42] [ii]

3. *'Schools provide structure and teaching beyond book learning.'* Inside school, "practicals" or tutorials mean students are often tethered to a desk for the duration of the lesson. By contrast, homeschooling allows more freedom, and more supervision so children can follow their interests under the watchful eye of their parents.

4. *'such as behaviours.'* While some Christian schools teach ethics or Christian religious classes during certain periods (in an attempt to instil Christian values), many classes fail to integrate the professed values of the Christian school. For example, english classes may not study the Bible at all. And science classes may not mention that God is the Maker of everything students study. In any case, classrooms certainly don't have a reputation for good behaviour.

---

[i] As previously noted, school children receive around seven minutes a day in face-to-face interaction with their teachers. Homeschooled children may get up to 300 minutes.
[ii] Also see meta-analysis by BJ Biddle and DC Berliner (endnote) whereby researchers say the overwhelming evidence is in favour of smaller classroom sizes – especially for younger age groups.

5. *'following orders, procedures, instructions.'* Following instructions at school continually, without self-directing your learning, stifles creativity.[43] Although all kids have great talents, we waste these talents ruthlessly. School children sometimes only learn how to do a task in a particular way by a teacher, instead of trying to figure out how to do the task themselves.

Understandably, schools find creative and critical thinking difficult concepts to foster because of time constraints and traditional teaching routines. They don't have time to let children find a way to do the task themselves. Instead, teachers demonstrate the way to do a task and have children follow their technique. Consider how this kills creativity! Sir Ken Robinson talked about how kids are willing to take a chance on something they don't know. But, by the time they get to adulthood, they've lost the capacity to have a go at things because they've been educated out of having a go. Instead, they do things 'the right way', and often fail to think creatively. Adults have become frightened of getting things wrong as they've been stigmatised for their mistakes too much.[44]

Robinson believes we are educating our children out of their creative capacities, capacities that we all once possessed. He says the trick is to *remain* creative, despite being in a school system that [unintentionally] discourages creativity. [45]

By contrast, the homeschooling environment facilitates creativity due to extra time and flexibility in the daily routine. Homeschoolers can spend hours every day with their parents learning how to think creatively. They can discover how to make decks, build sheds and sew patchwork quilts under their parents' guidance, and then find out how to modify the things they've learned on their own.

6. *'as well as participatory activities such as [sports, band practice and so on].'* At school, there's often little time left for honing sport or music skills because students spend so much time doing filler activities. After school, children are often so tired, they need rest. By contrast, homeschooling offers a far more flexible approach for the family, allowing homeschoolers to spend more time doing sports, band practice and so on. For group activities, homeschoolers can join with other homeschoolers (or even other school children) and create teams that enter the local sports clubs. More musically inclined homeschoolers can do choir practice with other homeschoolers and join existing community groups.

The Classroom Space

The classroom area can be a distracting study environment. Because of high noise levels and the disruption peers create, classrooms can be ineffective learning environments. Classrooms lack different types of spaces, such as stools, couch areas and open areas. Instead, many classrooms have only desks and chairs with limited room to move and stretch.[46]

Of course, classrooms are useful for teachers who must cram in the information governments and school protocol require them to teach. Therefore, teachers need students to sit still for extended periods of time, memorise facts for tests, do repetitive work and keep quiet. You might ask, 'Don't teachers know these activities are boring for kids?'

Yes, they know. Some even feel frustrated because they can't let children move around as they would like. One teacher showed her frustration, by talking about the amount of information teachers are expected to cram down students' throats in a short period. She believed teachers were no longer able to teach according to what they felt was developmentally appropriate because of the volume of information in the curriculum.[47]

ADHD in the Classroom

Perhaps this 'insane' pace contributes to some insanity of its own. Why are we surprised when one in ten children are diagnosed with behaviour problems?[48] Behavioural problems such as Bipolar, Oppositional Defiant

Disorder and Attention-Deficit Hyperactivity Disorder (ADHD) are more prevalent in schools today. ADHD rates have experienced a jump in recent years.[49] Some researchers believe this jump is attributable to the long hours children spend at school.[50]

These behavioural problems are diminished when parents provide an active, green outlet for hyperactive students.[51] [iii] For example, Joshua Hesford was diagnosed with ADHD at school when he was seven-years-old. His teacher didn't understand how Joshua was not like the other children who sat quietly in class, finishing their activities.

Instead, Joshua gazed out the classroom window, daydreaming and longing for recess. At recess, he could run, jump and kick a ball to his heart's content. He was so full of fidgets. Joshua also found himself lagging behind in schoolwork and became progressively frustrated at the homework building up. His teachers suggested *more* after-hours catch-up homework. But, Joshua soon became even more bored and despondent at school.

Eventually, Joshua's parents decided to homeschool. With a bit of help from his parents, Joshua raced through his schoolwork in three hours and escaped into the garden every day. With his father's woodworking advice, Joshua chopped down small tree branches and made miniature trains out them. He loved his new life. After he began homeschooling, there was never any suggestion he was unusually disordered.

As Joshua became an adult, he loved working hard and being active. His 'ADHD' became an advantage in soccer as he practised more often than his teammates. Joshua soon became a first-grade soccer player. At university, he excelled at his architecture course, often working until he was exhausted. Soon he got a job with one of the best architecture firms in the country.

Joshua found homeschooling gave him the chance to reduce his hyperactivity and channel his energies into his interests. Joshua's story is a common one, consistent with studies such as the one conducted by the

---

[iii] For more on environments that encourage children to learn see Chapter 13 on academic achievement.

School Psychology Review. Here researchers found children diagnosed with ADHD who were educated at home were academically engaged at twice the level as children educated in school, due to higher student to teacher ratios. [52] [iv] Although Joshua's fast-paced personality was seen as a disadvantage in school, in the real world, Joshua's 'ADHD' personality was a significant advantage.

Faith and Tolerance

Martin Luther once said, 'I'm afraid the schools will prove the very gates of hell, unless [schools] diligently labour in explaining the Holy Scriptures and engraving them in the heart of the youth'. In other words, schools need to teach the Bible diligently otherwise schools will become a thoroughfare to hell.

Psychotic or Energetic?

Dr. Robert Spitzer, the man who first identified Attention Deficit Hyperactive Disorder (ADHD), has admitted up to 30% of children diagnosed with ADHD may have been misdiagnosed. The exuberance the children display may be, he says, just the normal behaviour of a happy or sad child.[53]

Explaining and discussing faith and the Bible in a classroom can be difficult. It isn't exactly done in many Australian classrooms these days, except in Christian schools. Rather, teachers must teach about religion, instead of teaching students how to practice religion. According to Miriam Diamond's non-Christian book, *Encountering Faith in the Classrooms*, the teacher must avoid class mayhem which is common in classrooms

[iv] Results found homeschoolers were academically engaged for twice as long as public school students. They also had more reading and math gains. The key variable was identified to be student to teacher ratios between the two settings

with multi-faith students. Because students have conflicting worldviews, the teacher must discuss different religions inclusively. Teachers who teach *about* religion, rather than teaching students how to *practice* a religion, are teaching 'religious literacy'. Religious literacy also means teachers must teach *all* religions. This means little time is left for teaching Christianity in detail.[54]

Problems can emerge at educational institutions that prefer Enlightenment ideals over spirituality.[v] Institutions preferring Enlightenment ideals say, 'If you can't test something, it must be irrational'.[55] [vi] They say this despite running many subjects that they can't test empirically like ethics, philosophy, sociology and the arts.[56] [vii]

Even though spiritual ideas are labeled as irrational, school academics are told they must be tolerant and teach religion as well as agnosticism. Furthermore, they should give equal time to religious minorities as well as religious majorities. [57] The resulting curriculum weakly portrays most religions. The Bible and the Koran become all about love – because that's tolerant. Of course, the curriculum forgets about the truth – the bits in the Bible where God says to 'go and completely destroy the entire Amalekite nation--men, women, children, babies, cattle, sheep, goats, camels, and donkeys.'[58] In this way, schools only teach part of the truth. If schools *were* to portray all religions accurately, people might be afraid of what turned up.

It is only natural that secular educators want to warp Christianity beyond recognition and merge all religions into one. Christianity is a call to know the one and only true God, not the unknowable Allah, the 80 million Hindu gods or many others. They want Christian students to accept many

---

[v] Enlightenment ideals are said to be scientifically testable. Spiritual ideals are not and must be accepted by faith.
[vi] University lecturers who teach religion are told to disseminate information, but make no attempt to change the view of students after that. They should only advise students that 'understanding something is one thing, but believing it is quite another.' Diamond, MR, *Encountering Faith in the Classrooms*, pp. 7-9.
[vii] America uses the first amendment to claim that public schools should be free of religion and religious bias.

'different and valid' positions. They say Christian students find tolerance difficult – a difficulty 'compounded by the tendency to view anyone who offers an alternative vantage point as blind to the truth and a moral threat.'[59]

Some secular educators believe mature Christian students have hindered their intellectual growth due to their worldview. These educators think Christian students are 'inhibited from broadening their horizons' to alternative worldviews.[60] But, these teachers are the ones who inhibit other children from discovering the truth of Christ. By hindering students' walks with God, secular educators herd multitudes of school students to 'the very gates' of hell.

A Haven of Diversity?

> 'Many smart students are held back in that they easily complete the average class work load but they can't go any further in that classroom. These students are looking for an academic challenge, but not one that will draw attention to them. They don't want to do more than the other students, but will spend the rest of the lesson playing on their mobile phones or drawing pictures on their work and whispering.'
>
> *Kerry, Homeschool Mother and Teacher. (Correspondence, May 2016.)*

Critics of homeschooling believe homeschoolers are inept at socialising with people of different races and backgrounds. They say homeschoolers are given an incomplete social education at home. However, their alternative, public school, is not always a haven of diversity. Many schools have people who think alike and are of the same ethnic and socio-economic background. Take North Sydney Boys High School, a selective public school, in which the vast majority of students are from non-English speaking Chinese backgrounds. (This is unusual, given the location is in the middle of an English-speaking country.) Because so many of these socially advantaged Chinese students are attending this school (and other schools like it) and failing to spread themselves out between other local high schools, experts believe this is creating a situation where disadvantaged students such as refugees and indigenous people, clump together in 'residual' public schools.[61]

Christiana Ho, a researcher from Sydney's University of Technology, has studied ethnic segregation in inner-city public, private and selective grammar schools. Ho said she found it staggering that there is so much diversity between schools that are only a 10-minute walk apart.[62] Ho said there is significant segregation between white-dominated public school students with privileged parents and highly diverse public school schools with disadvantaged parents.

When we think about diversity in schools, we should also remember we are extremely selective when it comes to age. 100% of the students in just about every classroom are the same age, give or take a year. Furthermore, at recess and lunch, children are sometimes discouraged from mixing in different groups or genders because of shyness, contempt or different fears they hold. Although most children are not born in litters, we insist on educating them as if they were.[63] Dr. Peter Gray, a childhood research professor at the Massachusetts Boston College, wrote:

> *One of the oddest and in my view most harmful, aspects of our treatment of children today is our penchant for segregating them into separate groups by age. We do that not only in schools, but increasingly in out-of-school settings as well. In doing so, we deprive children of a valuable component of their natural means of self-education.*[64]

Because school children spend so much time with similarly-aged peers, many feel uncomfortable with older or younger people. When schools insist on grouping children according to their chronological age, they ignore much research showing that chronological age is a poor indicator of a child's readiness for school.[65] [viii]

[viii] Indeed, studies suggest if a child delays entering school for just one year, their learning ability is greatly improved. [See endnote.]

An Unrealistic Environment

School is an unusual and unrealistic place most people will never experience again. School's preparation for the real world is about as useful as trying to douse a house fire with a small, paper cup. Homeschool Mum, Fiona, went further and said school was detrimental for her children, 'When my kids were at home they were content in each other's company. But, as soon as they went back to school they wanted to socialise with kids their own age and lost their skills at getting along with others of all ages.'

School creates an environment where children are forced to learn information, much of which is rote learning. Students learn how to swallow lots of information for an exam, such as the National Assessment Program – Literacy and Numeracy (NAPLAN)[ix] or the High School Certificate (HSC) only for it to be regurgitated and promptly forgotten after the exam. Then they bring this limited learning style to university.

School children learn, not for their interest and pleasure, but for the end-of-year exam. Governments highly value exam results. Given that the Australian Government wants children to pass biennial NAPLAN tests, teachers must teach with the NAPLAN test in mind. Unfortunately, this style of teaching is not the best method of instruction. Dr. Justin Coulson, a parenting expert, said he won't be letting his children sit NAPLAN because NAPLAN causes stress and doesn't:

- Improve literacy
- Improve life skills
- Improve education
- Improve tertiary performance
- Make a difference to employment prospects
- Tell you anything about student achievement
- Create a positive and respectful school climate
- Help relationships between students, parents and teachers.[66]

[ix] NAPLAN tests are national standardised testing aimed at 'leaving no child behind'.

Others say similar things about the ineffectiveness of NAPLAN classroom testing:

> When teachers assess learning their focus is on providing a comprehensive picture of children's lives as learners and on monitoring, better understanding and supporting individual children's growth in learning. NAPLAN can never provide this detailed analysis... NAPLAN tests do not provide sufficient diagnostic information to identify areas of weakness or strength to support classroom learning.[67]

America also came to the same conclusion after they tested out a NAPLAN-style assessment system. American educators concluded they wouldn't be helping society if they got scores up, but didn't educate children.[68] Because NAPLAN testing is, at best, unnatural (in that it fails to teach children through their interests), NAPLAN testing stifles a child's ability to be creative and learn a diverse set of life skills.

NAPLAN testing also fails to teach a variety of ways to do a task. For instance, persuasive writing has been tested in Years 3, 5, 7 and 9. Assessment of only one type of writing has meant other forms of writing are forgotten, and teachers can't diversify their teaching to their students' needs.[69]

> "NAPLAN is not an educational instrument, it a is a political one where the government can justify its actions using children to achieve its goals."
>
> Kerry, Homeschool Mother and Teacher.
> (Correspondence, May 2016.)

Furthermore, NAPLAN testing, like HSC testing, causes too much nervousness and stress, with one survey showing 90% of classrooms had students that felt stressed before taking the exam.[70] In this way, the testing has negative impacts on children's wellbeing and quality of learning.[71]

Albert Einstein shared his thoughts on exams like NAPLAN, saying:

> *It is a very grave mistake to think the enjoyment of seeing and searching can be promoted by means of coercion and a sense of duty. To the contrary, I believe it would be possible to rob even a healthy beast of prey of its*

voraciousness, if it were possible, with the aid of a whip, to force the beast to devour continuously, even when not hungry.

School children are coached to learn in one of the most ineffective ways imaginable. These methods kill children's creative curiosity and embitter them toward learning. Children become frustrated at school, and their frustration is sometimes the greatest in schools when children are delayed or rushed in class, as we will see more clearly in Chapter 4.

4. Schools Have Time Issues

So much time is wasted at school... At school, you can elect to learn a lot about a specific area, but not a little of each as you would usually require in life.

Neville Hesford, Lawyer and Homeschool Graduate. (Questionnaire, June 2014.)

Wasted Time in Classrooms

SPENDING SIX HOURS AT SCHOOL EACH day is exhausting for students. Teachers must occupy children until they're collected in the afternoon. But, too often teachers choose boring and repetitive tasks to keep students busy. These sorts of tasks are known to increase fatigue, accounting for much of the students' exhaustion.[72]

This leaves students with limited energy to interact with parents. In this frame of mind, teenagers usually find monosyllabic answers easier than a normal conversation. Susan, a primary school teacher, explains:

> *A tremendous amount of filler is done because the day is too long and little children can't last. They do a lot of stuff just to fill in the time. I think it just wastes their lives away. Schools should compress the academic curriculum into a small amount of time. Small children benefit from being at home and spending time in play and activity, supervised in an unstructured way, rather than this artificial school day, where they come home, worn out, having done little academic learning and a lot of filler.*

Filler is as useless as stopping up a rat-hole with an apple dumpling. Children don't need filler in their education. Academically speaking, the top scoring countries spend about three and a half hours learning at school each day. Finland's school day is around four to five hours, with lessons running for three hours and 45 minutes (in between, pupils receive a healthy and tasty lunch). Compared to the Australian children, Finnish children spend less time in classrooms and score higher on international education indicators (OECD). [73] These students have one of the top performing school systems in the world.[74]

Comparatively, Australian school hours are needlessly long and exhausting. Children go to school for too many days in the year. Japan expects its children to go to school the most with 245 school days a year. Australia is close behind with 210 school days. But, 210 days is significantly above the average (even American students sit in class for only 180 days a year).

So, if statistics show students don't benefit from more hours and more days in school, why do we insist they attend school for so long? Is school just cultural or do we need a glorified babysitting service for working parents? Not only do parents have to work, but teachers have to work and child care centres have to work. Our whole society is structured around keeping the kids in school.

Do Countries That Require More Hours in the Classroom Produce Children with Better Academic Results?

Countries that score high on international assessments include Korea, Japan, Finland and Canada. But, do these countries score high because they spend more hours in study, compared to countries that spend less time in study?

Data from the OECD has looked at the number of instructional hours, rather than the days spent in school. It has found little correlation between hours spent in academic study and performance.

> 'According to the OECD, the hours of compulsory instruction per year in these countries range from 608 hours in Finland (a top performer) to 926 hours in France (average) at the elementary level... Of particular note, no state requires as few hours as Finland, even though Finland scores near the top of nearly every international assessment.'[75]

In other words, one of the top performing countries has the least academic hours. There can be no doubt school hours has little to do with academic results.

This is certainly true when looking at homeschoolers. Many homeschooling families spend only a few short hours in formal academic study. Yet, homeschoolers from all over the world, consistently outperform their school peers (see Chapter 13).

Rushed Students

'She's not one of those kids that get maths.'

Anonymous Parent

Some children just have to work at it. Not all kids are bright or talented enough to get everything the teacher says within the timeframe expected. These students may need more attention than teachers can provide to finish the task satisfactorily. Sometimes at the end of the class, slower students are caught unaware, feeling rushed, they don't complete their project. Then these students might feel anxious when hassled to finish quickly even if they were enjoying the project before they felt rushed.

Understandably, hassling happens for the sake of the class. Students cannot be kept waiting for long periods of time in the interests of the slowest in the class, lest the fastest ones get restless and anxious themselves.

William and Susan recounted the following experience about how the school handled their son's slow and particular habits at school. This experience was one factor that prompted them to explore homeschooling:

[Our son] found the teacher rushed him. He was a very slow and particular worker, doing a lot of artwork, like elaborate headings, with all his written work. But, he didn't have time to complete what he was working on. The teacher then made him stay in at recess to finish it. He found that frustrating and he wasn't getting enough time to do all that creative work that he loved to do. He loved reading.

In his classroom, the children were allowed to read once they had finished their work. But, because he was slow at his work, he never got a chance to read. So he never had reading time. He found that incredibly frustrating because he was desperate to read. He was finding the whole thing too overwhelming and miserable.

> These days many students have hidden learning disabilities that slow them down – eyesight disorders, eating disorders, middle ear processing, muffled hearing due to compulsory swimming lessons - all of which slow their performance time.
>
> Kerry, Homeschool Mother and Teacher.
> (Correspondence, May 2016.)

After William and Susan's son had started crying and refusing to enter the car and go to school, they decided to homeschool him. Their son's actions are typical of a common phobia, called school phobia.

School phobia is common among five-to-seven-year-olds.[76] This phobia is exhibited in children who fail to fit the school mould. Children with school phobia experience symptoms including nausea, diarrhoea, headaches, stomachaches and sore throat. Crying spells, tantrums, psychosomatic complaints and panic and self-harm may also show up.'[77] Homeschooling is a great cure for school phobia because children's symptoms disappear when allowed to stay home.[78]

Homework

Homework can hit students like a tonne of bricks after a long day at school. As if six hours of schoolwork wasn't enough, schools often heap students (sometimes as young as ten years old) with an average of one hour or more of homework every night.

So much time doing homework is exhausting for children and, some feel, likely even damaging to their physical health. Dr. Judith Paphazy has seen a steady stream of Grade Seven students with headaches, anxiety and insomnia. She believes these symptoms are due to the 'insane' amounts of homework students are expected to do. Paphazy also sees stressed ten and 11-year old students who have an hour of homework every night. This level of homework, says Paphazy, can cause serious mental and physical health damage.[79]

One hour of homework, however, is a breeze, compared to what some high school students are expected to do. These students average one to three hours a night.[80] In high school, the school and government's insistence on good grades are eroding valuable time teenagers would have otherwise spent with their family.

So, children have to do all this work for questionably useful results. Studies have shown homework has no benefit for high school students if homework time exceeds one and a half hours. Similarly, if middle school students spend more than 20 minutes a night on homework, the exercise becomes futile because children just switch off.[81] Even more damningly, a UK study found there was *no correlation* between academic performance and the time a primary school student spent on homework.[82] [x]

---

[x] Most similar studies suggest a small correlation between time spent on grades and homework exists, although they admit the difference is small.

Homework becomes more beneficial as students grow older and reach high school. And homework is sometimes more helpful for certain subjects such as mathematics. However, English, History and Science homework might not significantly increase a student's grades.[83] For these subjects, the relationship between homework and academic improvement is nonlinear. Indeed, the 'more time [spent] on homework in the early childhood years is found to relate to lower achievement.'[84]

> 'In high school each teacher assigns projects to their students without consideration for the total amount of homework hours required to complete them. I asked my students why they had not finished their homework I gave them. Their excuse was they had to do their chemistry homework first. I said my subject was more important, but the students said they were more scared of the chemistry teacher.'
>
> Kerry, Homeschool Mother and Teacher. (Correspondence, May 2016.)

Homework outcomes can be improved if parents help their children with homework. The more a parent helps their child, the higher the child's academic achievement. Not only do parents academically influence their children, they have a profound effect on their attitude to homework. Parents greatly influence a child's feeling of personal competence and ability to cope with homework.[85]

Of course, homework is critical in high school where assignments done at home are directly linked to HSC grades, so the role of parents is important if children are doing the HSC. However, the HSC is not needed if students want to enter tertiary education because portfolios are adequate, even preferred, in some cases.[xi]

[xi] See Chapter 18.

Think it's Family Time when You Get Home? Think Again.

Homework time cuts into valuable family time where parents can influence their children. However, family time is being eroded unnecessarily when homework time takes over family time.

5. Bullying and Sexual Pressures

And so seated next to my father in the train compartment, I suddenly asked, 'Father, what is 'sex sin'?'
He turned to look at me, as he always did when answering a question, but to my surprise he said nothing. At last he stood up, lifted his traveling case off the floor and set it on the floor.
'Will you carry it off the train, Corrie?' he said.
I stood up and tugged at it. It was crammed with the watches and spare parts he had purchased that morning.
'It's too heavy,' I said.
Yes,' he said, 'and it would be a pretty poor father who would ask his little girl to carry such a load. It's the same way, Corrie, with knowledge. Some knowledge is too heavy for children. When you are older and stronger, you can bear it. For now you must trust me to carry it for you.

Corrie ten Boom, The Hiding Place

Sex Education Doesn't Teach Abstinence

SEX OUTSIDE MARRIAGE NOW SEEMS TO BE a common part of school life in many schools.[i] Pre-marital sex or sexual thoughts are common today with 30% of internet searches related to pornography. Casual sex and sex

---

[i] There is no requirement for non-government schools to teach students about contraception, abortion, sexually transmitted diseases, or other 'safe-sex' information.

before marriage is now a part of life. Some students see sex as a way for girls and boys to receive recognition and satisfaction from each other.

Sex is common in school. In 2013, the *Australian Secondary Student and Sexual Health* study surveyed 2,100 students from 436 government, Catholic and independent schools. The study found a quarter of Year 10 students, a third of Year 11 students and half the Year 12 students were having sex.[86] [ii]

Premarital sex is common in schools because sex education is no longer about whether students should or shouldn't have sex. Rather sex ed is about how to apply a condom effectively to avoid Sexually Transmitted Diseases or unwanted pregnancies. Sex education is not about abstinence anymore because teachers assume most students will have sex. Therefore, schools don't promote abstinence seriously. They assume students will use each other's bodies at school.[iii]

Then the new fad of 'sexting', explicit text messages with sexual references, is becoming prolific. Protecting children from sexting is difficult enough inside the homeschooling environment (where everything is monitored), let alone outside the home environment.

Due to the addictive nature of pornography, sexting is becoming popular among school teens. More than ever, young people are sexting. According to the Australian Institute of Criminology:

> *In a survey of over 2,000 respondents, almost half reported having sent a sexual picture or video of themselves to another party, while two-thirds had received a sexual image. Sexting was prevalent among all age groups, with 13 to 15 year olds particularly likely to receive sexual images.*[87]

The practice is especially common among homosexual and bisexual students.[88] Some see sexting as 'modern-day courtship'. Parents are told

---

[ii] This said, 70% are sexually active in some way (oral sex, deep kissing or genital touching).
[iii] Christian schools are often more serious about sexual education and promote abstinence more.

they should not be disgusted at the phenomenon but should accept it.[89] Some think sexting among school children to be normal behavior.

Dr. Zoe Hilton from the National Crime Agency's head of child protection told Members of Parliament it was normal behavior for teens to text explicit sexual messages and photographs to one another. Hilton believed teens did this to copy stars like Kim Kardashian, who regularly posts explicit sexual images of herself on the internet. Kardashian, a popular role model for teens today, was blamed for encouraging teens in sexting.[90]

Sexting Among Teens

- 54% of students received sexually explicit texts
- 43% sent sexually explicit texts
- 42% received a sexually explicit or nude photo/video of someone else
- 26% sent a nude or explicit photo or video of themselves
- 22% used a social media site for sex reasons
- 9% sent an explicit or nude photo or video of someone else.[91]

When sexting progresses to a physical relationship, the relationship is not always wanted. Statistics reveal that when teenagers are frightened or drunk a third of them are pressured into unwanted sex by their friends or partners.[92]

Teen grooming by school peers makes teens more willing to engage in premarital sex. Grooming happens when teens say things like 'I can't believe she's a virgin!'. Or they glorify students who have sex. This sexual encouragement happens many years before a student has their first sexual encounter. Therefore, when they take the plunge, premarital sex has been normalised.

The normalisation of premarital sex in schools is concerning as this type of sex has dire consequences. Premarital sex leads to a plethora of other problems for students, families and communities. Abortion, for instance, causes the death of a baby and often causes much more depression and anxiety in the would-be mothers.[iv] [93] Christian parents need to know the consequences of pre-marital sexual relationships (such as the termination of a quarter of Australian pregnancies. One third of all Australian women now have an abortion).[94]

Parents also need to be aware that many secular teachers believe sexual relationships among teenagers are harmless.[95] Many are desensitised to the seriousness of the issue. Some teachers with corrupt lifestyles ignore student 'flings' because the worse immorality of students justifies the 'better' immorality of the teacher's lifestyle – 'I'm not as bad as them, so I'm okay.'

These teachers may turn their attention elsewhere because they don't value morality and are apathetic towards immoral actions among students, such as sexting. Professor Anne Mitchell of La Trobe University, is one such teacher. She said, 'While we need to be aware of the harm that might come if those messages (sexting) are sent out far and wide or misused, it doesn't appear to be doing harm to most kids.'[96]

Tots Taught Sex Ed

Toddlers will soon be taught about sex, sexuality and cross-dressing, according to Susie O'Brian from the Herald Sun. *Early Childhood Australia* is set to teach tots about cross-dressing using dress-ups. Teachers will also take these pre-schoolers on tours to the opposite sex's toilets as part of the Early-Start initiative.

Clare McHugh, the spokeswoman for Early Childhood Australia, said the program aims to reduce domestic violence as 'rigid views on gender' were associated with violence and domestic violence.[97]

Sexual Morals are Flexible

Ungodly sexual behaviour, such as premarital, intersex and homosexual behaviours are increasingly becoming accepted and promoted in many

---

[iv] A meta-analysis of women who had an abortion after an unplanned pregnancy compared to women who delivered their unplanned pregnancy revealed women with a history of abortion had higher rates of anxiety (34% higher), depression (37% higher), marijuana use (230% higher) and suicidal behaviour (155% higher). AfterAbortion.Org [see corresponding endnote].

Australian schools.[98] While this behaviour is encouraged in public school, a small percentage of those in power are even trying to decriminalise 'mild paedophilia'.[99] [v]

Australian society is moving further away from biblical morality, as was seen when a District Court Judge, Garry Neilson had his favourable ruling toward rape overturned by three NSW Court of Criminal Appeal judges. Neilson's (later overturned) ruling said that the repeated rape of a 15-year-old teenage girl by her uncle was only in the 'mid-range' of seriousness as the uncle didn't expose the victim to the risk of pregnancy or sexually transmitted diseases. (The uncle was de facto with his sister, the girl's mother, at the time).[100]

Pedophilia in Australian society appears to be more acceptable today.[101] Taylor Risetto (not his real name), is an atheist with a philosophy degree who teaches high school ethics classes. Taylor says he can think of no reason paedophilia should be unacceptable. He says, 'we can be immoral because God doesn't exist'.

Taylor is right. If no God exists, no morals exist.[102] [vi] If no God exists, our morals are changeable to suit a person's pragmatic cravings. And, with the ousting of prayer and godly teaching in American public schools in 1962, corrupt, atheistic views have been prevalent for some time.[103] [vii] In 2014, the Australian state of Victoria followed suit and banned teacher and volunteer

---

[v] The European Union seems to want to legalise paedophilia according to a booklet released by the European Union. Distributed and encouraged in Germany, the EU booklet called *Love, Body and Playing Doctor* was aimed at teaching fathers to sexually touch their children, particularly girls between 1-6 years, in inappropriate places. The booklet has been withdrawn due to criticism. [Source: see corresponding endnote.]

[vi] If there is no moral objectivity, everything (including deviant sexual behaviour) is open and fluid.

[vii] Prayer was banned in American public schools in 1962 after officials decided prayer violated the first amendment. STDs, divorce, cohabitation, drug use, violent crime, teen pregnancies, single-parent families, lower education scores and abortion have all increased significantly since, a result, some believe, of the banning of school prayer. See Star, P. (2014). *Education Expert: Removing Bible, Prayer from Public Schools Has Caused Decline*. CNS News. The top five complaints teachers had between 1940 – 1962 were talking, chewing gum, making noise, running in the halls and getting out of turn in line. From 1963 to the present, the top five complaints have been rape, robbery, assault, burglary and arson.

led lunchtime prayer groups in state schools. Will other public schools in other states adopt Victoria's policy soon?

Sexual Assault Among Peers

In 2015, there were 940 reports of serious sexual assault *among* children at school in Australia with some older students sexually assaulting their younger peers in school. In some schools, this assault is endemic.[104] The *Australian Bureau of Statistics* reports teenagers commit about 25% of rapes and 40% of child sexual assaults.

Often sexual assault in school is a result of boys pressuring girls for sex. A survey recently found boys are three times more likely to say 'pressure for sex isn't abusive' than girls.[105]

Incidences of blackmail and child grooming among peers have also surfaced. One report detailed how the perpetrator and victim remained in the same school together, *despite a report of sexual assault being lodged*.[106] In this case, the headmaster of an exclusive primary school told a mother that the sexual abuse against her son was possibly *normal behaviour* among boys of that age. Her son was forced to perform certain acts on other boys in his class. This mother expected the school had systems in place to discipline the guilty boys, but nothing was done. After moving her son to another school, she said people need to be more aware that these things can happen. The mother questioned the faith we place in school staff who are supposed to ensure our children's safety always.[107]

The sad thing is parents *are not* always aware of assault in their child's school. They find peer assault incidents hard to believe because many still think children are innocent – or too innocent to commit a crime. A child's fear may also prevent him or her reporting abuse, and there is a high possibility that abuse is under-reported.

But, even if parents are aware of the abusive situation, they are sometimes helpless to prevent another attack while their children are in the school. Indeed, when the boy in the above incident told his mother he was sexually abused by six-year old's in the school toilets, his mother told the police. But the police said nothing could be done because the perpetrator was below age ten and, therefore, no crime had been committed. The mother reacted to this saying because sexual assault of kids in school is not technically a crime, no one wants to talk about it.[108]

But, where do perpetrators as young as six, learn how to abuse other children? Some think the rise of sexual assault among young children is caused by exposure to:

- sexuality
- substance abuse
- violent family members
- child pornography and advertising
- problems at school and in the family and
- detrimental childhood experiences early in life like sexual victimisation.[109]

One in three perpetrators were victims in the past, according to research by the British Journal of Psychology.[110] Another researcher, Professor Freda Briggs, explained why, saying children tend to replicate the abuse they've suffered with other people because it releases some of the fear they felt at the event. Briggs fears that if children enjoy the power they get in this type of role playing, it may continue and become a habit.[111] Therefore, the cycle of sexual assault in schools self-perpetuates.

Bullying

'It was just the culture to get bullied.'

Lois, Homeschool Mother and Early Childhood Teacher. (Correspondence, November 2014.)

Australian schools have some of the highest rates of bullying in the world. One in six children at school are bullied *at least once a week*.[112] About two-thirds of children diagnosed with autism will be bullied once a week or more.[113] [viii] Perhaps it's ironic that while adults would never endure bullying on the scale we see in school, many think a bit of bullying is normal for the weakest members of our society.

> 'A survey of schools in about 40 countries found that Australian primary schools were among those with the highest reported incidence of bullying in the world...One in three students aged 10-11 years reported being bullied or picked on by peers.'
>
> *Child Family Community Australia*[114]

Vulnerable children make perfect victims because bullying usually involves a serious misbalance of power between the bully and the victim. Because bullies get a thrill out of having power, intimidating behaviour is often repeated and intensifies as time continues.

Some parents say bullying is good because 'it creates resilience.' But, this expression misunderstands resilience. Resilience is a person's ability to adapt to stress and adversity *properly*. Many victims are not properly adapting. They might change, but change isn't synonymous with proper adaption.

Far from adapting, bullying creates a host of psychological problems in both the bully and the victim.[115] Compared to non-bullied children, bullied children experience lower self-esteem, more loneliness, anxiety, unhappiness and insecurity. Bullies are twice as likely to experience depression and anxiety.[116]

[viii] Schools, not online, is the most likely place children are bullied according to a study by Reach Out Australia. [See corresponding endnote].

Additionally, some children themselves don't overcome these problems after school. Their feelings become internalised as they grow older. This internalisation causes anxiety, depression and low self-esteem.[117]

The effects of bullying can snowball, according to Boston Children's Hospital researcher and social psychologist, Laura Bogart. The longer a child is bullied, the worse the effects upon the child. These children will experience more psychological problems. One student, bullied over several grades, was Bill. Bill attended public school in the 1970s and experienced bullying during much of his school life. Bill now suffers from depression and low self-esteem. Bill shared his story:

My problem had to do with being 'better' than other students my age or older. The school I attended was only a small school and any kid with a bit of talent there was going to win everything. Because my Mum could race against Betty Cuthbert and Dad's side participated in all sorts of high-level sports, our whole family won all the age groups at every sport at that school. And I was the best in my family. I could beat kids two years ahead of my age group. I even won an under 12s hundred-yard race aged only ten at the interschool sports carnival one year.

Mostly my peers' siblings hated me. The more I tried to win their approval by working hard, the more I was picked on. Even my older brother didn't like me because I could beat all his mates, who took some of their anger out on him.

Being called 'Big Head', I used to look in the mirror and think my head must be fat or something. My peers could not understand I was not showing off as they presumed. God had simply given me more ability in that area. To me, as a kid, society appeared to promote athleticism as a good thing. It's in all strata of society – a contradiction if

Children who are bullied are threefold more likely to show depressive symptoms.

Centre for Adolescent Health: Royal Children's Hospital Melbourne ever there was one. We praise the winners and then can't wait to see them fail. We are 'one with them' as 'ours', but jealous at a personal level. But, how does a little kid work that out?

Reality Check

While protecting our children from harm should be part of every parent's makeup, our society has taught us to think protection is unnecessary by using the resilience argument. In a way, this toughness is useless because God plans to protect his people and teaches them how to respond to these situations *through* the godly council of parents. But, sin has marred parents so they are no longer perfect. Parents now have a distorted concept of protection, thinking protection includes allowing bullying, so their children become more resilient.

My peers loved when I brought back the trophies for the school but hated me for beating their brothers and friends. I threw all my medals away because I wasn't proud of them at all. By the time I was 15, I had figured it was better to lose and have friends than to win.

At that school, my memories are ones of constant hidings, being sledged, pushed and bullied by older kids – every day. The 90-minute bus trip home was hell. The Harrisons, the worst family of bullies, spent most of that 'giving' it to me. The two older boys, by several years, defended their little brother by serving it up to me. I got on well with the kid himself. On that same bus, my brother's mate, who was two years older than myself and much larger, also had a crack.

The school didn't help. They would put me in races and jumps in older children's age groups. In hindsight, my winning made the bullies look pretty sad. My brother would win, only just, then I came second. A long way back the others would come. I can see why they hated it, but the teachers surely could have been smarter. Wasn't it better for the school to lose a race and enter the slower kids in their age group! It should not have mattered if the school failed! The other children felt they had failed too.

Bill is reluctant to attribute his problems to his school experience. However, there are some things he wishes he didn't learn the hard way. He said, 'It does not pay to succeed at school or beat other students'. Sadly, Bill says, the knowledge of *how to survive school* did not come until after many years of bullying.

I don't play cards now because when I used to win – which was often – the other person became upset. I don't like competition anymore. Getting heckled by those who don't like you tends to make you not want to talk. I remember in that bus, whenever I tried to say anything, I was attacked immediately. Even the bus driver joined in because he had a son who was my younger brother's age, who also flogged the poor kid at everything. Bad form! Our school only had about 60 children. But we beat schools with 400 kids because our family won everything. My two brothers, my sister and I won almost every event. That was seven years of 90 minutes of hell every day aged only five to 12. It's got to mess with you. It's hard to talk about. It makes my heart race as I think and write about it. I dreaded school but had no escape.

Children take their experiences into adulthood, sometimes regardless of their upbringing at home. School can also turn lovely children into bullies. Even homeschoolers who begin attending school may turn into bullies, even if they don't want to be one. A homeschool graduate, Jessie, talked about his younger brother, who was earlier homeschooled, saying:

My fifteen-year-old brother goes to school [now]. He hates school because he feels like he has to keep up an image. The peer pressure is just enormous. You've got to be a tough guy. That's the sort of image he puts up. Because he sees many kids getting picked on, like the slower or nerdier. He's a nice kid, but he hates school because he feels like he's got to put other kids down to survive. You know – a kind of defence mechanism – attack someone else before they attack you.[118]

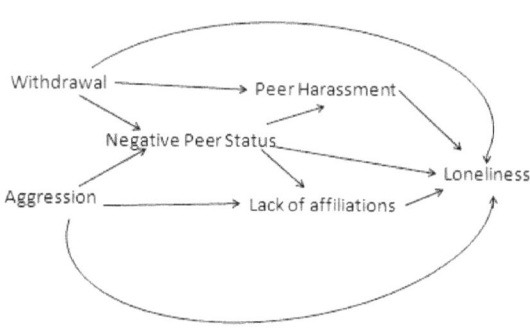

Social model predicting loneliness at school.
Juvonen & Graham 'Peer Harassment in School'

School can be a 'kill or be killed environment.' Furthermore, children are tempted to condone or join the bullying of weaker children. Without a constant counsellor, like a parent, bullying can become a way of life.

Children must be shown the right way. Just as fresh paint needs correct brush strokes to look perfect, teenagers need good influences to grow into godly men and women. If brush strokes are poorly applied, the paint job will be a disaster. Once the paint has dried, you can't change the painting; the paint is dry and inflexible. Likewise, children become harder and less teachable as time progresses. But, they'll always take their youthful experiences with them.

Peer Rejection

Peer rejection is damaging. When rejected, children are marked like a tree with a red X. The tree is chopped down when the woodchopper comes by. Rejected children become fair and easy game for bullies – fair game because 'nobody likes them anyway' and easy game because victims have few friends to defend them.

The peers won't protect victims, because by doing so, peers risk becoming marked with the red X themselves. Because other students won't consort with a dork, rejected children become more aggressive and withdraw. The longer the bullying lasts, the more victims report loneliness at school.[119] Bullied students also adjust poorly to school and one in ten drops out because of bullying.[120] [ix]

Girls (and sometimes boys) teased about their weight at school can become victims of obesity or anorexia. Sometimes their struggle is lifelong.[121] Often these children aren't even under or overweight – but, weight is a reason to tease, so bullies press these hot buttons in vulnerable children.[122]

Teachers Who Bully

Although teachers generally deserve the greatest respect for their work, some rogue teachers don't like teaching and sometimes only teach for the paycheck. These teachers can take out their ill humour on students, terrorising them and making their lives miserable. For instance, the behaviour of Bill's maths teacher, who disciplined students by flicking the contents of his nose at them, made his students fight for a seat at the back of the classroom. Bill said this environment was not a beneficial learning environment.

Although discrimination by teachers against weaker or 'less resilient' students is becoming less common today, discrimination still happens. Even principals are not immune to a bit of bullying, as the principal of Calare Public School in Orange demonstrated recently. The public and other teachers reprimanded this principal after he sent a letter to his staff making fun of weaker students in his care.

The letter referred to bullied students and students with mental health problems as 'morons', 'nut cases' and 'village idiots'. In the letter, the principal wrote, 'Please start identifying students at our school with the following characteristics: suffering from undue anxiety, lacking any

---

[ix] Over 60% of school children believe schools respond poorly to these crises. One in four teachers see no problem with bullying. 14% of children believe bullying has negatively affected their adjustment to school. One in ten highschool students drop out due to bullying. *DoSomething.Org* [See corre
sponding endnote].

resilience, poor socialising skills, two heads, webbed feet and village idiots. I will send out a well-scripted letter in Week 4 starting off '...*Have you bred a moron...etc. You might like to access the services of Calare's new initiative 'Operation Nutcase' ...etc etc. sign along the dotted line, or leave your thumbprint if you cannot write, etc.*"[123]

Conclusion

Ironically, we adults will not endure *workplace* bullying on the scale schools allow, yet we expect our younger, more vulnerable members of society to tolerate bullying. We realise workplace bullying is harmful and can cause damage to the worker. But, when we take our children to school, we call bullying 'resilience training'.

Children can do without bullying and sexual pressure. Therefore homeschooling is a preferable option to public, private and even some Christian schools. Homeschooling is important when we want to move beyond damage control of bullying and sexual harassment to developing sound moral principles and talents in our children.

6. Worldview Assumptions in School

But Peter and the apostles answered, "We must obey God rather than men."

Acts 5:29

AN ASSUMPTION IS A BELIEF THAT SOMETHING is true, despite having no concrete evidence to support it. Notwithstanding this lack of proof, people *need* to operate with assumptions, as assumptions help us fill in the blanks.

Everyone's assumptions affect their worldview. To make this clearer, I'll give you an example. You – a person who says you don't judge anyone – need a babysitter for your child because you need to attend a church meeting. Your pot-smoking next door neighbour, Ivan, offers his services. You politely reject his offer and hire 50-year-old Sally from the Friday night Bible study. Congratulations! You have just made an assumption.

Life is full of apparently unconscious choices. These unconscious choices are based on (often faulty) reason and emotions. These reasons and emotions are formed by many years of experience.

People have opinions on everything, even if they can't express them succinctly. They are not a blank slate (*tabula rasa*) as John Locke would have us believe (Isaiah 64:6). [124] Our opinions are based on reason from experience. For instance, have you ever wondered how you know what your shoes taste like? You know because you stuck it in your mouth when you were twelve months old. (Also, our opinions are based on our emotions and honed from our experience).

Why do men cringe when they see a soccer ball travelling quickly toward a man's private area? They cringe because they have experienced the feeling of a ball hitting this area before. But women have not – yet they still cringe watching this situation. This cringing is because people extrapolate out their experiences to fill in the blanks.

> *'There are no facts, only interpretations.'*
>
> Friedrich Nietzsche

> *'I am the Way, the Truth, and the Life. No one comes to the Father except through me.'*
>
> Jesus Christ

Consider a longer example. A man is told to enter an empty lecture theatre seating 500 people and take a seat in any place he wants. The man chooses the third chair from the aisle in the middle column on the 23rd row. Now, the man could have opted for any seat he wanted, but he chose the third chair in the 23rd row because of his underlying assumptions. His conscious brain forgot why he wanted that place; but, his unconscious brain remembers the lecturer looks like his maths teacher in sixth grade whom he didn't like.

We operate with these assumptions. We live by a worldview based on assumptions we have learned, have experienced and have been taught. We then extrapolate these assumptions to fill in the blanks. We believe our assumptions are rooted in truth. We feel we know it and have experienced it. Therefore it must be true. But, in reality, we're assuming it.

For example, Richard Dawkins assumes the earth is four billion years old because the 'evidence' (radiometric dating) tells him so. Creationist, Jonathan Safarti, presumes the earth is about 6,000 years old because the 'evidence' (the Bible – and science) tells him so. Christian evolutionists (thieistic evolutionists) believe in other 'evidence' that tells them so. Each accepts their own 'evidence' to prove their worldview.

Is Science King? What Does the Most Famous Scientist of All Time Say?

The **most famous scientist in history**, according to the Royal Society of UK Scientists, is the theologian, **Isaac Newton**. Newton outranked **Albert Einstein** in two polls with 61% of scientists saying Newton was more influential.

Of Newton, it was said, 'the overriding goal of his studies was to learn more about God'. Newton, himself, talked about science in his famous quote, saying, '**To myself, I am only a child playing on the beach, while vast oceans of truth lie undiscovered before me.**' Both Einstein and Newton were partly homeschooled.[125]

Following the evidence people accept is the question, 'Where do morals come from?' If your ultimate truth comes from anti-Christian books like the *Origin of the Species* or *Mein Kampf*, you'll think man is the final 'decider' of truth. If you hold the Bible as your ultimate source of truth, God will be your reference.

Given most teachers are non-Christians, it's safe to say these teachers will be teaching many anti-Christian assumptions. These beliefs can lead to a ruthless worldview where one man's belief, if consistent, is as valid as any other man's. In other words, the bully has as much right to bully, as the victim has not to be bullied. In the end, the stronger person wins  (survival of the fittest). Survival of the fittest should be a horrifying worldview.

But, no moral compass at school means no one knows what's right or wrong. A secular book on discipline had the following to say on morals:

> *You have probably wondered many times why people do undesirable things that seem to serve no useful purpose – why they are discourteous and disrespectful; why they try to harm each other; why they do not eagerly take advantage of the educational opportunities handed to them; and why at times they lie, cheat and steal. Because we consider these behaviours undesirable (or worse), we call them misbehaviour, or bad behaviour. Bad behaviour, just like good behaviour, is a product of ongoing interactions between psychological needs and socio-environmental influences that are part of the human condition.*[126]

Hitler and Eugenics

One of the greatest admirers of the eugenics movement was Adolf Hitler. Hitler, who praised eugenics in his famous book 'Mein Kampf', wanted to create an evolutionarily supreme race of humans.

In some schools, the moral compass is now so relative that right and wrong are decided by that which causes most frustration to school authorities. So long as you don't hurt anyone, you can do what you want. For instance, if gossiping doesn't hurt anyone, why should it be banned? As such, limits proposed by teachers are always moved. Under a relative worldview, limits are never static.

The Darwinian View

Darwinism is a prominent theory in many educational institutions, most noticeably in schools, universities and even many churches. Evolution is a popular biological theory developed by Charles Darwin in the 19th century. It says all species evolved from smaller, simpler organisms into higher, more complex ones through advantageous random mutation. The weak ones died off because they couldn't survive in an environment where stronger species are always winning the food or survival 'contests.'

Social Darwinism is human survival of the fittest. It tries to show individuals (or groups) get an advantage over one another because of genetic superiority. Strictly speaking, according to Social Darwinism, if one child belts another child to the ground, it's supposed to show the bully is biologically or genetically superior to the victim. Similarly, if a boy catches a puppy, swings it around by its tail, bashing its head into the concrete until it's dead then that act is a natural part of natural selection. It's just a part of showing one's superiority over other species. It's not wrong, but beneficial!

Darwin was deeply motivated by the people in his life. While the death of his daughter gave him the excuse he needed to believe a bad world is inconsistent with a good God, 'his devotion to the teachings of Charles Lyell was of far more significant influence. While Darwin travelled on his famed *Beagle* tours, Lyell's work was with Darwin as his 'constant companion.' Lyell's aim was to free men from the science of Moses.

Darwin was an anti-Christian man, even though he was trained for the priesthood. His philosophies lead (and have led) to dangerous ideas that cause pain and suffering that affect the weakest in our society the most. We don't protect and 'give justice to the weak and the fatherless' or 'maintain the right of the afflicted and the destitute' (Psalm 82:3) when we preach Darwin's evolution in our classrooms. Almost every science class teaches Darwinism as the ultimate theory of genetic upheaval and optimisation.

Eugenics

Darwinism spawned other amoral ideas like eugenics.[127] Eugenics is an investigation of the conditions under which 'men of a high type are produced.'[i] Eugenicists believe in making improvements to humans by cutting out or neutralising undesirable traits. The practice was most

---

[i] Francis Galton, English Scientist who coined the word, eugenics. Galton was also Charles Darwin's cousin.

common around the 1920s as the 'educated' started such abortion clinics as *Planned Parenthood*. Eugenicists decided what features were considered desirable in the new evolutionary human race. One of the movement's greatest admirers was Adolf Hitler, who applied eugenics theory in his famous book *Mein Kampf*.

In the early 20th century, forced sterilisations of men and women in America by the government were commonplace.[128] Targets included the 'feeble-minded' and the 'defective'. Eugenicists were convinced traits such as alcoholism, epilepsy and pauperism were genetic traits that should be wiped out from society, leaving only intelligent, wealthy and healthy individuals. Altogether, 60,000 children were sterilised in America under this policy.

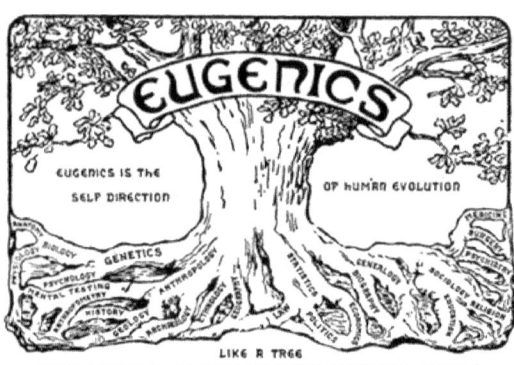

Eugenics Propaganda: Logo from the Second International Eugenics Conference, 1921.
[Source: Curators of the University of Missouri.]

In the 1930s, America's work so impressed Hitler, he asked for advice from California's top eugenicists on how to adopt the program in Germany.[129] Sadly, Germany took it even more seriously, and many horrific experiments were conducted on human beings who were considered genetically inferior.

As much as eugenicists denigrated inferior genes, superior genes were glorified. Baby Hessy Levinson (pictured) was thought to have superior genes. Hessy's picture was selected as the front cover for the Nazi's *Sonne Ins Haus* propaganda publication. Ironically, Levinson was (unbeknown to German authorities) a Jew.

The Nazi Party even financed a study by Dr. Earnest Rudin to prove the Aryan race was superior to other races. Hereditary health courts were set up, where children could be sent (by their teachers or doctors) to have sterilisations ordered. The health courts determined if children were genetically unfit. If they were found to be unfit, they were sterilised.[130]

As we know, the Nazis didn't stop at sterilisation; murdering defectives 'purified' the human race faster. Doctors were granted the power to order murders for Germans who were 'incurably ill', such as the senile, criminally insane and those with 'inferior genetics' like the Jews. Physically and mentally disabled people were also targeted.

The popularity of eugenics accelerated after Charles Darwin died. The theory, once adopted, created many disasters, culminating in the atrocities of the Holocaust and attempts to conquer the world through the 'superior Aryan race'. However, the public disliked the practice, and the programs were eventually abandoned. But, not before doctors had killed more than 50,000 children and babies.

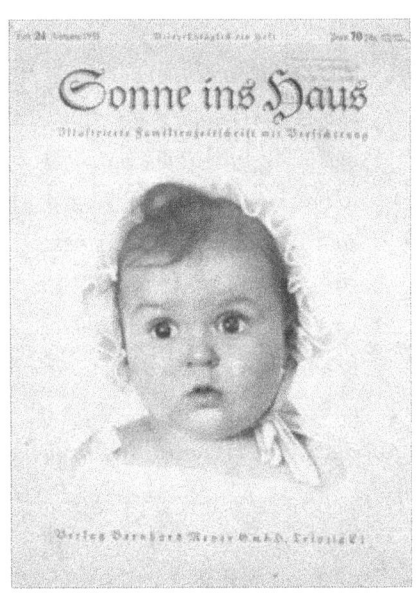

Today's society still practices eugenics. Eugenics can be seen when parents abort babies of the 'wrong sex' after a highly precise ten-week maternal blood test for fetal DNA. The test, which costs about $500, accurately predicts a child's sex and any genetic abnormalities.[ii] Doctors believe babies of the 'wrong' gender are being weeded out by unhappy parents at this

---

[ii] This test is, for a fee of about $500 (in 2015), done at ten-weeks and can determine the sex of a baby before the conventional ultrasound at 19-weeks.

time. Eugenics is also still being taught in both Christian and non-Christian schools, as schools promote the teaching of Darwinian evolution (which can lead to eugenics as has been shown). We've forgotten what eugenics does to human society. We've forgotten the horrors of WWII and the Holocaust.

Humanism

Humanism is a system of thought in which followers attach prime importance (or worship) to humans instead of God. This man-centered religion is widespread in Western society today with a large proportion of those with 'no religion' aspiring to humanistic thought. This brand of secular thought seems to pervade many of our public-school classrooms.

In Kevin Swanson's book *Apostate*, Swanson talks about the success of humanism, saying:

> *The problem with man as God is that he makes a terrible god. Humanist man makes his own laws and then proceeds to break them (Rom 2:14-15). His sole ethic is to attain happiness, but he struggles to define it and he is quickly forced to admit he doesn't have a clue as to what would produce it. He pretends to be sovereign, but he finds that he cannot even control his own wife. He wants to be the centre of life and worship but finds that nobody else worships him. He speaks with a voice of commanding authority, and the next day he is proven wrong by his two-year-old son. In his waning years, he runs out of money to provide for his own needs. Man makes a very poor god indeed!*

What is Truth?

Because a universe 'governed' by inanimate matter, motion and chance has no right or wrong, humanists have no good reason to accept any substantial values (and Christian values cannot be accepted or rejected). Humanists cannot tell good from bad. They must spin a roulette wheel and let chance decide. Therefore, evil can be good, and good can be evil.

According to humanism, morality is a choose-your-own-adventure novel. And just like the novels, if you pick the humanist pathway you can end up in deep water. Humanism claims to base its truth on man's reason. In this case, every person's view is equal and equally valid.

Our society operates like this. People decide what they think is right via democratic consensus.[iii] It's not based on higher authority because man is (apparently) the only reasoning being.

> **The New Tolerance**
>
> GK Chesterton once wrote, 'Tolerance is the virtue of the man without convictions.' This is because it's easy to be tolerant of things about which you have no convictions.
>
> For example, you can be tolerant of sexuality if you believe sexuality is determined biologically. But if you have objective convictions you're deemed intolerant.

For humanists, reason is based on pragmatism (what works for that person). And pragmatism is based on what feels the best for the greatest number of people. Therefore, if the individual making the ethics curriculum has lesbian feminist friends, they'll probably be sympathetic and include pro-homosexual and feministic literature in the curriculum. However, because these agendas are commonly subtle, it can be difficult for parents to recognise.

For example, a New York school student and lesbian, Jesse Bethel, joined with the American Civil Liberties Union to demand the school stop discrimination against homosexuals in their curriculum. District officials agreed, and as part of their agreement, officials showed pro-homosexual films and assigned homework about same-sex

---

[iii] This is not to say democracy doesn't operate well at times. As Winston Churchill said, 'Democracy is the worst form of government, except for all the others.'

families. Australia has recently shown signs of wanting to follow America's example.[131]

Another example shows rife blurring of gender boundaries. In California, students can choose which bathrooms they use depending on which sex they feel like on the day. This choice means girls can use a boy's urinal and boys can use a girl's toilet. The bill signed by the Californian Governor outlines how kindergarten children should be encouraged to *decide* what gender they are and then act accordingly. Again, Australia has taken steps to follow their lead.[132]

But, humanists have no good reason to reject (or accept) Christian values because a universe governed by matter, motion and chance can have no right or wrong. Humanists don't have a reason to teach ethics because human reasoning without God is empty. It's like studying a roulette wheel every time a ball falls into a pocket and trying to figure out an order. There isn't one.

Self-Actualisation

Self-actualisation is a theory and practice based on Abraham Maslow's work in the 1940s. The theory claims to be a positive psychology that leads followers on a journey to maturity. It's a favorite pedagogical philosophy adopted by many Western teachers today. To be the most 'fully human' being you can be, you must unleash the 'potentials' within yourself and walk the pathway of maturity.[133]

Maslow claimed he could separate people into categories where one person was more psychologically fit than another. Given support and opportunity, Maslow thought people would grow to maturity. His theory, which was based on his '*Good Humans*' study, showed different people have different needs. The more needs that are satisfied, the higher the individual reaches to peak experiences (see Maslow's pyramid).[134]

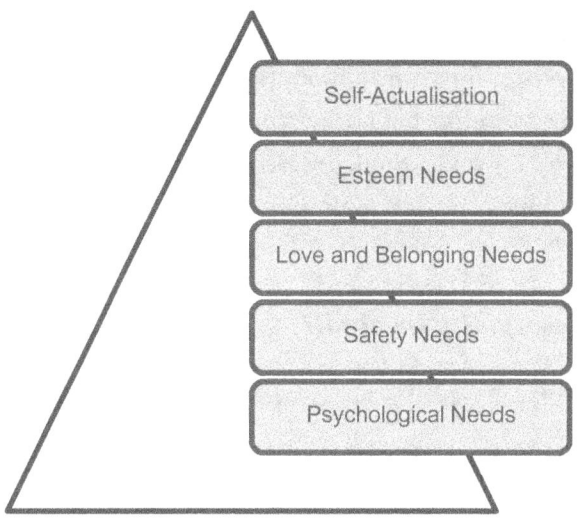

[Source: SimplyPsychology.Org.]

Schoolteachers are taught to aim for peak experiences in children. Unsurprisingly, there was even an eHOW page for teachers with instructions on how to create a self-fulfiled child.[135] It's paraphrased as follows:

Step 1: Provide food, clothing and shelter.

Step 2: Make sure children feel safe. Stop bullying or a bomb going off in the playground.

Step 3: Encourage socialisation.

Step 4: Promote self-esteem.

Step 5: You have the perfect human being who can give back to society. This person will be completely content and balanced, secure in their maturity.

Maslow's theory is dangerous for Christians because it completely fails to mention God. Self-actualisation a selfish and self-based ideology. Failure to fulfil a rung means self-actualisation cannot be reached. In other words, if you're put in prison for your faith and forgo psychological, safety, social and esteem needs, self-actualisation (or growth into maturity) will not occur. Christians, however, think differently. They find joy and maturity in trials and hard times.; in fact, trials are periods of personal growth (James 1:2-4).[136]

Is Anti-Homosexuality Immoral?

In the name of tolerance, schools are increasingly accepting ungodly behaviour, such as homosexuality. Steven Jay Gould, a renowned leader of the highly religious atheistic movement, said, 'Nothing is more dangerous than a dogmatic worldview – nothing more constraining, more blinding to innovation, more destructive to openness to novelty.' Gould dogmatically believes in 'not being dogmatic.' This contradiction is being adopted in many schools today.

> **'She's Just a Friend...Isn't She?'**
>
> If children see something accepted and affirmed, they tend to be quite influenced, especially if the advocates of the action are people the children trust. Because children are at a very impressionable age, teachers, parents and schools have the potential to affect student's identity and life choices. A prime example of this influence is seen in our society's propensity to affirm homosexuality.
>
> If children are always hearing about homosexual relationships, they may come to wonder if they are a homosexual. If a child has a best friend of the same gender that they have a strong affection for, they might be drawn towards homosexuality if their school, teachers or parents are continually accepting and affirming homosexuality as a good lifestyle choice.
>
> Many children naturally develop 'best friend' relationships in school which are usually of the same gender. But, an over-emphasis on homosexuality can distort a child's perception and make them question their identity.

Many public schools openly favour supporting homosexual relationships. Christian schools are also softening their stance by teaching that 'homosexuality is just another sin.' Although true, this statement has an undertone which suggests homosexuality isn't a grave sin.

The pro-homosexual worldview is making many schools adopt immoral lifestyle choices. The current secular thought being advanced today is that anti-homosexual stances are immoral. That is, if you believe homosexuality is immoral, *you* are immoral.

The National 'Safe Schools Program' (SSP), federally funded in 2013, is supposed to be an anti-bullying program in schools. However, some groups, like the Australian Christian Lobby (ACL), are accusing the program of using its generous funding to protect homosexuals against bullying and normalise same-sex attractions. [UPDATE June 2017: Although the Liberal Federal Government has cut SSP funding, some states, like Victoria, are protesting and insist they will still fund the program using state funds.] In June 2016, the Federal Labor Party committed to finance the SSP if elected.[137]

The ACL claims the SSP misappropriated $8 million in state funding to create a pro-gay activist campaign disguised as an anti-bullying program. The SSP forces children to accept the normalisation of transgenderism and homosexuality in schools. This, according to the ACL, is in line with the Australian Education Union's radical policy supporting normalisation of these things.[138]

The ACL claims the normalisation of homosexuality and transgenderism is done at the expense of ignoring other bullied children. Now, about 65 percent of LGBTI students get physically or verbally abused by other students at school. While nobody should be bullied at school, including LGBTI students, Christians cannot agree with the *forced acceptance* of:

- The act of 'coming out' in schools
- The promotion of LGBTI behaviour

- The repression of Biblical values resulting from LGBTI protectionist policies.[139]

Today, some state governments want to be overt when protecting homosexuals. The Victorian government wants to set up a school pride program in public schools. Its aim is to install support programs for LGBTI students in public schools.[140]

Not only has federal Labour promised to legalise homosexual marriage if it wins office (2017), but the Victorian Labour party is carrying out its promise to install a program that supports LGBTI students who 'come out' in every public school.[141] At Melbourne's annual Gay Pride March in 2014, the (then) Victorian Labour opposition leader, Daniel Andrews, announced Labour would install a 'Safe Schools Coalition' that would create a 'safer, more supportive environment for same-sex attracted and [gender diverse] youth.' This coalition (started in 2010) was previously in 120 classrooms around Victoria on a voluntary basis. Now Andrews is busily carrying out his plans. The program will become compulsory and hugely expand the transgender and pro-homosexual vision in Victorian classrooms.

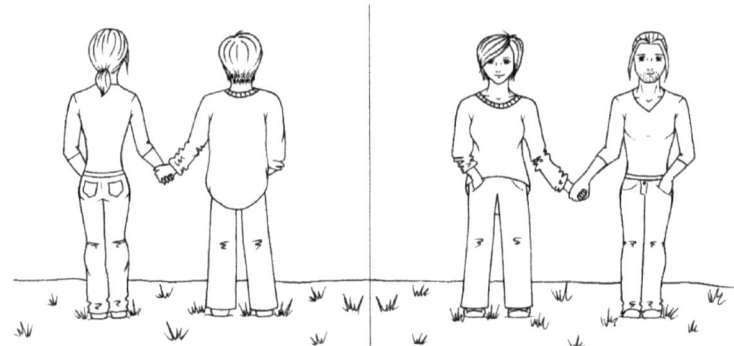

Godlessness

Whether children attend public or private Christian schools, they're almost always subject to the godless views of others. Because children absorb information like a sponge, they're easily influenced by their peers' views. Some of their peers' opinions come from anti-Christian parents and can have a strong influence on how children think about morality. The godless have no reason (besides the warm fuzzies inside of them) to follow God and do right (if they're consistent with their worldview). Non-Christians oppose Christians and sometimes believe teaching scripture to small children is warped and irrational – even abusive.[142]

One such person, Deborah Mitchell, who wrote *Growing Up Godless,* claims to hold an agnostic view. She offers advice to parents about how children can grow up without religion or God in their lives. However, Deborah presents several contradictory opinions. For instance, she says, 'We don't pray at the dinner table, but we are thankful.' The obvious question that follows is, 'To whom?' Mitchell says:

> *What does it mean to raise kids without religion? It means that, when kids ask why they shouldn't lie or why they should talk to the kid who is being bullied, you tell them, "Because it's the right thing to do, because you make the world a better place by doing the right thing." When you take god and religion out of the picture you place the responsibility on the shoulders of the children. "No", you tell your kids, "You won't go to heaven, but you can sleep better at night. You will make your family proud. You will feel good about who you are." When we help others 'because God wants us to,' we do not necessarily do it because we want to. Rather we have a prize in mind: God's approval, which translates into life everlasting. I suppose that morality backed by God is not a bad thing, but it can be a weak system.*[143]

Mitchell fails to realise naming something 'right,' means there is wrong in the world.[iv] This view comes, not from mere molecules floating in space, but from God, who decides all things (Rom 1:20).

After doing 'the right thing,' Mitchell says her children can sleep better at night. She believes doing this eases their minds. However, this philosophy is not consistent with many criminals who sleep soundly having just done some of the most atrocious crimes known to mankind. A good night's sleep is a bad motivation for doing the right thing.

And the question of what or who is to be the judge of Mitchell's right and wrong still exists (if people are just molecules as Mitchell infers). The reason 'because mother says so' is a poor reason to bring about child compliance that's purposeful and consistent – especially if your Mum doesn't claim to be God. Mitchell continues:

> *When you are raised without religion you tell the truth – while you are special to Mom and Dad, you are not special to the rest of the world. You are just a very, very small part of the big machine. Whether that machine is nature or society, the influence you have is very, very minute. No matter how important you think you are, the truth is, you're not. In the bigger picture, no one is important. The realisation of your insignificance gives you a true sense of humbleness.*[144]

Therefore, if a child loses his mother or father, there is little reason to continue living (if there was one before). This position also tries to replace God with friends and family. If friends and family aren't much to look forward to, hopelessness is a natural conclusion. It's the opposite of the Christian position which says that Jesus intimately cares for our every move

---

[iv] This is like the atheistic argument, 'I'm not going to believe in God because he let my son die. I can't believe in a cruel God.' This parent has just assumed God exists.

and thought. He cares for you whether you have a limitless supply of friends or not.

And Christ is always there as a friend, brother, husband, king and God. He supplies that which Christians lacks. Conversely, Mitchell believes:

> *When you tell your children there is no god, they begin to understand that family and friends are all they have, so they'd better treat them well. People depend on you. When you tell your children there is no god, they get a sense of immediacy, of how important and precious their time on this planet is. Yes, life is truly a gift. Blessed and lucky are interchangeable terms. They mean the same thing. You were damn lucky to be born and to be healthy and to have a life full of people who love and care for you.*[145]

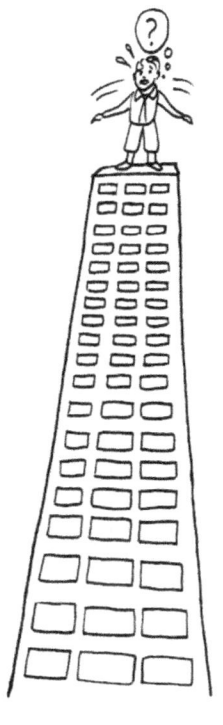

What Mitchell omits is that she thinks those 'unlucky' enough to be born into tragedy, without any hope, are then 'damn unlucky'. The 'gift' of life is no such thing if life is a hopeless spiral of anxiety and depression, as is the case for many non-religious youths today.[146] [v] This is evidenced by high rates of suicide among atheists in comparison to religious groups, as shown in a study by Kanitna Durvic et al. Durvic's study found that religiously unaffiliated (atheist or agnostic) people had significantly more suicide attempts.[147]

---

[v] Suicide was lowest during WWII and highest during the Great Depression.

Beyond the hedonistic enjoyment of their present lifestyle, atheism fails to create any hope for the unbeliever. Mitchell, the self-professing godless mother, says:

> *When you tell your children there is no God and something bad happens, they don't ask why God let this happen to them (after all, God loves them and how could he hurt them like that?) They understand that bad things happen and sometimes there is no reason. Tough luck. A bad break. Or, perhaps they see some sort of connection. X happens because of Y. But sometimes things just happen that are out of control.*[148]

The life of a non-believer offers no comfort. Things happen. Deal with it. Or don't. You can commit suicide. No one cares about you. You're worthless. You make no difference. Society might be better if you necked yourself. Then the world wouldn't have to put up with you. Except for God, there is no reason dictators such as Kim Jong Un, Sadaam Hussain and Idi Amin are morally wrong. With the moral compass spinning, who can tell right from wrong? Only God can show us the Way and point us firmly to the Rock (John 3:16).

A typically warped atheistic view is presented when Mitchell talks to her son about who created God, saying, 'As to answering his question about who made God, he would come to learn as he grows and matures [that] God is a projection of our ideal selves: strong, invincible, all-knowing.' If this is so, consistent atheist children become a narcissistic law unto themselves because they attempt to take on the characteristics of God himself. An atheist's view allows them to bully and gossip to their hearts content (so long as they don't invoke teacher punishment…but then, so what if they did?) They can be as bad as they want. Not only is God not the non-believer's Lord and Adviser, but they turn to mortals such as the astronomer, Carl Sagan, for advice:

> [Mitchell:] *Carl Sagan gives us a beautiful way to think of our recent arrival here. He said, "... the cosmos is also within us. We're made of star-stuff. We are a way for the cosmos to know itself." It is comforting in a sense to think of ourselves as offspring of the universe, where one day we will be returned, set free from the confines of the body and spread throughout the cosmos like a sneeze or even seeds... And awareness of this helps us to see Mother Nature as a friend to be respected and cared for, not as a foe to be used and conquered.*[149]

Perhaps we should discover who Carl Sagan is? Why should he be consulted? Carl Sagan's personal beliefs led him to a life where he was married three times and became a user and advocate of marijuana because it helped him with 'sensual and intellectual' experiences. But Sagan, although saying Christians were foolish for their belief in God, believed extraterrestrial life existed and researched it (with no results) to prove as much. One might wonder who the fool for his faith is: the person who has faith in God or the individual who has faith in aliens.

The Christian View

The Christian view is opposed to current Western pedagogical theories. Christianity assumes God exists. Christians hold to the position that all things are 'from Him and through Him and to Him' (Romans 11:36). Ultimate truth is based on absolute and purposeful morals, ethics and principles found in the Bible. This authority is from the everlasting and Ancient of Days who is omnipotent, omniscient and omnipresent. Other theories rest on whimsical, capricious and subjective opinions of sinful men with corrupt agendas, who run away from God (Romans 3:11). Only God can help people hold a genuinely purposeful view.

All Scripture is breathed out by God and profitable for teaching, for reproof, for correction and for training in righteousness.

2 Timothy 3:16

7. Preschools and Sacrificing Mums

Preschool

WHILE THE MANDATORY AGE FOR school attendance in Australia is about five-years-old, working parents sometimes send their young ones to daycare or preschool before this time. Primary care of children is done by the mother in the vast majority of Australian families, even more so within the Christian community; for this reason I will use 'mums' in this chapter. Because mums are often unwilling or unable to stay home with their infants, mothers return to work after this period and leave their babies in daycare. One mother said leaving her child behind was heartbreaking, 'I put my daughter in daycare at six weeks. I didn't have a choice because I had to return to work.'

This is a common refrain among working mothers who live in Western societies that say children don't need as much attention from their parents – an idea from Plato's *Republic*. Some educationalists and parents send their children to school as they still believe children ought to be socialised early.[150] Others are forced or inclined to send their children to school as they can no longer afford to stay home on a single income.[151]

Despite some educationalists advocating for early schooling, many researchers say later school attendance is better for children.[152][i] In his early childhood study, *Much Too Early*, Dr. David Elkind found children only develop the capacity to manipulate symbols when they are five or six. For

---

[i] David Whitebread, with 130 early childhood experts, signed the *Too Much, Too Soon* petition which called for children to start formal education at age seven as opposed to age four. This is in line with several European countries that have higher achievement levels. [See corresponding endnote].

this reason, younger children find math and reading harder than older children. A report by the Southwest Policy Institute has also warned parents that 'contrary to common belief', early schooling can harm children in many ways, namely emotionally, intellectually and socially. It can also cause them to become institutionalised as they become used to the school institution.[153] These institutionalised children develop many psychological disorders like fear, tension, developmental retardation, behavioural problems and other disorders.[154] Children need love and attention in their early years, not books and pencils.

Books and pencils so early in a child's life doesn't seem to work. Australian principals say children often need to repeat preschool because of cognitive immaturity on entry. Parents in Australia are beginning to enrol their children prematurely in school before children are ready. Parents do this as childcare costs are expensive and public school is 'free'. At $100 a day, the cost of childcare can tempt most parents into early enrollment. Wendy Hubbard, interviewed by *The Australian*, has a four-year-old daughter in preschool. Wendy said she is going to send her daughter to school for free as childcare costs $24,000 a year – money that could go on her mortgage.[155] Sadly, early enrollment means many children are entering schools before their fifth birthday.

Homeschool advocates Dr. Raymond and Dorothy Moore, suggest parents should let children decide what time formal education entry is right for them (see Chapter 13). The best learning environment for children is at home with their parents, which can ease their learning journey by providing help and access for children who want to explore the world around them. Parents far exceed a professional teacher's ability to give children what children need most – love and attention.

Sacrificing Mums

Donald Trump's 2016 campaign manager, Kellyanne Conway, said, after she refused to accept the role of White House Press Secretary, 'There are limits.' Conway was referring to women who take on too much at work and leave little time to parent. Conway said she could not accept the role as Press Secretary as it would be impossible to be a mother to four children *and* be

Press Secretary simultaneously. Conway addressed those who opposed her reasoning on the matter saying, the question shouldn't be, 'Would you take the job' but rather 'Would you want your wife to take the job.' Conway suggested women needed to learn there are plenty of opportunities out there for women, but there are limits as to what they can do. We must make wise choices, given our limits and opportunities.

Ph.D. Mother Gives Up Career to Homeschool

'My wife was very career-driven. You don't work for a Ph.D. in biomedical engineering without being that way. However, Angel has laid that aside to train our children...it's very challenging, but also very rewarding and I would encourage all parents to make an effort in this area. One hour a week at church cannot compete with 35 hours of government school and hours more of TV.'[156]

Chad Duty

Two things seem to significantly influence a mother's choice to be a career woman. The first is pressure from society telling mothers they are worthless and unsuccessful if they're 'just' stay-at-home mothers. The second is government pressure saying mothers must return to work.

While the world tells women they're unsuccessful contributors if they accept less than society offers them, the Bible applauds women who stay at home and look after their family.[158] Homeschool mothers make an immense sacrifice of their career when they homeschool. They sacrifice work, time and prestige for their children. In the past, staying at home was a natural

Are Mums Getting Older and More Educated?

The median age of mothers when they had their first child in 2010 was 31 years, up more than five years compared to 1971. By the age of 31, women have had a chance to develop and set up a career, making it that much more difficult to give up when motherhood calls. *The more they've invested in their career, the harder it is to give up.* According to the Pew Research Center, women in America who hold a bachelor's degree are 20% more likely to be working mothers than those who have not finished high school.[157]

part of motherhood. Now homemakers are viewed with derision because the status quo is to be a woman who 'contributes to society' by working *outside* the home.

Perhaps worse is how the government sees stay-at-home mothers. Women who stay home are viewed with hostility by the government. They're seen as inaccessible cash cows. The previous treasurer, Joe Hockey MP, seemed to reflect the government's opinion of stay-at-home mothers when he said, 'Another taxpayer cannot afford to pay you to choose to stay home.'[159] In 2013, the Commonwealth Treasurer said that after the youngest child turns six, mothers should head back to work. But, the idea that mothers are somehow a vast pool of untapped workers is warped and presumes stay-at-home mothers do no work.

This political message is already taking effect across the country. More mums than ever are heading back to work. In 2012, the *Australian Bureau of Statistics* reported almost eight out of ten mothers with children between six and 14-years-old participated in the labour force, a statistic that has increased over the years.[160] The way this arrangement works is by outsourcing childcare to daycare workers, grandparents, or other family members. This arrangement is supported in legislation with an increase in subsidies directed at working mothers. Simultaneously, subsidies aimed at family support in general, such as Family Tax Benefit B, have been cut. These entitlements were not supposed to be welfare but were compensation for income-tax deductions because of the burden of multiple children.[161]

These advocates for working mothers have short-term economic growth in mind when they rally mothers to work. Long-term economic growth is ensured by mothers with large families who produce good citizens.

The Australian government has demonstrated it has lost respect for stay-at-home mothers by cutting their entitlements (Family Tax Benefit B). But homeschooling isn't a burden on the state. Dotterweich and others (2013) surveyed homeschooled and private school children in the state of Iowa. They found significant tax saving compared to public school education.[162] Homeschoolers saved the state between $120 million and private school children $275 million a year. Homeschoolers and private schools provide a net benefit to public schools as they help pay for them. Because states can spend on average $12,000 a student a year, public schools can cost the government much additional money.[163]

In Australia, the NSW government pays $16,000 a year for each public school student.[164] Because the government says homeschooling is a valid educational option, Guy Tebbutt from the Home Education Association has suggested Australian homeschoolers should receive $10,000 annually a child.[165]

Homeschoolers save the government money. Initially, the government loses income tax when a parent begins homeschooling. The government doesn't save any money for the first child. But for every child after that, Tebbutt has recognised the family saves the state $16,000 per child per year! Tebbutt wrote, 'Given the government currently pays people to be unemployed, it seems logical and reasonable that it would be a better investment to support home educators that are actively raising and educating children to be quality members of our society.'[166]

Isabel Lyman, homeschool mother and codirector of Harkness Road High School, said homeschooling has produced literate students at a fraction of the cost of the public schools with minimal goverenment interference.[167] In this case, perhaps the government will consider scrapping public schools instead?

8. What About Christian Schools?

WOULD YOU STILL HOMESCHOOL YOUR CHILDREN if a good Christian school was able to meet your child's needs? While some Christian parents say they would be happy to use a school, others say they would homeschool no matter what. Their argument is that no school, no matter the quality, spirituality or opportunities offered, could create the personalised environment a loving parent can at home. Despite the availability of great Christian schools, no school can beat home.

School teachers, while they have affection for children, do not (and cannot) care for students in the same way loving parents do. Few people would take the steps a loving parent would to educate their children. Love is an essential part of a good relationship with children. As John Crudele, author of *Making Sense of Adolescence: How to Parent from the Heart* said, 'Kids spell love T-I-M-E.'

Another objectionable thing about Christian schools is that Christian schools are forced to teach in line with the government's curriculum. Although a Christian school's ethos and objectives often differ from a public school's (for instance, their mission statements often differ from public schools), they essentially teach the same material.

Parent disagreement with school policy and doctrine can also be a problem. Parents with deep convictions in different areas may not be able to teach their children effectively the subjects they're passionate about. Similarly, atheist parents with children in Christian schools must accept God is intrinsically involved in everything taught in the classroom.

But, even Christian schools sometimes separate education from religion. Teaching Christian religion and teaching other subjects are often treated as two different things (although this varies widely in Christian schools, some of which are better than others).

In a home school, however, Christian education is inseparable from family life. In this case, your Bible teacher is also your history teacher. At home, you might also learn history from the Bible, a rarity in many schools.

Also, while the ideology of Christian schools and their teachers are generally Christ-centered, the children flooding into their classrooms aren't always Christians. Problems with constant non-Christian influence arise when *peers* of Christian children in Christian schools come from humanist or other religious families.

Many religious institutions allow non-Christians into their schools, perhaps for the purpose of conversion. However, the reverse sometimes happens, and Christian children become converted instead.[168] Non-Christian parents often send their children to Christian schools as they want them 'experience Christianity' or 'become a moral person.' However, these non-Christian children bring the thoughts, feelings and morality of their parents to school. These views commonly include moral ambivalence, pro-liberal sins and other anti-God behaviour which Christians ought to reject.

While I was homeschooled for most of my school years, I spent three years in an Australian Christian school. I liked my teachers and, when I was older, I began to have adult relationships with some of my childhood teachers. I was impressed by their character and caring attitude toward their pupils. I believe they would have given their charges a godly example. However, these teachers said so many students they'd trained had not continued their relationship with God and had taken up worldly pursuits.

This outcome could not be blamed on these excellent teachers influence. But, what made their students derail? Charles Spurgeon wrote:

> *As a rule, the children of godly parents are godly. In cases where this is not the case, there is a reason. I have carefully observed and have detected the absence of family prayer, gross inconsistency, harshness, indulgence*

or neglect of admonition. If trained in God's way, they do not depart from them.

Kids Need Their Parents

I would say most Christian parents think Christian schools are not where their child gets their Christian education. This happens in the home. For young children we feel it is better in the formative years for their own parents to bring them through those years than a complete stranger who may (or may not) be a believer and struggling themselves with the faith.

William McAulay, Homeschooling Father. (Interview conducted August 2014.)

Spurgeon refers to Proverbs 22:6 which says, 'Train up a child in the way he should go; even when he is old he will not depart from it.' In short, Christian parents are not always training up their children in the way they should go, because seven out of ten children are walking away from churches after high school with only two-thirds returning in the next ten years.[169]

Many Christian parents are missing a crucial point. They are failing to train their children up in the Lord. Many are not taking the *time* to answer their children's questions and doubts about the faith. Why? Because the child is at pre-school, school or after school care, rather than being with their mother or father.  Teaching scripture to children diligently is hard when parents are separated from children because children are in school. And school usually provides little or no time to do these things.

PART 2: WHAT IS RIGHT WITH HOMESCHOOLING

Mark Demol's Story

From Student to Parent: How My Perspective on Homeschooling Changed

MARK DEMOL IS A RESPECTED MEMBER of his Baptist church and purportedly had some negative things to say about his homeschooling experience. As we talked, Marks warmth and gentleness made him likeable, personable and easy to respect.

Mark grew up in a large, Christian, homeschooled family of whom he is the second eldest. Mark is married to Deni and has two girls, a three-year-old and a one-year-old. He makes a living restoring historical planes and is extremely talented at the practical things in life (due in large part to his hands-on homeschooling upbringing).

Mark softly chuckled as he related how his wife, Deni, was 'educated' by her friends as to why she shouldn't date Mark. Deni's friends said dating Mark would not be wise because, although Mark was quite good looking, he was also homeschooled.

Rebbecca: Why did your parents decide to homeschool you?

Mark: They just weren't impressed by how we were turning out. There were a few teachers (well, one particular one) who they didn't like. When I had that teacher in primary school, I didn't learn anything (when I came home, all my workbooks were blank). And my brother was going to have that teacher, so they just kind of pulled him out straight away.

R: Did you like homeschooling more than school?

M: I didn't like school a whole lot. But for no particular reason (I had plenty of friends at school and was in good classes).

R: Did you miss your friends when you went to homeschool?

M: I missed my friends for a little while. For birthdays, we still had them over for a few years. I guess you just slowly move away.

R: What were your homeschooling experiences, especially what you found detrimental or harmful about those experiences?

M: I was trying to think of negative aspects, but looking back on it, I couldn't think of any. I think most of my memories have been positive. While I was going through it, there were things I didn't like as much. After I finished homeschooling and started working, I saw these people coming out of school, and they hung out with their school friends and *seemed* to have more stuff happening.

R: So, they seemed to have more of a social life?

M: Yeah, but I think that that was more to do with me and what I was doing at the time. When I moved out of home, it was different. I got to meet heaps of people, and that was fun. I could have just done that earlier and solved the problem. But I don't think that's an issue with homeschooling, although I perceived it was at the time.

> "Homeschooling has a bit of a negative image in our culture, which isn't a problem with homeschooling."

Looking back on my time as a homeschooler, there weren't that many negatives at all. Homeschooling has a bit of a negative image in our culture, which isn't a problem with homeschooling, but that can make homeschooling an unpleasant experience because *everybody thinks you're weird*.

R: Do you think there are negative things in your character that you would attribute to having been homeschooled? Or is that just part of your personality?

M: Well, looking at the social aspect of it, I'm very quiet...but, I don't think that's an issue with homeschooling at all. I think it's just that I'm quiet. That's just me. I tend to be a bit shy. I think that if I'd stayed in school I may not have been as quiet, because [the shyness] is forced out of you, such as when you're dealing with kids all the time. You're forced to get used to hanging out with other kids...otherwise, you will be by yourself all the time; *whereas if you're homeschooled and you're really quiet, you can just be really quiet. You're not forced to be social.* I guess you might not learn to hang out with a big group of kids your own age quite *as well*; but, I don't think that's much of a problem. I usually find homeschoolers can get along really well with people in wider age groups.

R: Do you think when you moved out of home, there were things about your homeschooling experience that didn't benefit you?

M: No. I think to the contrary. Homeschooling is good. Our family homeschooled with a Christian curriculum and Christianity was intertwined with everything we learned. Homeschooling was good because we were taught the right thing to do and the right way to live our lives in a godly way. Leaving home and working in a factory environment was a shock, but it's not like I was freaked out and wanting to follow what they did [peer pressure]. I actually knew the right thing to do, and I knew that's what I wanted to do. I think [growing up this way is a] better way.

> One of the biggest problems with school is the peer pressure thing. Basically, you have a few popular kids and everyone wants to be friends with them. If there is an awkward kid, it's fine to pick on them and it's funny. It really bugs me. The children aren't mature enough to see past that.

R: What do you think about Christian schools?

M: I think Christian schools are good...

R: Would you send your daughter there?

M: I would definitely prefer to send her to a Christian school over a public school. I don't know if this is entirely right or not, but I said to my wife the other day that *I think Christian schools make the best of a bad idea.*

I think today's schools are not such a great idea…whereas a Christian school is a better way to do a bad idea. From a Christian perspective, you have the values you want to teach your children…and with schools you have all these kids coming from everywhere and kids whose parents don't always care what the children do. These days, kids can do what they want, and they're encouraged to be independent and are allowed to get away with anything. They're thrown together – and your kids are in among it.

One of the biggest problems with school is the peer pressure thing. You have a few popular kids and everyone wants to be friends with them. Picking on the awkward kid is fine (and seen as funny). It bugs me. The children aren't mature enough to see past that.

R: What's your view on maturity? Do you think homeschoolers should be sent to high school?

M: Not necessarily. I'm not sure why you would unless you were worried about the academic side of things.

R: So, what you're saying is that, when it comes to homeschooling younger children you aren't worried about the academic side of things, but then in high school you become worried at that point?

M: No, I guess not. But in my head, that's possibly the only reason you would send them back…but I don't know why.

R: At the high school age would you say they are mature enough to go?

M: I think they're still too immature. It's probably generalising a lot, but I think children don't have the experience and are still too immature for [Years 10 or 11 of] high school. Maybe not in Year 12, because, at that point, students might be worried about their career and want to do well. But in the other years, they still just want to be cool and hang out with their mates and fit in.

R: How is letting homeschoolers out into a university or work life different to letting them out into a high school environment?

M: I think peer pressure is entirely different in those situations. People are more accepting of you for who you are, and there isn't this pressure to fit in at work. It seems like people make friends at uni more easily (therefore, it's a different situation there).

R: What do you think about the socialisation argument? That is, if you homeschool, you're not going to be properly socialised because you haven't had the benefit of relating to other children throughout your life.

M: In my experience, I haven't seen that at all. I haven't seen homeschoolers at all struggling to fit in with whatever they decide to do next. Sometimes parents choose to homeschool because their child does not fit into school for whatever reason. Socially they might not be as comfortable. Often that's why homeschooling gets that image – because the children are maybe like that anyway (though none of my friends struggled with this).

R: How has your view of your parents' choices of education changed from what you thought of homeschooling as a teen?

M: When you have children of your own you look at things differently. When you're a teenager, you're only thinking about yourself. You think, 'I'm not able to do this and I think it's because of homeschooling.' When you're a parent, you just think about doing the best thing for your child. As a Christian, you're worried about your children learning these bad things at school and you don't want

> *When you're a teenager, you're only thinking about yourself. You think, 'I'm not able to do this and I think it's because of homeschooling.' When you're a parent, you just think about doing the best thing for your child.*

that for your child because you love them. It's more about them. Being a parent forces you to think about it that way.

9. About Homeschooling

HOMESCHOOLING IS A LEGAL, MINORITY educational choice that provides an alternative educational pathway to traditional school. Homeschooling is most often chosen by parents who don't like school or who feel they can educate their children more effectively compared to schools. Unlike school, home education looks different depending on different faith groups and parenting styles.

Is 'Homeschooling' Just School at Home?

Homeschooling isn't just school at home. The word homeschooling should be called 'home education' as most homeschools don't look like schools. They don't involve copying school-like structures in a home environment. For most homeschooling parents, the reason home education is good is that it isn't like school. That's what parents were trying to get away from in the first place!

Replicating school at home seems to create too much stress for many parents. In *Write These Laws on Your Children: Inside the World of Conservative Christian Homeschooling*, Robert Kunzman relates how Cynthia, a homeschooling mother, tried to replicate the public-school curriculum at home. Cynthia tried to create 'public school at home' and found it was a disaster. Instead Cynthia opted for a premade homeschooling curriculum from *Sonlight*, and found the experience far less stressful.[170]

In 90% of homeschooling households, Australian mothers are the primary educators and fathers are the breadwinners.[171] Homeschooling parents seem to have a similar, or perhaps a little below average, income compared to the overall population.[172] In America, researchers have found home-educating families earned a similar wage to all married-couple families with children under age 18 and 'homeschool parents are somewhat above average in terms of their formal educational attainment.'[173]

A father and mother's personality is often reflected in the homeschooling curriculum. Parents who prefer more structure in their lives tend to favour a more organised curriculum. Those who prefer looser educational approaches are happy to take a more unstructured approach.

HOMESCHOOLING STYLEs

LIBERAL

Radical Unschooling
Child decides their educational (?) pathway with little input from their parent

⬅➡

STIFF

School at home
Mimicked school structure at home. Parent decides curriculum entirely with no input from child.

The graph below exhibits the extremes of home education. From my observations, I feel Christians who sit in the middle have the best approach to homeschooling. I say this as I've seen severe burnout with Christian homeschooling parents who try to structure things too formally; homeschooling parents who fail to structure at all seem to go against Deuteronomy 6:7. But, it appears that some families make things work that other families cannot.

Strict and inflexible education at public and private schools has also meant homeschooling is becoming more popular among 'free-living' families (known as 'hippies'). Other families that prefer homeschooling include Christian parents who object to secular schools and see problems with Christian schools.

The massive rise in homeschoolers (almost doubling every one to two years in some areas like the Hunter[174] is reflected in the decline in Australian public school enrollments. Public school enrollments are slower than ever today.[175] This decrease is due to dissatisfaction with the education system because of:

- bullying,
- religious factors,
- bad school culture,
- poor learning environments,
- boring or unchallenging curricula,
- lack of good character development,
- and dissatisfaction with how schools treat mentally or physically disabled children.

Many parents send their children to non-government schools, while a small proportion choose to homeschool. Homeschooling parents often believe they can do a better job of educating compared to non-government schools. Around half of all homeschooling parents homeschool after experiencing problems with school. Hence, many homeschoolers have spent some years in the school system before their parents realised homeschooling might be better.

How Many Homeschoolers Are There?

Homeschooling numbers vary depending on the country or state. This variance is caused largely by the legal position a government takes on homeschooling. Because homeschooling is legal and encouraged in America and Australia, these countries have relatively large populations of homeschoolers.

Some countries like Brazil, Germany and China outlaw homeschooling (except under extenuating circumstances). In many of these countries, religious exceptions are rarely considered. Places like the UK and Russia are making

---

Every Family Homeschools

Many parents say, 'I wouldn't know how to homeschool.' However, they don't realise they're already doing it. They homeschool their children outside school hours, from 4pm to 9am. Parents teach their children during meal times. That's why many parents, when they finally start homeschooling, seem to know what to do. They know because they were doing homeschooling all along.

Therefore, it doesn't make sense when a parent says they don't like homeschooling because that parent homeschools every day!

homeschooling almost impossible. Australia and America are relatively free to homeschool.[176]

In Australia, an estimated **30,000 – 50,000 homeschoolers exist (about 3-4% of the school-aged population).** In America, there are an estimated three million homeschoolers (about 4% of the school-aged population). Homeschooling is growing quickly with a **40 percent rise in just four years** (between 2010 and 2014).[177] Extrapolated out, this would be about a 30-fold increase since 1985.[178] [i]

This rise in Australian homeschooling numbers is smaller than America's rise which has been a **40-fold increase in American homeschoolers** since 1985. Now there are about two million homeschoolers, making up 3% of the population of school-aged students.

This growth is partly because homeschooling families have more children than other families. Researcher, Dr. Brian Ray, said homeschooling families have 60 percent more children than other families, with an average of three children.[179]

Germany has mostly outlawed homeschooling and only has 400 homeschoolers – not even close to 1% of the school-aged population. In Brazil, homeschooling is illegal. In Russia, homeschooling is difficult because the government pressures citizens to attend traditional schools.[180]

The NSW government has also been domineering in comparison to other state governments in Australia. This is reflected in the relatively strict curriculum expectations put forth by the homeschooling authorities. NSW homeschool registration is sparse because many homeschooling parents reject the

"In our homeschool group, we were the smallest family with only three children. The average in our group was five."

Joshua Hesford, Architect & Homeschool Graduate.
(Questionnaire, June 2014.)

---

[i] This number has been extrapolated out based on a 40% increase in homeschoolers between 2010 and 2014.

government's domineering education requirements, especially compared to other Australian states. Parents and the NSW government don't see eye-to-eye on curriculum issues, and each believes they're ultimately responsible for a child's education. [181] In 2014, the Home Education Association estimated there might be between 3,000 to 20,000 homeschoolers in NSW alone. [182] [ii]

Famous Homeschoolers

Scientists: Isaac Newton, Albert Einstein, Pierre Curie George Carver, Margret Mead and Thomas Huxley.

Writers: Hans C. Anderson, Pearl Buck, Agatha Christie, Charles Dickens, C. S. Lewis, George Bernard Shaw, Bret Harte, Beatrix Potter, Blaise Pascal, Mark Twain, Christopher Paolini and Laura Ingalls Wilder.

Inventors: Alexander Bell, Thomas Edison, Orville & Wilbur Wright and Benjamin Franklin.

US Presidents: John Quincy Adams, William Henry Harrison, Abraham Lincoln, James Maddison, Franklin Roosevelt, George Washington and Woodrow Wilson.

Artists: Leonardo Da Vinci and Claude Monet.

Actors, Composers & Singers: Taylor Swift, Lindsay Lohan, The Jonas Brothers, Hillary Duff, Wolfgang Amadeus Mozart, John Philip Sousa, Charlie Chaplin, Whoopi Goldberg, The Hanson Brothers and Jennifer Love Hewitt.

Religious Leaders: Joan of Arc, Jonathan Edwards, Philipp Melancthon, John Newton, Hudson Taylor, John and Charles Wesley.

Others: Florence Nightingale, Julian Assange, Bertrand Russell and John Travolta.

[ii] Homeschoolers must register, although they may be exempt if an exemption is granted. However, this exemption seems to be, in many states, just as easy to get and maintain as a homeschooling registration.

Should Parents or Governments Have Legal Control of Homeschoolers?

The state and the homeschooling fraternity disagree about who has the higher duty and responsibility to educate children. The Bible is clear parents have the responsibility to bring up children properly (Prov 22:6). And, even the *NSW Education Act* says parents own this duty.

However, states have the right to make laws on education and can change laws whenever they wish. The state is also, according to Romans 13:1-5, our governing authority to whom we are to be subject for our good. As Christians, we must be careful to remember this passage in Romans alongside Proverbs 22:6 and Deuteronomy 6:7.

Reasons Parents Didn't Register for Homeschooling in NSW

According to the NSW Parliamentary Inquiry (2014) the top reasons parents didn't register were due to:

- Philosophical objections.
- Prior negative experiences with the regulatory system for homeschooling.
- Perception that registration offered no benefits to the family and is quite onerous.[183]

Governing authority is enforced by government inspectors in most Australian states. These inspectors oversee registered families through home visits, reviewing the homeschooler's curriculum and quality of work. They are one of the main reasons parents don't register in NSW.

Failure to register is particularly noticeable in government states that have stricter education requirements, such as NSW. Those with fewer homeschooling requirements, such as Victoria, seem to experience higher rates of registration.

It seems that if parents and states don't see eye-to-eye on homeschooling issues, parents solve the problem of the power imbalance by homeschooling illegally. At the same time, governments appear to turn a blind eye to illegal homeschoolers by ignoring their illegal activity. Indeed, only one vocal case of illegal homeschooling has been prosecuted in Australia to date.[184] [iii]

> 'Inspector visits were one of the most stressful times of the year!'
>
> Bill and Antoinette Hesford, Homeschooling Parents. (Correspondence, April 2014.)

But, why do these parents risk prosecution? They take that chance because they don't believe the government has the right to impose 'domineering education requirements'. They don't register because they don't wish to be monitored by supervisors. Furthermore, there is usually no punishment for parents who fail to register.

Supervision is a tough issue because both parties cross swords about who has the higher duty and responsibility. States argue children without supervision are at risk of abuse. Parents claim they shouldn't be monitored unless school children are also monitored. These parents argue monitoring assumes homeschooling parents are guilty of abuse (or other things) and need to be watched.

Homeschooling parents say they are judged incorrectly, as the government begins by assuming parents are guilty of abuse until proven innocent. This assumption is repugnant to many homeschooling parents as parents have always been the ones to protect their children when the school system failed – not inspectors.

[iii] Bob Osmak, of the Home Schooling Association of Queensland educated nine children. He is the only one who has been prosecuted for illegal homeschooling in Australia. He was issued a measley $300 fine and had to pay the prosecutors legal costs.

Child Abuse in Schools and Homeschools

By looking online, you would think far more homeschoolers are abused, compared to public, private and Christian school students. This view is overwhelmingly supported by blogs and underwhelming supported by evidence.

The silence is almost deafening because the only research conducted on this matter shows public and Christian school students are abused more often than their homeschooling peers. Below are some relevant papers on this issue:

National Home Education Research Institute STUDY

(2016)

American homeschooling researcher, Dr. Brian Ray, conducted a rigorous study examining the above question. He surveyed 9,369 participants. To increase integrity and validity, Ray purchased a national, independent business study of 907 participants to act as the baseline of his study.

Ray found there is no evidence saying homeschoolers are abused more often than school children – quite the opposite. Ray found 'those who were homeschooled were significantly less likely to have been sexually abused as minors than were those who were public schooled and those who attended private Christian schools. Further, there was no significant difference in the rate of having been sexually abused as a child between those who were homeschooled and those who attended private non-Christian schools.'[185]

Homeschooling's Invisible Children ARTICLE

(2015)

While a pro-homeschooling organisation produced the study above (the *National Home Education Research Institute* or NHERI), only one other published article has been conducted on homeschooling, using available public data and government statistics.

This article is from an organisation called *Homeschooling's Invisible Children* (HIC). HIC doesn't claim to promote or denigrate homeschooling – it only appears to want its regulation in American states.

HIC concluded, 'the rate of death from child abuse does not appear to be lower among homeschoolers than among families who are in the public school system.' Unlike the study by the NHERI, the HIC article was only a review of data, not a rigorous study, backed up by an independent, control study, like the NHERI study.

Also, the HIC article is confusing because, while HIC claims 'preliminary research suggests that homeschooled children are at a greater risk...', they produce no evidence of the fact. Their actual findings showed there was no difference (something we are only told towards the end of the article).

Unless HIC is biased against homeschooling, I fail to see why they should mention their preliminary 'findings' when these findings are erroneous (based on their own data).

Also, HIC claims to get their evidence by looking at cases in their HIC database of abused children and government statistics. In case you missed it, this is like taking statistical data on overall teenage criminal behaviour from only the juvenile prison population![186]

Conclusion

Homeschoolers are less abused than school children. Based on limited research, it seems homeschoolers are safer at home than public schools or Christian private schools.

Reasons People Homeschool

People with little exposure to homeschoolers, often think homeschooling is practised mainly by people with extreme religious views. Although many homeschool parents are religious, many homeschoolers (especially Australian homeschoolers) don't have a religious bone in their body.

Why do homeschooling parents homeschool? The NSW Board of Studies asked this question in their 2013 survey of homeschoolers. Outlined below are the reasons parents choose homeschooling:

- 17% said they chose to homeschool for philosophical reasons,
- 14% special learning needs,
- 5% religious grounds,
- 3% bullying,
- 25% other reasons and,
- 37% declined to respond.

The religious percentage seems quite small in this study. The Parliamentary Homeschooling Inquiry Committee commented on this study, saying, 'whilst only five per cent of applicants completing registration forms for homeschooling nominate religious reasons for homeschooling, 17 percent nominate philosophical reasons and a further 36.5 percent gave no response. It is reasonable to assume that that true number opting for homeschooling on this basis is higher than the five percent disclosed.' [187] [iv] This indicates the percentage of parents who homeschool for Christian reasons could easily be around a third to half of all Australian homeschoolers.

The Inquiry also found a heightened sense of responsibility on parents' behalf was common among the cohort of homeschooling mothers. Homeschooling mothers desire to play a bigger role in their children's development than schools allow. These mothers don't believe their children will necessarily adapt to life well without as much parental influence as homeschooling allows.[188]

What Influenced You to Homeschool?

"We listened to a set of recordings with the school [our child attended], and they asked the question, 'Why do we educate our kids?' Most people responded, 'We educate them to grow up and get a job.' But that's not the important thing for us; it's growing up and getting a Christian character.

So, we homeschooled because we thought the development of a Christian character in our children was more important than just gaining information - not that non-Christian school doesn't focus on character, but their primary focus is to inform. So we thought our children are not going to get [much Christian character at school]. "

Steven and Barbara Fraser, Homeschool Parents. (Interview conducted May 2015.)

[iv] Worldwide, homeschoolers present different pictures. A study conducted on American homeschoolers found most homeschoolers are Protestant Christian while many others are atheists, Jews, Muslims, Buddhists or Catholics. Many of these religious groups homeschool because they think they can do a better job of passing on their religious convictions and beliefs, compared to public or private school education.

Homeschooling parents want to reclaim the control over their children's lives that they feel schools take away. Rather than schools, parents want to be the major carers of their children. Homeschooling parents want to start participating more in their children's lives – as much as they did before school or daycare started.

From the interviews conducted for this book, it seems many homeschooling parents often started homeschooling because they notice their children becoming unhappier and changing for the worse at school. This can sometimes be brought on by bullying. Bill and Antoinette noticed a change in their children's behaviour and character when they attended school:

> *The kids were always happy. They always played together happily before they went to school. But, almost as soon as they went to school, the eldest child, Joshua, would be crying. He'd have his arms lifted up towards us as if to say, 'What are you doing? Why are you leaving me here? I don't want to be here. I want to be with you – I'm always with you.' But, we were stoic; we thought it was best to leave him with them.*

Even though children might be dreadfully unhappy at school, many parents persist in sending their children to mainstream schools, because going against the flow and trying homeschooling is thought to be detrimental or just too hard. Many feel they must go with the majority and provide a good education by encouraging their children to go to school. This pressure causes parents to question themselves about whether they're qualified to look after their child's education in a homeschooling environment. Consequently, some resent the school system for the widely-held assumption that schools are 'better qualified' to take care of their children. After all, there must be some reason very few Christians are homeschooling.

The thought of homeschooling is terrifying for almost everyone who has never done it (author included!) But, courage can be propelled when Christian parents run out of alternatives. Lack of options made the McAulay family think about homeschooling after their seven-year-old began struggling at school:

The main influence was that our son was miserable about school. In the morning, he was crying and didn't want to get into the car to go to school. So we had to look at alternatives. That's what got us looking at homeschooling.

A parent's concern for their child who is flailing at school is one of the main things that helps parents overcome their fear of homeschooling. Those who were afraid of the consequences of homeschooling realise how effective homeschooling can be and embrace home education.

Parental Reasons to Homeschool (By Grade Level)

The spiritual and educational needs of children change with age. Younger children tend to have different issues with school that propel their parents to homeschool, such as character development concerns. Older children tend to encounter more bullying problems as they go through puberty or change schools.

Homeschooling researcher, Guillermo Montes, asked if parental reasons to homeschool vary by grade. Montes wanted to know if there was a correlation between the age school was stopped, and the particular reason parents had to stop schooling.

Montes found younger homeschoolers in grades K-3 were twice as likely to homeschool because of parental objections to school teachings. K-3 parents seemed more concerned with what their children learned (especially morally) than those in later grades.

Many homeschooling parents who were originally unwilling to let their young children attend school let their teenagers decide if they wanted to attend Year 11 and 12. Homeschooling mothers and fathers felt their teenagers were now mature and prepared enough to handle bad influences at school.

Younger K-3 children were three times as likely to be homeschooled. Parents of these children believed their positive influence was vital for their offspring's proper growth. Half of these parents said their objections were religiously based. But, even the other half of homeschooling parents (who identified as non – religious) had a significant proportion of parents who said they wanted to develop character and morality in their children (60% of non-religious parents).[189]

The table on the next page is an abridged version of those in the Montes study and details the reasons parents homeschool by grade level.[190]

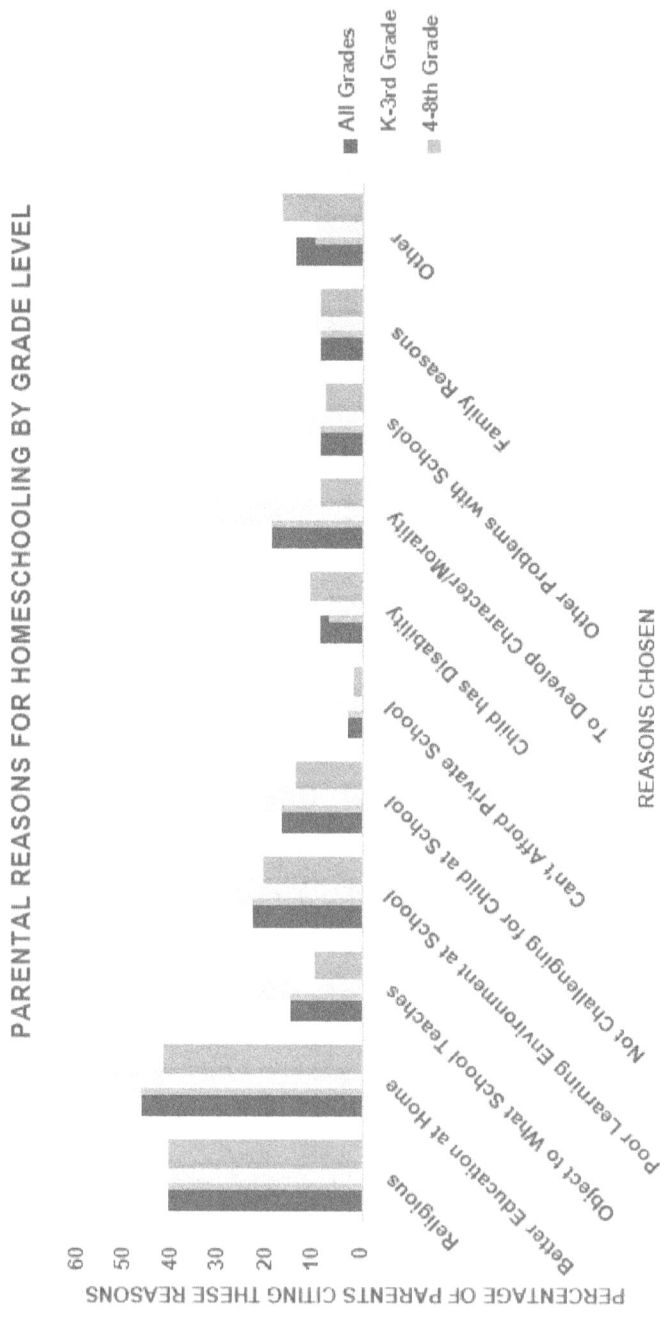

A significant reason parents with younger children homeschool has to do with their increased protectiveness and sensitivity to younger children. Parents feel children are more vulnerable and malleable to incorrect curriculum teaching at younger ages. Many of these parents homeschool from day one.

Parents with older children (4-8th grade) begin homeschooling more often as they notice how much school peers are influencing their children. Many previously well-behaved children change for the worse as they learn to copy naughty kids around them. This becomes more obvious in later years when many parents withdraw their children from school.

When schools fail to teach children properly (even after parents have tried many solutions for many years), parents decide to give home education a chance. Many ask, 'How could it be any worse?' Others choose to homeschool after hearing about how effective homeschooling is at teaching children according to their strengths.

A Good Reason to Homeschool

Homeschooling has a significant influence on a child's choice to follow in their parent's footsteps. The Gen2 study found homeschooling educations meant children were much more likely to follow their parent's beliefs compared to children in public, private or Christian schools. They also found school adversely affected a student's satisfaction with adult life, their Christian beliefs as an adult and the amount a child would follow in their parent's footsteps.

Ray, B. (2015). Gen2 Survey.

In older children, many parents reason homeschooling can work to the strengths of their children and reduce stress in disabled students. The Montes study chart shows more parents withdrew their disabled children when they were older. This is partly because some disabilities like hearing loss, are not detected until later.

At any time, parents can start homeschooling as they travel around the world. Homeschooling makes travel easier. Parents who start travelling and therefore begin homeschooling sometimes find their children are happier and succeeding academically. Therefore, some of these parents keep homeschooling their children after their time of travelling ends.[191]

10. Homeschooling and Christianity

IN THE WEST, CHRISTIANITY IS BEGINNING to decline. Christianity is being replaced with two religious camps: one is religious, humanistic thinking, the other is radical Christianity as defined by the Bible.

As we have seen, the first religious camp, humanism, is taught in public schools.[i] Public schools, first invented for 'social efficiency, civic virtue, and character, rather than mere learning or advancement of sectarian ends,'[192] were originally Christian. However, as public schools began to turn away from Christianity, Horace Mann, an American educational reformer and politician received responsibility for the Massachusetts Education Portfolio in 1827 and then represented more secular educational concerns on in the House of Representatives. Mann, a Unitarian,[ii] was commonly known as 'The Father of the Common School Movement'.[193] Under his leadership and the leadership of non-Christian men, public schools were 'debarred by law from inculcating the peculiar and distinctive doctrines of any one religious denomination'. Public schools began allowing all religions and all types of 'Christianity', including the popular and heretical Unitarianism position.

This is how public schools first started in America. Soon, the principle of debarring Christianity in public schools spread to Western nations like

---

[i] Humanist Manifesto I, signed by John Dewey, one of the public school entrepreneurs, says, 'So stand the theses of religious humanism.' Thereby, humanists admit humanism is religious by design. The Manifesto advocates replacing the Christian religion practiced by their forefathers with humanist religion.

[ii] Many considered Unitarians to be apostate Christians. Unitarians (literally 'one who rejects the doctrine of the Trinity') believe God is one person, not three. Unitarianism also strips Jesus of full divinity. Examples of Unitarians are Jehovah's Witnesses and Christadelphians.

Australia and public schools became places to teach secular religious thought to future generations.

In America, a hundred years later in the 1960s, those who disliked the rigid educational ways of public schools started homeschooling. Many of the early homeschoolers were free thinkers who were considered hippies. These hippies pioneered the way to homeschooling. Soon Christians saw they could teach their children Christian ways, without having to be involved in the godless public school system.

Therefore, the second religious camp is serious Christianity, distinguished from the old, slowly-fading cultural Christianity. Serious Christianity is fostered in Christian homeschools around the world, whereas the hollow form of nominal Christianity, is dying out and being replaced with humanism. Humanism's entrance has been made easier by the relabeling of humanism as 'Christian Humanism', a philosophy of thought that has nothing to do with Christianity. Rather, this philosophy is called Christian Humanism because moral aspects of the philosophy are supposed to resemble the good deeds of Christians.

Christian Humanism is likely what many schools mean when they use the title 'Christian' in their school name, without directly teaching the gospel at school. These schools want the Christian morals, but don't like the gospel or the observance of God's Word.

In many cases, these Christian schools don't greatly affect students' Christian values and behaviours compared to non-religious schools. Many are no different to public schools. Linda Gorman, writer for *The National Bureau of Economic Research*, talked about how little religious schools affect student behavior, saying private schools appear to reduce teenage sexual activity among girls but not boys. Only among boys do they reduce smoking, arrests and cocaine use. Furthermore, private schools have no apparent positive behavioural effects on children from single-parent households.[194]

Researchers noted a striking result of their study between schools was the similarity between religious and non-religious schools, 'there are no statistically significant differences between the various school types'.[195] They say that once family background, religiosity and other controls were included, the school effect of evangelical schools was like other sectors. Therefore, behavioural outcomes had more to do with family factors than school factors.[196]

In other words, if you put a non-Christian child into a Christian school, they won't be affected by Christian values any more than a public school student would be influenced by Christian values. Hard to believe, but that's the verdict.

But do Christian home schools more effectively pass on religious Christian values compared to religious schools? Since 1988, the *Nehemiah Institute* in America has been conducting an ongoing study measuring student understanding of the Christian worldview among homeschooled, public school and Christian private school children.[197] The Institute's test identifies a student's worldview on political, economic, educational, religious and social issues (PEERS test).[198] The PEERS test consists of a series of statements to which students agree or disagree. Depending on how the questionnaire is answered, the student is deemed to have a Biblical theistic, moderate Christian or secular religious worldview. The results, surveying 28,147 students, are displayed in the chart on the next page:

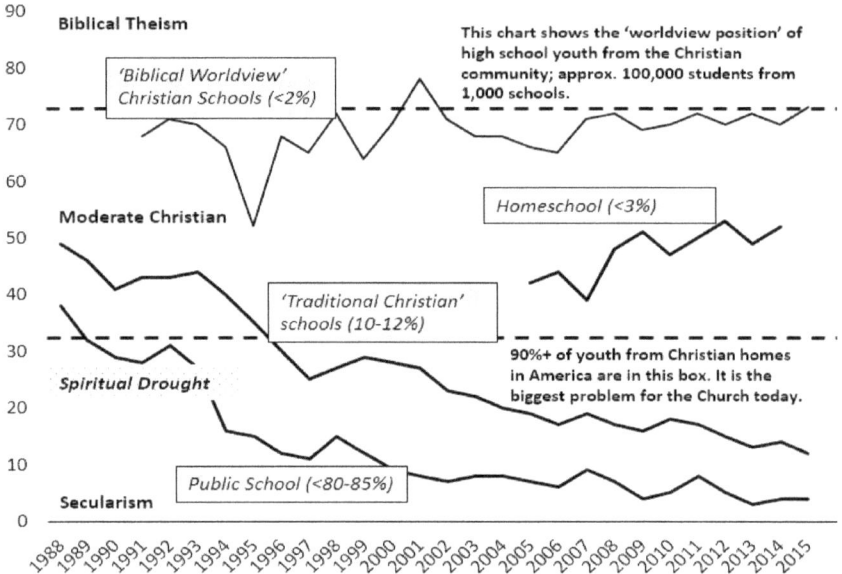

Students having a:

- Biblical theistic worldview scored 70 - 100.
- Moderate Christian worldview scored 30 to 69
- Secular humanist worldview scored 0 to 29.
- Socialist worldview bottomed out and scored 0.[iii]

Home schools score well on the PEERS test coming second to 'Christian Worldview Schools'. It's important to recognise homeschoolers that claim to be Christian can score better or worse depending on the Biblical worldview their parents teach them.

By Grace Alone

Homeschooling will not make your children Christians. It may help encourage them in their faith but homeschooling does not have the power

---

[iii] In America students are more likely to identify as a Christian because it's cultural to identify as a Christian. Australians do this, but to a lesser extent. So the statistics could be a little different if the same study were conducted in Australia.

to save. As much as any Christian parent would love to 'make' their child a Christian, it is not possible. There is no procedure, no step-by-step protocol they can follow. Only God's grace has the power to save. Unfortunately, Christian homeschooling lends itself to works-based Christianity as some see it as a method to work themselves and their children to heaven.

Over the last few years, my heart has bled as I noticed a disturbing trend among some homeschools where parents seem to trust more in their religious works to save their children. Often children from these homeschools become resentful and frustrated by the amount of sheer rules their parents, heap upon them. They heaped a burden on their children that they themselves could not follow. In short, many homeschools have forgotten about the gospel and the message of grace.

Instead, these families raise children in strict, religious environments, stuffed with rules, regulations and overly-strict punishments for transgressors. This doesn't have the effect of making them better Christians. Rather these religious homeschools breed resentful children who reject the gospel and/or their parents. At the very least, these homeschooled graduates reject homeschooling as they blame their woes on this method of education instead of their parents rejection of the gospel in favour of works.

These religious homeschools are reminiscent of the Acts 11 'circumcision party' who heaped rules on people and expected them to follow them as the Old testament believers did under the Old Covenant. They forget we live under a new covenant of grace. As parents, they strictly mandate obedience and are quite ungraceful when children, even occasionally, go against their wishes.

I believe it's easy for any Christian to fall into the trap of works – especially Christians who are seemingly doing everything 'by-the-Book'. It's our sinful nature. That's why we must be constantly reminded of the gospel. The gospel forgives the repentant sinner, despite their having contributed nothing to grace. As such, we too must be parents who forgive our children and teach grace above works in every area of our homeschool – especially if we want to call our homeschool a Christian, gospel-centered homeschool.

Empathy, Altruism and Pro-Social Behavior

The aim of Christian teaching is to train children in the way of the Lord. Part of this involves training children to behave in a godly manner, with empathy, altruism and generosity. Parents have the primary role of instilling these traits in their children. But, are Christian homeschooling parents better at cultivating these qualities compared to other Christian parents?

Kingston and Medlin (2006) are researchers who compared homeschoolers and mainstream school children in these measures of empathy, altruism and pro-social behaviour. Empathy, according to the researchers, encompassed taking the perspective of others, sympathetic concern for others, feeling distressed at others' misfortunes, and becoming emotionally involved in books and movies. Altruism was defined as a willingness to help others even if self-sacrifice was required. Pro-social behaviour was defined as 'honesty, cooperation, generosity and other positive traits'.[199]

Do Fewer Christian Homeschoolers Abandon the Faith?

There seems to be some evidence that positive relationships with parents and parental attitudes toward Christianity correlate with lower apostasy rates among Christian teenagers. Therefore, teens who spend more time with parents are expected to have lower apostasy rates. So homeschoolers with strong parental relationships will experience lower apostasy rates.[200]

Before children were measured, researchers looked at their Christian parents' values and religion. They asked parents to give a score to the following questions:

- My religious faith is important to me.
- Religious faith is very important to my child.
- I attend religious services two or three times a week.
- It is very important to me to provide religious instruction for my child.
- My child agrees with my values.
- My child's school reinforces the values I try to teach him/her.

- It is very important to me to teach my child the values I believe in.
- I want my child to decide for him/herself what values to believe in.

For all questions, except the last, Christian homeschooling parents' scores were higher than Christian public school parents, indicating homeschooling parents 'were more concerned [about] teaching their children their values and religious beliefs, and more convinced that their children's education reinforced this endeavour, than public school parents'.

When researchers measured different characteristics between homeschoolers and public school children, researchers found public school children were inclined to be less altruistic and to showcase themselves in a positive light more than homeschoolers.[201]

Homeschoolers were thought to be motivated to be more altruistic, because of they wanted to follow their parents' teachings more than public school children (this desire is maybe what caused homeschoolers to be better behaved, compared to school children, in this study). Concerning these results, Kingston and Medlin said:

> *Do these results mean that homeschooled children consistently behave more morally and altruistically than other children? Not necessarily, even though their parents suggested they do. Advanced moral reasoning and sincere altruistic intent… do not always lead to principled and unselfish acts.* [202]

Kingston and Medlin continue to say the motivation to behave well and be more altruistic is possibly different among homeschoolers and public school children. This may translate to homeschoolers describing their behaviour more realistically, in contrast to 'public school children [who] were more likely…to present themselves in an exclusively positive light.'[203]

Christian homeschoolers are not less *intrinsically* sinful compared to their school peers (Rom 3:10). But, Christian homeschoolers have compelling motivations that change their behaviour to be more altruistic compared to their public school peers who don't have these motivations.[204] These homeschooling motivations include a desire to please their Christian parents, by harmonising their values and beliefs with the example set for them.

Although homeschoolers were more altruistic, they were not more empathetic. Empathy scores between homeschoolers and school children were on a par. Kingston and Medlin discussed the higher altruism but equal empathetic scores, saying:

> **Homeschoolers More Pro-Social**
>
> In Kingston and Medlin's study, homeschoolers exhibited more prosocial behaviours such as honesty, cooperation and generosity compared to public school children
>
> Kingston, S and Medlin, R. (2006), pp. 1-10.

> *These results could mean that homeschooled children more readily translate empathetic thoughts and feelings into altruistic intent than public school children. Or perhaps altruism is based not only on an empathetic understanding of others but also on an ethic of unselfishness* parents teach their children…*perhaps homeschooling parents teach standards more successfully than public school parents.*[205]

By looking at their morally mature parents (rather than their immature peers), homeschoolers can better learn altruism and unselfishness. Learning from parents means children will more often copy their parents in everything, including faith.

Are Homeschoolers More Likely to Keep Their Faith?

The home environment gives parents a better opportunity to train children in Christianity without having outside distractions that vie for a child's heart and soul. One researcher, Tracy Romm, concluded parents' primary motivation for homeschooling was to was to facilitate the transmission of values to their children. [206] [iv]

[iv] Romm's study was a case study of eight Atlanta homeschooling families. Romm intensively interviewed these families and directly observed their home lives.

Christian families, according to a 2005 survey, make up at least 70-96% of homeschool families in America.[207] The percent of Christian homeschoolers in Australia is thought to be much less. Still, Christians seem to make up a substantial proportion of Australian homeschooling parents, many of whom hope their faith will be passed on to the next generation.

Is there any evidence homeschooling can more successfully pass on Christian values compared to public, private and Christian schools? Let's look at the *Gen2 Survey* by Brian Ray. This survey was an in-depth look at homeschool graduates with an average age of 27. The purpose of the study was to 'understand the key influences that either encourages or deters [millennial homeschoolers] from believing or practising the faith of their parents'.[208] [v]

The following graph is an abridged version of the results from the *Gen2 Survey*. It illustrates the correlation between the method of education and certain other outputs, such as orthodoxy, Christian behaviours, satisfaction in adult life and similarity of beliefs to parents.[209]

---

[v] Although many homeschoolers participated in the study, a special effort was made to encourage public, private and Christian school children to take part in the study. The study looked at 9,369 subjects, 70% of whom were female. An independent business study with 907 participants was used as a baseline to enhance integrity and validity of the larger study's results.

Key

Degree of Influence	Positive	Negative
Trivial	+	-
Small	++	--
Moderate	+++	---
Large	++++	----
None	+/-	

Adult Life Outputs	Orthodoxy	Christian Behaviors as Adults	Satisfaction in Life as an Adult	Beliefs similar to Parents
Strong Relationship with Parents	+++	+++	+++	++++
Attend Church at Early Age	+++	+++	++	+++
Attend Church at an Older Age	+++	+++	+++	+++
Homeschool*	+++	+++	++	+++
Christian School*	--	--	+/-	--
Private School*	--	--	--	--
Public School*	---	---	--	---

*Comparing children educated for at least seven years in their particular education system.

In this graph, we see homeschoolers take on their parents' beliefs more readily than any of the school children, even Christian school children. Homeschoolers appear to be much more influenced by their parents compared to school children, especially in the areas of Christian behaviour and orthodoxy.

Ray's findings are consistent with Tracy Romm's qualitative study that found all eight homeschooling families interviewed had cultivated strong character traits in moral and religious beliefs. Romm attributed the gaining of these traits to homeschooling.[210] [vi]

Another researcher, Wayne McEntire, wanted to see if homeschoolers fulfilled the religious and behavioural expectations of their parents. McEntire surveyed Baptist General Convention of Texas (BGCT) church students in grades 7-12. In his study of 3,795 participants, McEntire found 80% of homeschooling students in the Washington State got the highest orthodoxy score possible, a reflection of the high amount of religious material they studied in their books and curriculum materials.[211]

McEntire also cites a study by Smithwick in 2001, which found Christian private schools and Christian home schools affirmed a biblical worldview in more than 50% of the issues addressed. In contrast, public school students from the same evangelical denominations held a biblical worldview in only about 17% of the same issues.[212]

What about Christian school's influence compared to Christian home schools? Wayne McEntire's study of Grade 8-12 students were analysed for their responses to some questions developed by Josh McDowell's Ministries. The questions looked at children's behavioural, dispositional and attitudinal answers to the questions posed.

Significant results are as follows:

[vi] Romm's study was a case study of eight Atlanta homeschooling families. Romm intensively interviewed these families and directly observed their home lives. [See endnote.]

ITEM	PERCENT WHO ANSWERED YES: *Homeschoolers/ Christian School Student*	STATISTICALLY SIGNIFICANT: Yes - .000 No - .004 (2-tailed).[vii]
Watched MTV at least once a week	16% / 43%	.000
Used an illegal, non-prescriptive drug	2% / 10%	.004
Lied to parent, teacher, or other older person	66% / 79%	.050
Attempted suicide	0% / 4%	.004
Drank enough alcohol to be legally drunk	2% / 12%	.000
Gambled or bet money on something	13% / 25%	.030
Stressed out	34% / 55%	.006
Angry with life	4% / 18%	.000
Confused	28% / 53%	.001
Always tired	29% / 50%	.004
Seeking answers	45% / 71%	.001

McEntire's study shows homeschool parents are succeeding at influencing their children behaviourally and morally, to a greater extent than other Christian parents. Christian homeschoolers are participating in less harmful

---

[vii] A 2-tailed significance of less than 0.05 shows a result deemed significant (or meaningful). If it is above 0.05 the result is deemed to have possibly come about as a result of 'random chance'. Scores of more than $p=0.05$ were omitted from the graph here, but can be found in McEntire's study.

and risky behaviours compared to their Christian school peers. These results show homeschoolers are significantly different from their Christian school peers in many ways.

The influences affecting homeschoolers' positive behaviours are attributed to parents, according to McEntire. In contrast, Christian school children engaged in riskier behaviours because of the negative influence peers exerted on Christian students during their six to eight hours at school each day. McEntire found homeschoolers display less risky behaviour because their parents have the opportunity to weave moral precepts into their children's curriculum. Parents teach in a pro-Christian environment as opposed to a hostile environment; this supportive environment can reinforce positive values.

McEntire also suggested children would have better morals modelled to them in a Christian homeschool because homeschools were more likely to have two parents in the home who foster better behavior among the youth. The researcher said homeschooling parents may make more accurate assessments of their child's likelihood to do wrong and, therefore, these parents may be better prepared to correct their children's behavior pro-actively.[213]

It seems McEntire is suggesting homeschoolers behave well because they are continuously monitored and taught the right things to do by their parents. They can be appropriately corrected at home, whereas teachers have less authority to discipline other people's children.

Throughout the study, homeschoolers described themselves as less busy, not as tired, less stressed and less angry at life. A low-structure, high-flexibility environment were likely contributors to the less stressful homeschooling environments. Because homeschooling parents provided a more loving and less stressful environment, students were not as tense as their school peers.[214]

Dispositionally, homeschooled students showed more of a solidified Christian worldview as they were less likely to describe themselves as confused or seeking answers.[215] A coherent or less confused worldview is helped when children have quality, purposeful relationships with parents as opposed to a confusing lot of competing value systems.[216]

Critics say homeschoolers have a warped worldview as they haven't been exposed to the diversity of worldviews and backgrounds most children experience at school. Critics believe homeschoolers are indoctrinated and subject to intellectual enslavement under the instruction of their parents. But, having like-minded parents teaching the same worldview is a positive thing because while Christian homeschoolers are not exposed to a diversity of beliefs and backgrounds, they do learn about different beliefs from a Christian worldview. [217] [viii] They meet others of diverse backgrounds through their socialisation in church, homeschool groups and other community groups. For example, Christian homeschooled girls are taught by their parents that many boys from different backgrounds want girls due to lust. Good homeschooling parents tell their girls to beware boy's advances. Parents watch their girls in these interactions and address any potentially harmful situations directly.

This way of learning is cleaner and less hurtful to children compared to being exposed to different views of sexuality at school and having to pick for themselves. Of course, Christian homeschooling parents choose the child's way of teaching and methods of socialisation but having loving parents pick these things is better than having the politicians, government schools, or even children themselves choose.

A Christian homeschool can ground highly emotional and impressionable teens. Homeschooling gives parents an opportunity to teach their teens how to give an answer for the faith they have while protecting them from confusing and harmful worldviews.

[viii] Researchers defined pro-social behavior as 'actions that evidence honesty, cooperation, generosity and other positive traits.'

11. Can I Afford to Homeschool?

IS HOMESCHOOLING AFFORDABLE? Affordability is a huge concern for parents interested in homeschooling as education must be affordable to work properly. After all, the average family pays taxes to the government and, therefore, many parents think they should send their children to public schools, so they don't have to pay for their children's education twice.

Homeschooling will probably never be cheaper than public school. But homeschooling is affordable. Home education is as expensive as you want to make it. When buying into homeschooling, parents can choose a variety of plans ranging from free to expensive curricula.

One advantage of educating at home is that parents have a choice to buy, rent or borrow books from friends or libraries, depending on their budget. These books are often reusable with following children.

Homeschooling Resources Online

Free, online resources are everywhere. Curricula, eBooks and printable worksheets are constantly being written and available for homeschooling parents willing to search for them. Some are past patent

You Might Have Bought Them Anyway

Many necessary educational expenses would have been gained if parents sent their children to school because some textbooks must be purchased irrespective of education choice.

protection and can be downloaded legally for free.[ix] Free online software also exists.[x]

Many of these resources are high quality, such as those from the Khan Academy. Some parents believe homeschoolers can complete most of their education at the Khan Academy. The Academy encourages this and has placed videos on the effectiveness of homeschooling with their resources. (Check out *Start Homeschooling with the Khan Academy* at the footnoted web address[xi]).

Are Prepackaged Curricula Any Good?

While most mothers criticised packaged curricula, pre-made curricula can be a good idea for flustered first year homeschooling parents who feel they don't know what they're doing.

As parents develop teaching skills, many will find they can plan or modify the curriculum later.[218]

Homeschool Coalitions

To make homeschooling even cheaper, families can volunteer their time in homeschool coalitions. Homeschool coalitions are simply groups of homeschooling families that pool their resources to get more bang for their buck (and for socialisation reasons). For instance, four families might hire a tutor to teach their children languages. Or one parent might teach art lessons for a term and then take a break the next term as another parent takes over and teaches their unique skill.

[ix] These can be found in the public domain.
[x] For example, free typing programs are available from freetypinggame.net.
[xi] https://www.khanacademy.org/resources/parents-mentors-1/homeschool-with-khan-academy/a/start-homeschooling-with-khan-academy

Planning Your Curriculum

Designing a curriculum is less overwhelming than it was years ago. Many websites suggest what things Australian parents should teach as their children reach older milestones.[219] Some websites also spell out government requirements and how to fulfil them. [xii] If you're worried about the government requirements in your state, join the local homeschooling groups and ask parents how they manage these issues.

Homeschooling Cost Breakdown

The cost of homeschooling depends on the curriculum you choose. While there are plenty of free online resources, private tutoring and music lessons can make your costs rise quickly.[220]

The cost of homeschooling varies with each child's talents, interests, disabilities, and giftedness. If your youngest has a fondness for books, they might be content curling up with a borrowed library book. If your eldest has a fondness for electronics, you might spend a little extra buying gadgets.

Michelle Morrow, homeschooling mother of four and author of the *Homeschooling Downunder* website, estimates educating your first child is more expensive than following children. As parents find their feet and learn how to reuse old materials, homeschooling costs drop.[221]

Morrow did a rough outline of how costs decrease with subsequent children depending on the educational provider:

- Distance education provider will cost
    - $2500 AUD for the first child and
    - $1900 for the second
- Designing your curriculum
    - $2000 for the first child
    - $1500 for the second child

[xii] For a state by state look at homeschooling laws, see Devitt, R. (2017) *Australian Homeschooling Laws*. Why on Earth Homeschool from
https://www.whyonearthhomeschool.com/aussiehomeschoolinglaws.html.

- Natural learning
    - $1500 for the first child
    - $1500 for the second child. [222] [xiii]

Other homeschooling writers suggest you can homeschool on as little as $250 USD per year, per family![223] However, some say homeschooling is the most expensive form of education because it requires a parent to forgo another income.[224] Of course, the cost will also be highly dependent on what you and your children value in an education.

Pulic School is Pragmatic

If choosing schooling is just about the cost, parents ought to choose public school. However, if you want the *best* Christian schooling, consider homeschooling.

Is School More Expensive than Homeschool?

Private Schools

Homeschooling is a very cheap option compared to private school. Most private schools are expensive and can cost as much as $35,000 a year.

Prices among states and territories range widely. Victoria is the most costly and Canberra is the most affordable. At Canberra Grammar School, parents pay a comparably modest fee of $20,140 per year for Year 12 students. Geelong Grammar in Victoria will make you cry as you cough up a whopping $35,721 a year.[225] But, this annual fee is just the beginning. A parent will pay an initial enrollment fee of about $500 to $6,000 to register their child for private school on top of the five-digit annual fee.

More charges arrive as the reoccurring cost of uniforms, textbooks, excursions, bus fees, special programs, computer equipment, musical

---

[xiii] 'With a budget of $725 per year you could include: a maths program and an online maths subscription ($80); an english program ($175) plus reading books ($200); a science program, such as Apologia ($120); a history and geography resource ($150). Reusable resources can greatly reduce costs for the second child to around $300.'

instruments and annual building levies pile up. After all, those pristine lawns the students aren't allowed to walk on must be maintained.

How much does private school cost in total for an average family? According to *The Australian Expatriate's Gateway*, it will cost more than $500,000 to send two children through an Australian private school.[226]

Christian Schools

Christian schools used to be affordable. Now they are far less economical with prices rising constantly. Rising costs are perhaps not the school's fault entirely as augmented government funding for private schools has meant the gap must be made up by paying parents. Schools determine funds based on tuition fees, fundraising levies, building contributions, annual class fees, subject levy fees and a one-off enrollment fee.

The following list outlines the costs of some Australian Christian schools in 2016:

- Tyndale Christian School (Sydney, NSW): $5,470 Junior; $6,840 Senior
- Illawarra Christian School (NSW): $5,904 Junior; $8,225 Senior
- Maranatha Christian School (Victoria): $5,769 Junior; $8,423 Senior
- Trinity Christian School (QLD): $6,234 Junior; 8,852 Senior
- Kingsway Christian College (WA): $5,450; $7,775 Senior
- Marrara Christian School (NT): $3,440; $5,600
- Christian Schools Tasmania (TAS): in 2007 fees were 'from $1200 Junior'; 'from $3,925 Senior'
- Leighland Christian School (TAS): $2,500 Junior; $5,975 Senior
- Canberra Christian School (ACT): $ 3,930; $4,460 Junior
- Brindabella Christian School (ACT): $ 4,672 Junior; $7,788 Senior.*
  *Prices according to school websites.

On average this works out to be $4,456 per junior student and $6,786 for a senior student each year. Of course, additional costs apply. One school included over $800 in additional costs on top of annual school levies.

Homeschooling Mothers Saving the Government Money

The government says stay-at-home mothers should start working because the government can't afford for them to stay at home. However, it seems homeschooling stay-at-home mums save the state a lot of money.

If a public-school student costs around $12,500 per year of taxpayer money and females pay an average of $11,500 in tax* the cost of one public school child in school a year is more than one mother would contribute in tax. Therefore, homeschooling saves the government $1,000 in tax if just one child is homeschooled with a stay-at-home mother.

Some argue the economic impact of an extra $33,500 ($45,000 minus $11,5000) floating in the economy is of more benefit. They must remember that homeschool families have an average of three children per family. If these three children went to public school (costing taxpayers $37,500 per year) while their stay-at-home mother went to work, the economic impact would likely be nullified by the very high cost to taxpayers of sending three children to school.

Of course, the above argument fails to consider the positive economic impact of good (and plentiful) citizens. Citizens raised by homeschooling parents seem to make excellent citizens by almost every measure and study.

Asking homeschool stay-at-home mothers to go to work doesn't seem to be a smart idea for the government. Perhaps they should reconsider their position on this issue regarding homeschooling families.

*$3,572 plus 32.5c for each $1 over $37,000. Women earn an average of $45,000 per year.

More Time at Work to Pay for School

An ethical problem remains for Christian parents here. It seems many parents have to spend more time at work to pay for expensive Christian or private school fees. Longer hours at work mean parents spend less time with children. Although spending time with children is a Christian action, Christian schools make this harder and harder with their high school fees. It might not be the fault of the schools themselves, but the reality of Christian schools is they are expensive and reduce family time together as parents work more to pay for such costly education.

Public Schools

Every year, the Australian government pays about $12,500 per public school student on a parent's behalf.[227] This fee doesn't include additional school costs like those mentioned above. Although public schools are spruiked as free, many will cost parents significant sums. Sophie Cross from MotherInc.com estimated high school children will cost about $4,000 per annum for every child at a public school. This sum is inclusive of fees, lunches, uniform and extra-curricular activities.

This would make the cost of educating a homeschooler comparable to the cost of educating a public-school child. Also, if you homeschool three children or more (instead of sending them to public school), you will be saving taxpayers a considerable amount of money (see above/below).[xiv]

School Costs You Didn't Foresee

And there's more to school costs than just the fees. If you've got kids in school, get used to spending that cash – especially if your kids go to private school. School has hidden costs like those driven by peer pressure (keeping up with the Joneses). 'Mum, I'm going to look like a total dork in those pants. I need Levi's!' So you buy the Levi's.

Conclusion

Happily, homeschooling isn't just for the wealthy. Homeschooling works out cheaper than private and Christian schools. But, is homeschooling all about the money? Barbara Fraser, a homeschool mother, didn't think so when she said, 'Can you afford to send them to school and not have them grow in Christ?'

Barbara gets at the heart of finances. How we spend our money reflects greatly on what we value in life. Our actions also speak volumes to our

---

[xiv] This saving is attributed to the taxes the government might glean off another working parent (generally the mother). The taxes from one parent are less than what would be spent by the state on the children if more than three children were to go to public school from the same family.

children. Homeschoolers know they're more important to their parents than money and new clothes because those from second-hand stores are sufficient. Homeschoolers are more important to their parents than movies at the theatre because rented movies for $3.00 are adequate. They're more important to their parents than computer games because old board games are sufficient. They're more important to their parents than meals at fast food restaurants because home-cooked meals are sufficient.

By being frugal, families with only one income can still give children expensive instruments and other luxuries. Christian homeschooling parents make their money go further because they're serious about their children's education and spiritual lives- even if they're not spending $250,000 per private school child.

12. What About Socialisation of Homeschoolers?

BY NOW, THE SOCIALISATION QUESTION HAS BEEN KILLED, gutted, boiled, flayed alive and set to roast in coals several times over. On countless occasions, researchers have tested this issue statistically, only to find homeschoolers are *better* at socialising than their school peers. Even though the wider public still view homeschooling negatively, the general view towards homeschooling has improved. This is largely due to the flood of pro-homeschooling studies and literature on socialisation and other successful homeschooling prospects.[228]

One reason homeschoolers are so well socialised is that many Christian homeschool parents are acutely aware of the socialisation question. In fact, negative views on this issue have stopped many parents from homeschooling earlier than they otherwise would have. For this reason, many Christian homeschooling parents painstakingly ensure their children are well socialised because they realise the vital importance of socialisation with many people, Christian and non-Christian.

> 'My kids were much better at getting along with people of all ages when they were homeschooled and were able to be cheerful and outgoing in public and get along with their peers and friends. They learnt to interact with the world in a much more real way than being expected only to know how to communicate with other kids their age.'
>
> Jenny Allan, Homeschool Mother.
> (Questionnaire, March 2014).

What is Socialisation?

Before we look at the evidence, we must define socialisation. According to the Collins dictionary, socialisation is 'the modification from infancy of an individual's behavior to conform with the demands of social life.'[229] A longer, more descriptive definition from Dictionary.com says socialisation is 'a continuing process whereby an individual acquires a personal identity and learns the norms, values, behaviour and social skills appropriate to his or her social position.'[230]

Socialisation is important as it allows children to interact with their society in harmony with other members. Perhaps our society has underestimated the role parents play in this process, and simultaneously overestimated the role school staff and other children play in socialisation.

Does Socialisation Require Work?

Acutely aware of the socialisation question, many homeschooling parents go to enormous lengths to ensure their children are well socialised.

But, school children's parents often think socialisation comes with the territory. That is, stick your child in a group of other children, and they'll automatically learn good values, how to behave and to develop their personal identity.

God tells us good behaviour doesn't magically come about but is trained by constant prayer and meditation in the Bible (Psalm 119).

As Theodore Roosevelt said, 'To educate a man in mind and not in morals is to educate a menace to society.'

Are Christian Homeschoolers Socialised?

Are Christian homeschoolers socialised as per the above definition of socialisation? This book will argue they are generally well socialized according to the observations of homeschooling researchers and my own generalised observations.

The Christian homeschooler develops a *personal identity* when they sit, talk and walk with their godly parents regularly. When parents teach children to set their eyes on Jesus, Christian homeschoolers find their *personal identity* in Christ Jesus. Godliness is instilled using the Bible, which provides objective truth or *norms*.

The Christian homeschoolers' *values* are taken from the Bible. Their *behaviour* is modelled off Christ and their parent's Christian example. They learn *social skills* from the Bible as well as their parents' godly examples and society as a whole. Their *social position* is that of a servant, and a brother or sister in Christ.

It appears Christian homeschoolers are well socialised according to the dictionary's definition of socialisation. But, how do public school children stack up to the dictionary's definition?

Public School Socialisation

According to the above definition, many public school children are not well socialised. They suppress their *personal identity* by conforming to be like those around them. They often hide who they are until they can reveal themselves without criticism. Unless they have the will to resist the school's religious teaching, they gain their subjective *values* from humanism and their peers and teachers, many of whom are secular humanists. A humanist religion means *norms* have no objective basis and are fluid, therefore, unable to be established.

In general, public school children's *behaviour* is modelled off peers more than their teachers, especially in the latter years. [xv] Their *social skills* often become that of a person who

> **School Only About Socialisation**
>
> According to the public school social engineer and philosopher, John Dewey, school has little function besides socialisation. Dewey is quoted saying, 'Apart from participation in social life, the school has no moral end nor aim.'
>
> *Dewey, J. Moral Principles in Education, p. 11.*

[xv] See Chapter 2 on Peer Pressure.

appears to love the popular and ignore the unpopular. And, without Christian influences, public school students get their *identity* from humanity, not God.

Researchers seem to back up these assertions. Plenty of studies have shown homeschoolers are well-socialised compared to public school children. For instance:

1. Dr. Michael Slavinski reported that mass school socialisation has caused a proliferation of 'delinquent behaviour' among youth. Slavinski says student bodies are becoming increasingly filled with drugs, violence, illiteracy, promiscuity, comtempt for authority and peer dependancy.

2. Dr. Michael Mitchell found conventional schools promoted materialism, aggressive competition, 'being popular' and self-confidence. Mitchell's study showed these ideals are discouraged among homeschooling families. Instead, they encourage their youth to emulate integrity, responsibility, respect for others, biblical soundness, trust in God and an amiable disposition.

3. Dr. Thomas Smedley found homeschoolers have superior social skills (see graph). In his [American] *Vineyard Adaptive Behaviour Scales* test (a test to measure maturity and well-adapted behaviours in children in 1992), homeschoolers ranked in the 84th percentile, while public school children were only in the 23rd percentile. In the graph, the Mean Adaptive Behaviour Composite score of 115.55 for the homeschooled children is in the 84th percentile compared to the national norm: homeschoolers scored in the top 16%.

4. Dr. Larry Shyers administered the *Direct Observation Form of the Child Behavior Checklist* in a study designed to identify 97 problematic behaviours in homeschooled and traditionally school children. Those who were traditionally schooled exuded eight times more antisocial traits compared to their homeschooled peers.[231]

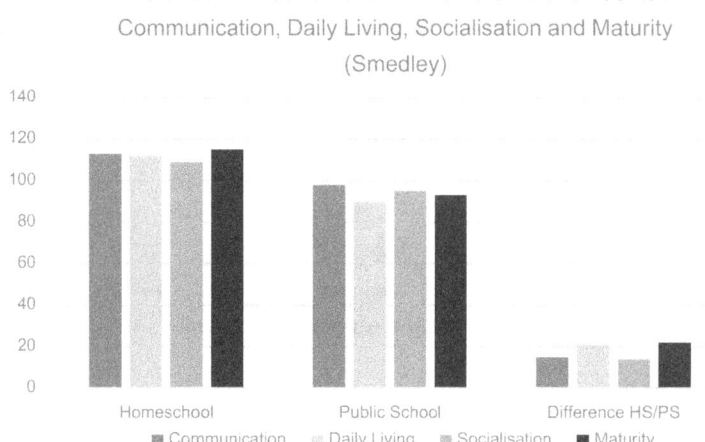

This data shows exposure to school life does not lead to proper socialisation. Indeed, school life seems to lead to a litany of bad behaviours and adverse consequences.

But aren't we being a bit biased, where are all the studies done by pro-school organisations that compare homeschoolers results? Surely, they would add to a fair discussion. It turns out, in one case homeschoolers were being tested by authorities, as officials compared them to public school children; but results were so embarrassing, the authorities decided to put and end to the situation: 'After a few years of suffering public embarrassment from press reports of homeschoolers outperforming public school students, officials started giving homeschool students different tests so that a direct comparison was no longer possible.'[232]

Socialising Difficulty in Remote Areas

In rare cases, socialisation is a problem for geographically isolated homeschoolers. To be clear, this problem is more often due to remote isolation, rather than inherent homeschooling factors (such as hiding children away from the world). In these cases, parents often choose to homeschool. This may be because of poor or absent school facilities, such as many missionaries experience.

In these cases, socialisation can be an issue. Although remote isolation means fewer people for homeschoolers to socialise with, according to the dictionary's definition, remote isolation is no excuse to produce unsocialized children, as parents should be the primary instigators of socialisation.

That is, Christian parents will teach their children about norms, values, behaviours, and identity, regardless of rural isolation. But even most families in rural homes find *some* social connection possible.

Deliberate Isolation of Homeschoolers

Those who deliberately isolate their children appear to make up only a small minority of homeschooling parents.[233] These parents deliberately separate their children from other families, often, because they fear all outside influence on themselves and their children.

When homeschooling parents deliberately isolate their children, despite having appropriate socialisation opportunities, homeschooling can be a nightmare for children. This nightmare is recounted in numerous anti-homeschooling blogs. These blogs show Christian and non-Christian

---
The Amish Rumspringa

The Amish rumspringa is a rite of passage into the Amish community after an Amish teenager decides they want to stay in (or leave) the Amish community.

During Amish rumspringa, the rules governing Amish youth are relaxed. Amish adolescents can engage in rebellious behaviour and defy parental norms.

Because they're not baptised (and the Amish Anabaptists only encourage baptism after teens have matured), many go out into the world and misbehave. Misbehaviour can be wearing non-Amish clothes, buying a car, television, going to the movies, nightclubs or bars.

After a time, the youth are encouraged to choose between the Amish community or the world's community. Most choose the Amish community.

parents are equally involved in homeschooling isolation.

A small minority of Christian homeschooling parents make the mistake of thinking other people, even Christians, equal bad influences. These parents forget members of the Christian body, such as their own homeschooling children, die if cut off from the Christian body.

Previously isolated homeschoolers sometimes become rebellious, and resent their parents for isolating them too much. Some of these homeschoolers suffer and go astray when 'released' into the real world as they are not used to, and cannot deal with the new pressures they face. Perhaps this is akin to the Amish practice of *Rumspringa* where Amish parents release their teenagers into the world, saying, 'Choose between them or us.'

Although I admire the Amish for many of their convictions, isolation for long periods is unscriptural. Isolationists give only two choices for people, both unbiblical. Firstly, they say we must be in the world and of the world (i.e. non-Christians). Secondly, they say we must be out of the world and not of the world. But this goes against Jesus commands to be in the world but not of it (John 17:15).[234]

Large Homeschooling Families

Jesse (the second eldest of 10 children) and Benjamin (the eldest of four) are in their mid twenties and grew up together in a home group.

Ben and Jesse were best friends and were in a close-knit group of four boys (one of whom was Ben's brother). To this day, Ben and Jesse are firm friends. They continually spend time together and are close with each other's families. When asked if they would describe their relationship, they said their relationship would be more like cousins. This intimate socialisation among home groups is standard.

Jesse Rose and Benjamin Buckley, Graduate Homeschoolers. (Interview conducted May 2015.)

Research and Testimonies on Socialisation in Homeschoolers

Socialisation is a great reason to participate in homeschooling groups. Studies show most homeschoolers socialise in an average of five different social settings regularly, such as their church, Bible study, hobby clubs and sports teams.[235]

Constant socialisation among homeschoolers was noticed by Dr. Brian Ray of the *National Home Education Research Institute*, who said, 'Home educated [children] are doing well. They're typically above average, on measures of social, emotional and psychological development.'[236]

Greg Cizek, Associate Professor of Educational Research at the University of North Carolina, also said, 'If anything, research shows that because [homeschooling] parents are *so sensitive* to the charge, they expose [their children] to many activities.'[237]

Emily-Jane talked about the social interaction her homeschool family had with the community:

> *We were really involved with the Armidale homeschooling group. Once a week we would go to an ice rink owned by one of the homeschool families. We also went to the art gallery every fortnight. Here we would copy art pictures on the wall onto a sketchbook. Sometimes they'd have hands-on, interactive things and different projects set up for school groups, like sculpting. Some homeschoolers lived on farms, so we went blackberry picking and yabbying in their dam. Then we came to Canberra and joined another homeschool group with 12 families. When I was 12 years-old, my sister and I started 'Mothers of Preschoolers', where mothers could come together for a Bible talk while we minded their children.*

Apparently, Emily-Jane didn't suffer from a lack of socialisation. Melissa, another homeschooler, had a similar story:

> *My parents went to great lengths to socialise us. We had church every Sunday, and my father started a youth group to encourage meetings with young Christians. We met weekly with a homeschooling group, and six of us had regular classes in dance, music and languages. My parents were*

completely dedicated to our education, but frequently socialising ranked higher in our family's priorities.

Peer Pressure in Homeschooling?

Ask almost any homeschooler, and you will find serious peer pressure is amazingly rare among homeschoolers. When interviewees were asked if they had experienced peer pressure while homeschooling, they said the only time they had experienced peer pressure was when they were doing activities with school children. Melissa, a homeschool and Criminology Honors graduate, addressed this, saying:

> In ballet classes, I was with other school children around my age. If I didn't do what they wanted, there was a weird sort of peer pressure. But I didn't conform to what they wanted me to do. Apart from ballet, I didn't experience peer pressure. I certainly didn't experience this at church or in my homeschooling group.

Jay, another homeschool graduate and university science student, chuckled when asked if she had experienced peer pressure when she was homeschooled:

> Homeschooling gave us independent minds, and I never had any peer pressure from my family. My sisters would say, 'Do this with me,' and I would do it because it was fun. But I never really did anything I didn't want to do. If all my [school] friends were doing something at youth group and said, 'You've got to do this,' I would say, 'No. I'm not doing that – that's stupid.'

Christian homeschoolers are not any more special or resilient than other children – it's just that parents have more time to give them support and encouragement to withstand social pressures when they're young and vulnerable. This support gives them the confidence to stand up to peer pressure and develop strong moral characters.

Even though Melissa's family valued socialisation more than education, her family scored well in the 20th percentile in their studies.

Homeschoolers and best friends, Ben and Jesse, also described the homeschooling families they grew up in, saying, 'We grew up together in a homeschooling group with four or five large families. Each family did their own thing [academically] and then we socialised together through the week. We all knew each other through church.'

Other Research Explaining Why Homeschoolers are Well-Socialised

An Australian homeschooling researcher with Monash University, Glenda Jackson, found homeschoolers are generally well-adjusted and have high self-esteem. [238] Although some ex-school children missed their peers, they can see that the benefits of homeschooling outweigh school because homeschooling allows students to learn at their own pace and doesn't isolate students when they're ideologically different.[xvi]

This non-judgmental environment has positive effects on children, according to homeschooling expert, Steven Kelley. Kelley points to several studies that find the psychological self-concept[xvii] of homeschoolers is higher than that of public school children.[239]

> **What would you say to parents who say, 'I don't want to homeschool my child because they won't be properly socialised'?**
>
> Home educators, William and Susan, responded to this question, "We agree that we want our children to be properly socialised; that's why we homeschool. Homeschooling enables the kids to socialise properly. They grow up with people all day long and grow up with people in their homes, with people down the street and in the supermarkets. That's why they're well socialised."
>
> *William and Susan McAulay, Homeschooling Parents. (Interview conducted August 2014.)*

[xvi] In my experience, most homeschoolers say they miss their peers during the first year of homeschooling, and then they miss their peers less as time progresses and they form closer bonds with their family. We will call this 'school withdrawal'.

[xvii] Self-concept is a general term used to refer to how someone thinks about, assesses or sees themselves. For example, a person who thinks they are fat when they are skinny has a warped

A high self-concept was attributed to higher levels of love, support, involvement, independence, responsibility and the reinforcing of self-worth at home. Other elements affecting psychological self-concept were reduced anxiety levels and more contact with parental love.[240]

When Kelley looked at homeschoolers' academic self-concept, he reported homeschoolers had a healthy self-concept ranking in the 72nd percentile, a score that was above the national [American] average. In many studies, he found homeschoolers had higher self-esteem and, contrary to popular belief, were not isolated, but active and contributing members of society. Kelley said 98% were involved with other people in various age groups, like church. (Everyone in Kelley's study attended Baptist churches).

Homeschoolers were less concerned and influenced by their peers compared to private school children. Homeschoolers viewed their parents as primary authority figures, more so than private school children. After communication skills were evaluated, Kelley found homeschoolers in his sample were significantly better socialised and more mature than children who attended public schools.[241]

Don't We Need Social Glue to Hold Society Together?

Some opponents of homeschooling feel homeschooling is dangerous because it fails to foster social cohesion or 'social glue'. [xviii] Critics argue that because homeschooling has a different brand of social glue than you see in schools, homeschooling creates free radical adults who upset the traditional view.

The Minority Is Always Weird

Homeschoolers are in the minority. Those in the minority will always be a little weird. The chances are good that if school children were in the minority, they would be seen as weird.

(and negative) self-concept. Self-image is highly influenced by the individuals closest to a person, such as peers.
[xviii] Lack of social cohesion is the same reason Germany gives for banning homeschooling.

If we have a look at school's brand of social glue, it has numerous problems. Firstly, it is inconsistent as it sticks some people together tightly, yet fractures other relationships; school's social glue is accepting of other children in the same year group – so long as they are 'normal'. However, whenever others are perceived to be 'different', the glue breaks down. It even creates fractures in some relationships, alienating brothers from sisters and parents from children.

John Holt, a schoolteacher and homeschooling author, noticed how defective school's social glue was, because of the glue's rigidity. Rigidity or tight control in school leads to immaturity because immaturity is the only control school children have over their already tightly controlled world. Holt believed school children deliberately deprived teachers and parents of their [the child's] intelligence, and act stupidly – thereby rebelling passively against the authority figures in their lives:

> *By putting on a mask, by acting much more stupid and incompetent than they really are, by denying their rulers [or teachers] the full use of their intelligence and ability, by declaring their minds and spirits free of their enslaved bodies.*[242]

Therefore, we need another glue that isn't based on rebellion to authority figures. Homeschoolers respect authority figures more which leads to stable families and families that contribute to society. This 'home-brand' glue is quality and leads to a healthier concept of how to contribute positively to social cohesion in wider circles in adulthood.

Are Homeschoolers Socially Awkward?

Homeschoolers may be seen as socially awkward when they are young because they don't have school's brand of 'social glue'. But, if homeschoolers are awkward around others (and many are not) it's sometimes because they're unsure how to act around immature school children.

> 'In her collection of essays, *The New Left: The Anti-Industrial Revolution*, atheist and capitalist Ayn Rand accused John Dewey's philosophy of stressing irrational, collectivist behaviour. Feminist writer

> Patricia Sexton described public education as an overwhelmingly effeminate environment...By rewarding feminine behaviour, such as sitting still and passively listening... the existing structure of education produced 'the impotent female' and 'the feminised male', timid, passive, uncreative, unfeeling.'[243]

Because homeschoolers are more mature than school children (a fact backed up by numerous studies) they may struggle to relate to others who they think should be more mature.[244] Homeschooling parents, Steven and Barbara, noticed their homeschoolers struggled to relate to other school children in their youth group because of the maturity gap:

> *Our kids found it difficult to relate to school children because of their different maturity level. The comment they had when they came back from youth group was, 'The kids talk about rubbish all the time.' The school children's excitement for the day was what our kids thought was rubbish.*

Conversation topics homeschoolers prefer are often more mature, as homeschoolers are given more responsibility and freedom at home compared to their peers in school – who are raised in a heavy, rule-based institution that allows them less freedom. Homeschoolers are treated with more freedom at home as the rules are relaxed and children are given more freedom to be children. Many are given adult responsibilities at young ages as they step up to the challenge. This increased freedom at home causes asynchronous maturity development between homeschoolers and school children.

Increased maturity in homeschoolers is reflected in researchers' conclusions, some commenting homeschoolers were able to 'converse with adults with more ease and poise' than their public school peers.[245] Homeschoolers happily speak with more ease and poise because they don't fear adults as authority figures. Their authority figures were always their loving parents, teachers and often their best friends; if your best friend is your teacher and authority figure, education is less stressful.

Socialise with Parents First

Gordon Neufeld and Gabore Maté think children don't even need other peers until they have properly learned to socialise with their siblings, parents and other significant family members. Before this time, Neufeld and Maté believe socialising children with their peers is of little benefit:

> *To be sure, socialising plays a part in rendering a child capable of true social integration, but only as a finishing touch...The real challenge is helping children grow to the point where they can benefit from their socialising experiences.*[246]

Neufeld and Maté continue to say premature and indiscriminate mixing with peers, without adult involvement as primary attachment figures, may cause fighting or cloning. In this environment 'each child seeks to dominate the other or has to resist being dominated, or cloned, as a child suppresses his sense of himself for the sake of acceptance by others.'[247]

Radically, these researchers question the necessity of early socialisation at all, aside from family socialisation, saying, 'until children are capable of true friendship, they really do not need friends, just attachments. And the only attachments a child needs are with the family and those who share responsibility for the child.' As we absorb this new research, perhaps we should reconsider our children's primary attachments, especially when they are young.

This said, homeschooling parents seem to be as committed to socialisation as other parents, especially in later years. Furthermore, because the issue of homeschooling socialisation tends to be overblown, homeschooling parents are very alive to the potential pitfalls of failing to socialise their children.

13. Better Academic Performance and Mental Health

HOMESCHOOLERS ARE NO SMARTER or more naturally skilful than other children. They are just homeschooled. Research has found homeschoolers with higher academic scores than their school peers, would be at the same academic level, had homeschoolers attended school![248] [i] Higher academic scores among homeschoolers were found to be caused by increased periods of academic engagement. Because homeschoolers are academically engaged *more than half time*, compared to public school children (who are academically engaged only *one-fifth of the time*), homeschoolers score higher than public school children.[249]

Almost all studies on academic achievement conclude that homeschoolers regularly perform above average.[250] Dr. Brian Ray found homeschoolers in Canada and America score 15-30 percentile points higher than their public school peers.[ii] [251] Homeschoolers taking SAT and ACT tests outperformed their public school peers.[iii] Australia has studies suggesting those who homeschool all the way through primary and secondary education outcompete school students (and partially homeschooled students).[252] Anecdotal evidence given to the NSW Parliamentary Inquiry in 2014 also suggests Australian homeschoolers have similar positive outcomes regarding academic achievement and employability.[253]

---

[i] Homeschool parent's attention, involvement and tutoring were accounted for in this study.
[ii] Here, percentile is where a person sits on a chart, relative to others.
[iii] These tests, sat by students across America, indicate how well a prospective student will fare at university.

Dr. Ray said his [American and Canadian] tests indicated homeschoolers 'are performing well in college. In other areas of adult life, they're showing themselves to be hard-working and independent-minded, living off their own earnings and contributing in a positive way to their society and families.'[254] Even the vehement, anti-homeschooling academic, Robin West, confirmed as much in her article *The Harms of Homeschooling*.[255]

Academic success appears to hinge partly on academic flexibility. Wilfred Aiken writes of an eight-year study, conducted by Harper and Brothers, where 1,500 children were educated in conventional classrooms, while another 1,500 were trained in flexible classes or not taught at all. The children in the second group, who had adults to answer their questions only, outperformed the first group on every parameter! These measures included grades, leadership and on-the-job attitudes. Children with no teaching had the highest score of all the groups.[iv][256]

Why did this happen? It seems that when children are interested in a task, they tend to work harder on it. Homeschoolers who follow their passions and interests work harder on material they're interested in than children given work they're only mildly interested in and haven't chosen themselves. Because curiosity is the key to learning, self-led study inspires children to drive their own learning. Furthermore, we tend to remember information we've sought out ourselves more than information we are told to collect.

Children educated in their area of interest learn more. Therefore, wise home educators will warmly facilitate reasonable requests to study a homeschooler's area of interest. For instance, if a homeschooler asks, 'How do trees receive food and grow?', a photosynthesis study might be ideal.

Younger students benefit from more flexible learning programs. Some researchers, such as Ray and Dorothy Moore, believe children benefit when they're withheld from formal schooling until ages 8-10.[257] As a parent, you might worry your child won't be able to 'catch up', but, the Moores suggest

---

[iv] Obviously, children ought not to be left to their own devices and study whatever they want (e.g. forget maths); but, children learn best when they're interested in a topic.

children learn a lot faster than we think and have an amazing ability to catch up when they're behind.

The Moores say that **all the learning that is necessary for success in high school can be done in only two or three years of formal study**. Furthermore, if parents delay compulsory instruction in the basics of education until Year 9, many students might enjoy academic success they may not have experienced had they attended school from Kindergarten.[258]

Children don't need seven hours of structured learning a day![259] This point is imperative for us to understand for the sanity of homeschooling parents and children. Our children's vulnerable little brains are simply learning too much for too long. Look at the time Australians expect their children to be at school – 10,710 days for their primary and secondary days in total. Compared to almost all the other democratic countries (OECD countries [v]), *Australia has the largest attendance requirement*. But, children from Hungary spend only 6,054 days at school during their primary and secondary education and achieve higher academic scores than Australian children.[260] Margery Evans, a teaching expert, shows more time doesn't equal better performance. Evans says:

> *It might be assumed achievement would be higher in countries where children spend more time in school compared with countries where children spend less time in school. Analysis of 2012 PISA data indicates*

School Not Student-Directed

'It has been ten years after school has finished. Most memories at school are just a wash of classrooms and schoolyards. I can't remember driving my learning or learning something I was genuinely interested in. You just had to do it.'

Tristan Devitt, Graduate Student K-12. (Interview conducted October 2016.)

---

[v] The Organisation for Economic Co-operation and Development (OECD) is a coalition of 34 countries. They are committed to democracy and the market economy.

this is not necessarily the case. For example, the ten countries where children spend the greatest amount of time in school have a mean PISA score for mathematics that is 20 points below that of the ten countries with the lowest amount of instruction time. [261]

The time a child spends on his homework isn't correlated to how well he does in the exam. But, a child's time at school does teach them something – how to ace tests, do homework and copy notes. Ivan Illich, who has been described as a 'maverick social critic', proposed school makes students, 'confuse teaching with learning, grade advancements with education, a diploma with competence and fluency with the ability to say something new.' [262] Illich also believed homeschooling did the opposite. Homeschooling allows children to pick and study things they find interesting. Homeschoolers, he thought, learn, not for a diploma or grade achievement, but more for the joy of learning.

Achievement Related to Homeschooling Years

When academic outcomes of homeschooled students were measured, 'overall performance was more highly related to the number of years they had been homeschooled than to the number of years they had attended conventional schools.'

Medlin's results are consistent with the Australian Board of Studies research on the academic achievements of homeschooling.[263]

Not only do homeschoolers feel the joy of learning, but parents do as well. Homeschool parents can be fellow learners with their children. When parents teach their children, a parent's own drive to learn is awakened. When parents revisit old subjects they studied at school (often decades before), they take joy in learning the material from a new perspective. Their joy is infectious and motivates their young ones. Indeed, researchers, DeMille and DeMille, report that when parents teach their children, their own latent desire for learning awakens. This desire then motivates parents to become life-long learners.[264]

Curiosity and learning are inseparable. Kip and Mona Lisa Harding discovered this among their own children. In *The Brainy Bunch: The Harding*

Family's Method to College Ready by Age 12 the Hardings describe their children's remarkable journeys to college by age 12.[265] [vi] Most children in this unusual Catholic family started college younger than age 12 (some started at age 10). Kip and Mona Lisa insist their children are not exceptionally gifted – they're just average children who could follow their interests.

Homeschooling: A Mould for Every Child?

Parents commonly turn to homeschooling when they believe classroom expectations are unreasonable or unsuitable for their child. They perceive their child is drowning in homework, or getting bored by dry tasks and decide to try something new.

Ben was one such student. He was diagnosed with dyslexia at a young age and found school dull and boring. Due to his photographic memory, Ben scored at the top in every test. However, he *never* learned how to write. Eventually, his parents removed him from school. Ben was thrilled.

When I interviewed Ben, he explained how homeschooling gave him opportunities he wouldn't have had at school:

> *I got to play with my hands doing a lot of woodwork and explore a whole lot of things. But, there was no woodwork in school. There was painting – always crummy painting. It was the old water painting which was horrible. I usually enjoyed painting, but not that style. Not with bad paints. I never got to do woodworking [at school] either.*

Ben liked studying early in the morning. He usually woke up very early and finished all his homework before 6:30 am. 'I'd do all my maths before about 6:30 and then the day was all mine!'

Benjamin Buckley, Graduate Homeschooler. (Interview conducted May 2015.)

For example, their eldest daughter, Hannah, started college at age 12 and was full-time at age 13. She finished her Bachelor in Mathematics by age 17. Rosannah, at age 23, was the youngest architect in the *American Institute of Architects* and completed her five-year architecture course at the tender age of 18. Serennah, 22, decided God called her to be a physician, so she took

---

[vi] Note also that college is America's equivalent to university.

the SAT at age 11 and started part-time at Auburn University in Montgomery. The remaining ten children in the Harding family are equally remarkable – even though their parents insist they're just average children. From what I know of homeschoolers, this is not unusual.

The homeschooling environment facilitates these educational leaps and bounds. Extraordinary feats for school children are more easily accomplished for homeschoolers due to the immense amounts of spare time in which students can continue self-directed study or start other projects. At home, students can find their niche subject and often excel at these topics, working hard to finish their project.

Better Mental Health

Homeschooling parents have much more control over the physical and emotional health of those in their care. If parents are loving and caring, homeschoolers will blossom. The opposite happens when abusive parents homeschool – and homeschooling can make abuse easy.

However, most parents love and care for their children. This love means children can blossom in an accepting environment. Because they feel accepted, their inhibitions and reservations melt. They can be themselves and do what makes them happy.

Therefore, homeschoolers seem at ease with who they are and many of them are glad they were homeschooled. The Gen2 study shows 67% of homeschoolers said they 'strongly agreed' they were 'glad they were homeschooled' while only 4% 'strongly disagreed'. The home educating parents interviewed in this book all revealed how pleased they were with their children's ability to ignore the outside world and decide what was right. Many homeschoolers are sure about their skills and abilities and happily express their opinion on many topics.

Studies also show, the longer a child is homeschooled, the better their sense of self-concept.[266] [vii] This correlation was shown when more than half of the 224 homeschoolers sampled in the *Piers-Harris Children's Self-Concept Scale* ranked in the top ten percent when compared to their peers at school. Researchers accounted for homeschoolers high self-concept because homeschoolers have:

- High support levels
- High parent involvement
- Independence from peers
- Low anxiety levels
- A sense of responsibility
- High contact with parental love

These factors are attributed to an absence from school and a loving home environment.[267] Many homeschoolers, like 26-year-old Emily-Jane, feel this way:

> *I think homeschooled kids are less likely to be bullied at home or rely on others opinions of themselves. Therefore, I would homeschool my kids because homeschooling produces better results than the school system. By results I mean academically, besides mentally and emotionally.*

This loving home environment is important for parents who want to develop healthy and happy children. Because mental health is important and sometimes dependent on the time a parent spends with their children, homeschoolers receive great support from parents who are around their children constantly. Love is spelt T-I-M-E; a homeschool parent can give far more time to a child than a teacher.

We know teachers can only spend a very short period each day with each pupil in personal exchanges. According to the Moore Foundation, teachers average only seven minutes a day in personal exchanges with their students.

[vii] Self-concept is an idea of the self we hold combined with the responses of others about us. This study looked at students in grades four to 12. A randomised sample of 224 qualified participants were picked from the mailing lists of the two biggest national homeschooling agencies. 77.7% of all homeschooled children sampled ranked in the top quartile of the test.

This averages out to two personal responses a day for each student. The Moores found homeschoolers spent much more time in personal exchanges with their teachers – about 100 to more than 300 minutes a day.[268]

This time allows parents to dedicate their energy to learning their child's interests and quirks. Parents are better able to appreciate their children might be bright in some fields and need more help in others.

Sleep

Because homeschoolers don't need to rise early, they are usually less tired than school children. In a study examining homeschooled and traditionally schooled students, researchers discovered half the Christian school students described themselves as 'always tired'. Homeschoolers, by comparison, described themselves as 'always tired' *less than a third* of the time. This extra time sleeping means homeschooled students are more alert and happy compared to mainstream school children.[269]

Dr. Lisa Metlzer, a sleep psychologist at National Jewish Health in Denver, conducted a study on the sleep habits of homeschool teenagers and their (public and private) school peers. Metlzer suggests teenagers need more sleep than schools are often letting them have. They need nine hours of sleep every night. When they get an average of only seven hours a night, by the end of the week they're ten hours behind on their sleep schedule, which impacts 'every aspect of functioning'. Metlzer's study showed homeschoolers slept an hour and a half longer each day compared to school children. Indeed, school children were in class 18 minutes before most homeschool children even awoke!

And before you think, 'Can't teenagers just sleep earlier rather than staying up until midnight?' you'd better pause for thought. Many teenagers cannot simply sleep earlier to solve their sleep deprivation problem because sleep-regulating hormones stop them from doing this. Metlzer says:

> *Melatonin, the hormone that helps regulate our sleep, shifts by about two hours during puberty. So, even if they wanted to get to sleep earlier, teenagers are battling biological changes in their bodies that are nearly impossible to overcome.*[270]

Metlzer continued to say some adolescents cannot physiologically fall asleep earlier. In other words, expecting a teen to fall asleep at 9pm is like expecting an adult to fall asleep at 3pm. Therefore, teens must sleep later.[271] Homeschooling gives adolescents a fantastic opportunity to rest more and get the rest they need to be productive. This extra sleep assists homeschoolers to think more critically and creatively, as we will see in the next chapter.

14. Critical Thinking and Broadened Creativity

JOHN TAYLOR GATTO, AN EDUCATIONAL AUTHOR and speaker, once wrote, 'Genius is an exceedingly common human quality, probably natural to most of us.' Many of us can shine in a particular area, even if we're terrible in other areas. In homeschooling, these areas are focused on and magnified. Although homeschoolers don't have a higher proportion of geniuses among them, the home education method brings out genius more often than regular school allows (hence why homeschoolers have a name for being so smart).

Homeschooling brings out the genius in many students by providing the support children need to concentrate. It also gives homeschoolers time to develop their ideas or projects to their full potential. As they create these things, their confidence increases and their creativity broadens.

As homeschoolers become more comfortable with their lifestyle (now free from the restraints of mass thinking in mass education) they begin to think more critically. Jonnie Seago remarked on this process in her study, saying homeschooled families became comfortable with a more 'self-determined' lifestyle after a few years. They often began to broaden their social and political views. [272] This allowed them creativity in many areas of art, religion, politics and education.

I Can Teach Myself

Before we wonder how we will teach our children to think critically and be creative, we must realise homeschoolers are largely capable of leading their own studies. When homeschooling mother, Antoinette, is asked how she taught her children, she often replies, 'They taught themselves.' Galileo Galilei echoed this sentiment when he said, 'We cannot teach people anything; we can only help them discover it within themselves.'

Tiffany, a homeschool graduate and music teacher, started her music studies early, after she identified a passion for music:

> *After begging Mum for trumpet lessons, I had my first recorder lesson on my sixth birthday. I played recorder for five years, doing recitals with the homeschooling group. When I was 11, I transferred over to the clarinet and played the clarinet and saxophone simultaneously. When I was 19, I auditioned for the Australian National University (ANU) School of Music and was accepted into a (clarinet) music degree.*

In a way, Tiffany directed her own study by following the musical pathway she found interesting. She became successful because she spent hours practicing clarinet at home, something homeschooling fostered. (Indeed, among my own homeschool group, there was several talented homeschooled musicians and singers.)

Flexibility

A relaxed and flexible homeschooling lifestyle creates a low stress environment, in which families can grow happily. A relaxed lifestyle means schoolwork is completed more easily and efficiently. Methods like the 'school-at-home' method can be replaced with less formal learning to decrease stress and create a friendlier learning environment.

> Homeschooling allows children to develop their own creativity and not be stifled by mass education.
>
> Fay Robertson, Homeschool Mother.
> (Correspondence, January 2016.)

Flexibility means homeschoolers can do activities most school children are unable to do (due to time restrictions). Melissa, a homeschool graduate, talked about these opportunities, saying:

> *If there were an activity during school hours we thought was great and educational, we would be able to do that instead of being in school. I was involved in a lot of classes outside homeschooling activities, including dancing and language. I was also involved a lot with the local theatre productions where I got to meet a few school children.*

Flexibility also assists Christian parents as 'there is no separation of church and state.' This means parents can freely 'teach the doctrine intertwined in the way they want to, while teaching courses such as history or biology.'[273]

Flexibility is great for parents too. Homeschool parents, William and Susan, value the flexibility homeschooling offers:

> *Flexibility was great with the curriculum – with outings, shopping, housework, holidays and sleep-ins. We had freedom to read anything we chose to our children without being restricted by grades or individual texts. If our child went to school we could still read to them, but when they got home, we were restricted because they were too tired and worn out. Homeschooling flexibility was also great for holidays – just to function as a family without other people impinging on you and telling you how you'll do it and what your children are going to do.*

Timetable flexibility is a great advantage in homeschooling. No longer do mothers have to fight other mothers in SUVs during the morning school rush or work their shopping trip around the 3pm school rush. They're able to make other events work with their schedule because they're the boss of their calendar.[274]

Employability, Business Skills and Extra-Curricular Activities

> 'We went out to coffee shops regularly and all the café workers knew me well. I spent a lot of time at hardware stores which I enjoyed. We were building a house at this stage so we were always getting new plumbing parts. The hardware store always challenged me on maths because I had to convert plumbing measurements in inches to plumbing measurement in metric. I would have to solve the problem in the store. I became good at that.'
>
> *Benjamin Buckley, Graduate Homeschooler. (Interview conducted May 2015.)*

Homeschoolers are highly mature, responsible and experienced in many areas before they reach TAFE or university. This maturity has led many homeschoolers to entrepreneurial ventures, usually long before their mainstream school peers.[275]

Many homeschoolers have a practical understanding of everyday life. They pick up skills by watching their parents regularly balance a budget, maintain their family home or run a family business. The drive to achieve these things is possible because children have grown up wanting to copy their parents' example. Simultaneously, they have learned useful and necessary business skills. The NSW Parlimentary Inquiry recorded:

> *There is an increasing number of young people who have never attended a mainstream school but have been educated at home and are now employed, running their own business or undertaking further studies.*[276]

Employer Favours Hiring Homeschoolers

One American company has recognised maturity is a common trait among homeschoolers. Chick-fil-A, an American fast food restaurant, recruits 30,000 front-line workers which service 1,000 restaurants across America. They mostly hire teenagers around 17 years. One recruiter, Andy Lorenzen, says Chick-fil-A prefers to tap into the homeschooling pool of college-aged kids to find reliable employees. The recruiter believes homeschoolers are smart, ambitious, very driven and have plenty of loyalty to the company and a good work ethic.[277]

Entrepreneurship

Typically, a person learns to become a consumer of ideas and products. But, the homeschool environment is an exception to the rule. Following the exodus from the school system, (and often after a time of bewilderment), homeschool parents start looking at what they are doing educationally. As parents start to think creatively, their children follow them and also begin thinking creatively.

Choosing your own homeschool curriculum is the beginning of entrepreneurial thinking for the whole family. Taking charge over your children's lives gives you the confidence to take charge in other areas, such as finances. A surprising  number of homeschooling families run a family business or teach their children a trade.[278] This has created a market for conferences such as the *AME Youth Entrepreneur & Vendor Program*, run by Christian homeschooling pastors and parents in America. These conferences, open to homeschoolers from 13-years-old, include lectures, business plan contests, training workshops and youth vendor exhibit areas for keen, young entrepreneurs.

All children are natural entrepreneurs, and homeschoolers are no exception. If entrepreneurial learning is fostered, children will be wired to create their own ideas throughout their life and think creatively. This is what we see in the following list of homeschool entrepreneurs. They include the founder of:

- the Bank of America, Amadeo Giannini,
- the *New York Tribune*, Horace Greeley,
- the Honda company, Soichiro Honda,
- McDonalds, Ray Kroc,
- the Giordano clothes brand, Jimmy Lai,
- *Success* magazine, Dr. Orison Swett Marden,
- *The New York Times*, Adolph Ochs,
- Kentucky Fried Chicken, Colonel Harland Sanders,
- MuggleNet, 12-year-old entrepreneur, Emerson Spartz,
- and Wendy's restaurant chain, Dave Thomas.

Another well-known homeschool entrepreneur is Palmer Luckey. Palmer grew up in California, the eldest of four homeschool siblings. He credits homeschooling for allowing him to explore and develop virtual reality (VR) technology as a teenager. His VR technology was a product of years of home study with different materials.

Palmer loved tinkering with various tools and materials. He began engineering other gadgets but had a soft spot for VR technology. When he was 15, Palmer entered California State University and began studying journalism. But his heart was with gadgets because he simultaneously ran an online forum called Mod Retro. Then, when Palmer turned 17, he got a job at the army's VR lab in Playa Vista California.

While Luckey dreamed of having a virtual reality gaming world, he thought the technology had already been discovered or was too expensive for most people. When he eventually found VR technology didn't exist, he set about making it himself. With a tenacity and maturity common to many homeschoolers, Palmer created a new product. He was business savvy and able to think outside the box at a very young age. This skill enabled him to sell his VR technology to Facebook for a whopping $2 billion – all at age 21.

Many of the homeschoolers interviewed in this book showed brilliance in different disciplines and exhibited an ability to think critically. Melissa is an example of one such homeschooler who, before age 20, completed an astonishing amount of study and work experience. Melissa managed to compile an amazing portfolio before most mainstream school students have finished their second year of university. Melissa chatted casually about her experiences, saying:

> *Educationally, I never completed Year 12 or achieved my HSC. But, by age 20 I have a Bachelor of Social Science with half my debt paid, a scholarship to complete honours this year and connections to prospective jobs. I have also gained experience in five different jobs. If I had attended school, I doubt I would have accomplished this much.*

For those who are willing to persevere, the internet makes things easy. Business opportunities abound. Homeschoolers have plenty of time to do business because most have plenty of spare time, (most having completed their homework in just a few hours).[i]

---

[i] Homeschoolers interviewed in this book did an average of a three hours of homework a day. The least any student did was one hour; the most seven hours.

The internet can offer many opportunities for keen students who want to learn business. A homeschooler can quickly learn how to start a business online. Palmer Luckey made pocket money by buying mobile phones, unlocking them and selling them back online.

Political Lobbying

Because homeschoolers are taught to think critically, many find themselves lobbying the government for political change. Politically-savvy homeschoolers understand how they, the [future] voter, have the power to change a politician's mind.

And because homeschoolers have plenty of time to learn about social and political issues that interest them, they lobby governments more than the average student. Daniel Golden wrote about this in *The Wall Street Journal*, saying homeschool parents have become pros at wielding enough clout to block political actions that disadvantage homeschoolers. Even though homeschooling groups have small numbers, they always make their agenda heard. Golden says homeschooling families overwhelm Congress and state legislatures with bombardments of emails, phone calls and visits. This ability to wield so much power (as a conscientious objector) has meant homeschoolers are exempt from many compulsory education measures.[279]

Australian homeschoolers are also tenacious advocates when lobbying for homeschooling, as was evidenced by the plethora of positive submissions to the *NSW Parliamentary Inquiry into Homeschooling*.

In this Inquiry, laws on homeschooling regulation came up for review in 2014. Many homeschoolers wrote to the committee, expressing their support for less homeschooling regulation and more acceptance via legislative support. The sheer volume of submissions in favour of homeschooling has forced the government to look at homeschooling seriously and confer more with homeschooling parents when making decisions.

Leadership Development

Home is a good environment to learn leadership skills. As homeschoolers watch their fathers lead their family through life, they learn good leadership, provided the father is a good leader. Homeschoolers copy the way their parents show leadership in the family. Older siblings then demonstrate and practice leadership around younger siblings as Jonnie Seago discovered. Bass (1960, cited in Seago) supposed future leaders came from homes:

- that were harmonious,
- that emphasised positive incentives,
- that didn't baby children or push them too rapidly,
- where they were treated as functional at their level of maturity,
- where children were not left to their own devices, but were stimulated,
- that encouraged children with many interactive problem-solving senarios. [280]

At university, research found homeschooled students often took a leadership role in group assignments. They wanted to ensure the group completed the task competently and received good grades for the effort they produced.[281] Researchers Bolle-Brummond and Wessel found:

Nearly all [homeschoolers] were largely prepared through homeschooling to be academically and socially successful. The students indicated homeschooling equipped them with organisational skills and self-motivation in their studies. While they had to adjust to a formal educational setting and different teaching styles of their professors, this did not negatively affect the students' ability to learn and succeed.[282]

In other words, although homeschoolers were 'behind' because they needed to learn the universities' method of education, they still managed to attain leadership positions and achieve good marks. They could do this, according to homeschoolers themselves, because they had a homeschooling upbringing.

15. Close Family Ties

> I trust my parents more than I trust anyone else. Even as a teenager I respected and valued their input. My sisters are also my best friends. When I was 13, many of my school friends talked about how much they hated their siblings, particularly their sisters. I remember thinking that was sad. I didn't understand why they hated them, because, to me, sisters were friends that I lived with.
>
> Emily-Jane Fraser, Homeschool Graduate. (Correspondence, February 2015.)

CHRISTIAN HOMESCHOOLERS HAVE CLOSE RELATIONSHIPS with their parents, according to over 9,000 homeschoolers who completed the Gen2 Survey. Consequently, homeschoolers 'strongly' described themselves as having beliefs similar to their mother or father.[283] [i] They also described themselves as having a strong relationship with both their mother and their father.

Close family relationships come about when families spend plenty of time together. Melissa spent a lot of time with her siblings and parents when she was homeschooled. Growing up in a close-knit family of eight, Melissa tells how she enjoyed spending time with her family, 'I was blessed to be homeschooled. A large family was a big part of this, as we were never alone.

---

[i] The survey was an American survey of 9,369 homeschoolers. It had some shortcomings that included participants being made up of 70% females and 30% males. The findings are flagged as preliminary. Participants were an average of 27 years of age.·

It was evident how much our parents cared for us and invested in us. We were a family and not just people we saw each night.'

I Dread School Holidays!

Many families lose the ability to spend time together harmoniously when they spend so much time apart from each other. When school holidays approach, some parents get increasingly anxious, saying 'I just don't know *how* I'm going to keep them occupied! Maybe school holiday camps?' When school resumes and children return to the regular babysitting services, parents feel relieved.

Professor Lisa Rivero, who wrote *The Homeschooling Option*, said parents who might enjoy their children's company, were considered clingy and controlling if they looked forward to three months togetherness in school holidays.

Homeschoolers, who spent time in traditional schools before homeschooling, said their homeschooling experience had strengthened their family unit. These homeschoolers often preferred to go to the movies with their parents instead of their friends.[284] Tristan, who was a prefect over a hundred private school students, said:

> *During my teens, the thought of going to the movies with my parents was not at all appealing. But now I've matured I would have no hesitation going with my parents. I was just a product of social expectations…it wasn't cool to go to the movies with your parents.*

Homeschoolers disprove the common idea that parents and siblings cannot be good friends. For them, it is common that their best friend is their mother or father. They learn to copy what their parents do. They even copy their mannerisms, like school children do with their peers. Jay, a homeschooler, talked about her siblings fondly, when asked about her family relationships:

> *I definitely have better relationships with my siblings than if I'd been to school. I know most of my friends didn't get along with their siblings when they were younger and only get along with their siblings a bit now. Homeschooling with your siblings forces you to get along with each other.*

Of course, in our family, there were fights – definitely fights – but being homeschooled meant my sisters were my best friends. So, we got on better and weren't picky about who we talked to.

Cats in the Cradle

When a small child is dropped off at a nursery at 8am, and picked up at 5pm, they may assume their parents regard children as a low priority in the parent's busy schedule (whether true or not). When older, the child thinks nothing of dropping their parents off at the nearest nursing home.

If adults were ignored as kids, they will ignore their old and 'useless' parents. After all, their parents taught them how to prioritise family.

Conversely, homeschooling can teach children great family values. Because children notice and value their parents' attention, they will always treat their parents respectfully if parents have treated children respectfully.

Homeschoolers are inherently fallen and argumentative like school children. However, homeschoolers have more time to work on making their family relationships better. Practice makes perfect.

Relationships Require Family Time Schools Can't Give

School children don't have the time they need to spend with their families to cultivate good bonds. School doesn't let children have time to make family relationships work when children spend so much time away from the family.

School children must wake up early in the morning, brush their teeth, eat a quick breakfast and find their way to school. After spending seven hours in study, and peer socialisation, they pile back into the bus go home.

Children arrive home exhausted. At this point, their mother expects them to chatter about their day when all they want to do is sit in front of a media screen and zone out. Hardly in the mood to answer questions about their day, preschoolers react to parents by crying, and teenagers appear rude and sullen. The poor parents don't understand why their children are behaving the way they are.

Child Compliance

Paul says that in the last days people will be abusive, ungrateful, lovers of themselves, without self-control and disobedient to their parents.[285] We see this in many children today (even if we don't consider adolescent behaviour). Some toddlers are downright abusive to parents – something some parents try to overcome using compromise, bribery and coercion.

Children become more obedient as they grow older – a process helped by good family socialisation. Sharick and Medlin, homeschool researchers, commented on this trend, saying:

> *As children grow older…willing compliance to parental directives improves. Although [a child's] need for self-determination increases with age, so does self-regulation and their internalisation of their parents' standards. Their maturing cognitive, linguistic and physical skills also enable them to [obey] more readily. Although they may not always choose to do so, older children are better able to respond to unwanted parental directives without open conflict, an ability that parents are eager to cultivate.*[286]

Sharick and Medlin are convinced the primary place to socialise should be the family. More family time means better socialisation and behaviour as children are more willing to obey parents who are responsive and treat their children with respect. Respect and cooperation are inadvertently modelled by parents when parents responded warmly to children's reasonable requests.

Similarly, Grusec and Davidov found children with parents who are often available and supportive in times of need are better able to accept their parents' directives as indications of the parents' caring and goodwill.[287]

The question, however, is about homeschoolers. Do homeschool parents have what it takes to produce obedient and compliant children?

In a study analysing 24 homeschoolers, Sharick and Medlin, discovered homeschoolers obeyed their mothers 'most times'. Researchers suggested that, in conjunction with other research, homeschoolers are 'certainly no worse' and 'probably better' than their traditionally schooled peers. In the end, researchers felt confident to conclude that, despite limitations, 'the compliance level [of homeschoolers] was found to be so high that it seems safe to conclude homeschooling parents are successfully teaching their children.'[288] [ii]

Children from religious backgrounds were also found to be more self-controlled, have better social skills and learning methods compared to children with non-religious parents. Researchers accounted for this result using the following explanations:

- The social interaction religious parents received because of their religion improved their parenting skills.
- Religious people have positive, pro-family and pro-sacrificial values.
- The sacredness and significance placed on the families by the religious organisations.[289]

On these results, a sociologist involved in the study said, 'Getting their kids into heaven is more important than getting their kids into Harvard.' [290] Although no parent can 'get their kid into heaven,' parents who are with their children regularly can encourage them in the Lord's ways and give them a great foundation to follow God.[291]

[ii] Researchers hypothesised this may or may not have been representative of the larger population of homeschoolers.

16. Arguments Against Homeschooling Refuted

UNDERSTANDING HOMESCHOOLING STEREOTYPES helps us understand objections to homeschooling. Some homeschooling stereotypes are true, while other are false or outdated. Many of these latter labels are difficult to remove from our community's traditional conception about homeschooling. Some incorrect labels include students with little resilience, academic shortcomings, overprotective and possessive mothers with no professional qualifications to teach.

Perhaps more accurate stereotypes exist about why parents choose to homeschool. These fall into three categories. Stereotypes on:

1. religion,
2. students with disabilities and
3. students who have been expelled from school.

The last two stereotypes include families who are often forced to homeschool because school/s may reject or teach their children poorly. Those with disabilities often homeschool because they fail to physically or intellectually keep pace with their peers. Others are forced to homeschool because the school finds the child so disruptive, they are expelled.

The first group are those who proportionally receive the lowest amount of media attention. These children have parents who think they can do a better job of teaching compared to school. They consist of the clear majority of homeschoolers and homeschool for social, religious or political reasons.

Because homeschoolers with good reasons for homeschooling receive less media attention than those with other reasons, homeschooling has a poorer name than it deserves.

According to many Christian homeschoolers in the Gen2 Survey, homeschooling gives students a good academic and social experience as outlined in the graph below:

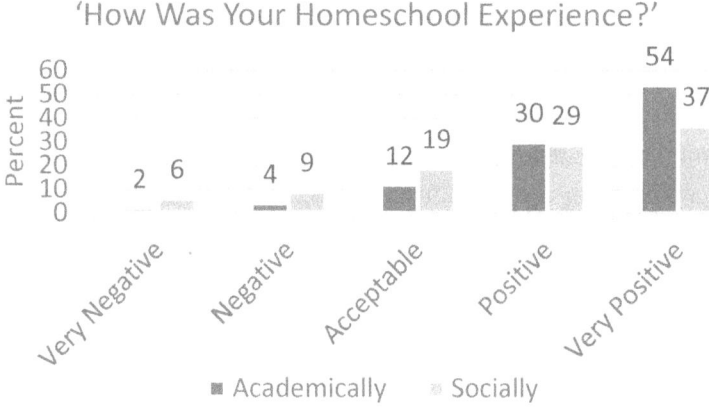

Notaries Who Oppose Homeschooling

Homeschooling doesn't have the best name, despite the data presented in this book showing how well homeschoolers perform in every area.[i] Despite positive data on homeschooling, some Professors like Robin West of the Georgetown University Law Center, remain opposed to homeschooling. Many, despite the data, boost the negative image of homeschooling.

West says homeschooling education is harmful, despite using little data to support her views. [292] The professor speculates parents can neglect education and subsequently create illiterate children. Revealing her anti-Christian bent, West says, 'If you want to teach them from nothing but the

---

[i] Pie graphs from data presented in Brian Ray's Gen2 study on 9,000+ graduate homeschoolers.

Bible, you can.' This idea promotes the [wrong] presumption that many homeschooling parents do just that.[ii] West continues, 'in unregulated States, parents need not teach their children a thing, if they so desire. Religious parents can teach nothing but the Bible and nothing but a literal interpretation of that.'

West likens homeschooling parents to criminals and homeschoolers to class drop outs. She alleges homeschool children are at higher risk of abuse, and pose a threat to public health as 'they might not be routinely vaccinated.'

West seems to believes homeschoolers are abused because no 'safe-haven' from the 'intensity of a parent's love' exists. She also thinks homeschoolers are not respected for who they are. West asserts authoritarian leadership (as she assumes is enforced by homeschooling parents) creates an immature recognition of the need to obey (West calls this 'ethical servility').

The Three Groups of Homeschoolers

There are three groups of homeschoolers that homeschool for very different reasons. Some receive disproportionate amounts of media attention compared to others.

1. Religious, social, political reasons
    a. Majority
    b. Low media attention
2. Disabled
    a. Minority
    b. Medium media attention
3. Expelled
    a. Minority
    b. High media attention

[ii] A parent's opportunity to be neglectful does not imply parents will. This is like saying every Dad has the ability to beat his children. Just because they can do something, doesn't mean they do it (indeed, the vast majority do not). Exceptions exist but are the minority.

Homeschoolers Equally Empathetic and More Altruistic Compared to Public School Children

In a study aiming to compare empathy, altruism and moral reasoning in homeschooled and public school children, researchers looked at 80 children in grades 3-5. Researchers found the following results:

- *Homeschooled children and public school children did not differ in empathy,*
- *In general, children who were more empathetic were also more altruistic,*
- *Homeschooled children were more altruistic than public school children,*
- *Homeschooled children endorsed a slightly higher level of moral reasoning to justify their solution to a moral dilemma than public school children,*
- *Public school children were more likely than homeschooled children to present themselves in an exclusively positive light,*
- *If public school children responded similarly on the other measures, their empathy, altruism, and moral reasoning scores may have been inflated, causing smaller differences between the two groups of children than would otherwise be the case.*[293]

West also raises concerns about some hardcore homeschoolers headed by a patriarchic, sole-breadwinning father. These families, she claims, live in trailer parks, on borrowed capital from others. West says homeschooling families teach each other few valuable skills and provide society with no overall economic growth.

However, West provides no proof homeschoolers are abused, unvaccinated failures living in trailer parks. Her article is more a rant about what *could* go wrong with homeschooling, rather than what is statistically proven and substantiated.[294] [iii]

Another professor, Michael Apple of the University of Wisconsin-Madison, seems to think homeschool parents start with 'meritorious' intentions, but their actions are less so. He laments because he says homeschoolers are so politically vocal and 'socially and culturally retrogressive'. Conservative homeschoolers, Apple says, are fueled by 'nostalgic and quite romanticised' past idealisations where previous generations would learn 'real' education. [295]

Apple says homeschool families cocoon and shun 'cultural and intellectual diversity, complexity, ambiguity, uncertainty and proximity to 'the Other.''[296] He seems to suggest parents are wrong for wanting a 'safe and predictable' environment for their children. According to Apple's estimation, homeschoolers are undemocratic because they propagate individual personalities that fail to create shared experiences, which, he insists, are highly necessary for 'mutual understanding, empathy and social cohesion.'[297]

Apple compares homeschoolers to online communities who don't want to interact with people of different ways and opinions. This customization, he says, radically undermines 'the strength of local communities, many of which are woefully weak.'[298]

Arguments Encompassed

West and Apple's objections to homeschooling are commonly held arguments against homeschooling. To become familiar with the discussions, we will look at an anonymous letter submitted to the *NSW*

[iii] Kate Brunner [cited in the endnote] says West seems to blatantly misquote statistics to support her argument. West says 97% of child abuse reports comes from school officials. However, the *United States Department of Health and Human Services Report, Child Maltreatment 2007* records only 17% of cases were reported by school officials. Indeed, most reports were of children younger than the lowest age at school. So, there couldn't have been 97% of child abuse reports coming from school officials.

Parliamentary Inquiry into Homeschooling (2014) that proffers many of these objections. The submission reads:

Dear Committee,

I have been a teacher for over 30 years, in government and private schools, in Australia and overseas. When I heard about this inquiry today, I decided to use the opportunity to share thoughts that I have been harbouring for a while.

In brief, I have found the following issues with homeschooling:

1. Homeschooled students were considerably behind, academically.

2. Homeschooled students have very little social resilience and mostly abandon an attempt at school after a short time, to go back to the comforts of home for their schooling.

3. Homeschooling mothers are generally overprotective and possessive of their children, making them fearful and dependent. This at times borders on child abuse.

4. It has always been a mystery to me, how a parent can possibly take on the job of several professional teachers, as well as the complex school administration - and succeed at it. The inspections by the Board of Studies appear to be rather superficial - or the students would be better prepared for life.

5. I concede that in some situations, like in remote areas, homeschooling is an appropriate option. However, if a school is nearby, it should not be an option for parents. The 'learning by life' philosophy might appeal to some - but I think we moved away from that a couple of centuries ago. As even homeschoolers are required to teach the Australian Curriculum, the argument really seems to be about the location, rather than the content.

6. There are also questions about children's rights and the definition of boundaries between the family and the society. I believe our society has an obligation to keep children at school and away from possible dangers, like abusive situations and religious fundamentalism. I have often found that the school rings the alarm bells, before counselors, DOCS, police, etc. become involved. If this option was taken out of the equation, children could be doomed in an abusive situation, with no protection by the public.

In summary, I suggest

* *To limit home-schooling to areas, where schools are too far to travel to. Online services will soon be available for those families.*

* *To increase BOS control and regular visits by liaison officers. It is important that this is not a purely bureaucratic act, as it is with the registration of Independent Schools, but that the families are actually visited, work is sighted, children are interviewed and tested, etc.*

* *If there was to be a push for more home-schooling, I would suggest that parents need regular training, to justify them functioning as teachers.*

Yours Sincerely

Anonymous[299]

This letter contains many common myths about homeschooling, so we will deal with arguments systematically:

'Homeschooled students were considerably behind, academically'

The writer's statement goes against the common perception that homeschoolers are actually over-achievers. As Ian Slatter, Director of Media Relations at the HSLDA put it in 2009, 'Today, you would be hard pressed to find an opponent of homeschooling who says homeschoolers, on average, are poor academic achievers.' We must have done well because we found one.

In this letter, the writer gives no evidence homeschoolers are academically behind *as a whole*. (Perhaps the writer had one or two homeschoolers in his/her class who were behind academically, and so has tarred the entire homeschooling population with the same brush.)

Studies by many organisations show homeschoolers perform well above average in all subjects. The *National Home Education Research Institute*, an American research group dedicated to homeschooling research, found the vast majority of studies prove homeschooling is a great academic environment for children.[iv] In Australia, the NSW *Board of Studies* (BOSTES), found homeschoolers performed better than their peers in 19 out of 20 measures. (The last measure was not deemed statistically significant.)[300] [v]

> **We Aren't Consistent**
>
> You can only get away with verbal and physical assault at school. At work, you would get a lawsuit. So why do we let our weakest individuals deal with these attacks?

'Homeschooled students have very little social resilience.'

While homeschoolers are not used to bullying, and don't like being intimidated, we should realise bullying is not normal behaviour. Bullying is offensive behaviour. Homeschoolers are not used to bad behaviour because they are usually raised in loving environments, with no or little bullying. This lack of harassment at home occurs as (most) parents observe and stop bullying in the family as soon as it happens.

In school, children wrongly tolerate the same bullying behaviour adults wouldn't think about tolerating! But, school children often do more than tolerate bullying as they learn to insult when they are insulted and hit back when they are hit. They learn to react badly when bullied so they can protect themselves, even if protecting themselves means hurting someone else and learning bad behaviour. Hurting or insulting others becomes their shield

---

[iv] See Chapter 13 for more on the topic.
[v] In measures where homeschoolers (who had been homeschooled their whole lives) were compared with school students, they did better in 19 out of 20 measures. Homeschoolers who went to school performed more like school children, depending on how much time they spent in school. Only one measure was not statistically significant, even though homeschoolers also got a higher score in this test [see endnote].

against insults. As adults, we forget we would never tolerate the same behaviour against us!

Homeschooling adults who enter employment quickly adapt to their new social environments. Like other homeschoolers, Ben had no problem adapting to his workplace. He commented on the argument that says homeschoolers have little ability to do so, saying 'I think [homeschoolers] will learn resilience when they're older and they start work. My first job was in labouring...and you learn how to fit in very quickly. I had no problems catching up.'

The letter writer also fails to comment on school children's ability to adapt to work situations. There are teething problems for some teenagers who are given little or no responsibility at school and then expected to take on, in some situations, extreme responsibilities suddenly.

'Homeschooled children mostly abandon an attempt at school after a short time, to go back to the comforts of home for their schooling.'

At school, children are less free and less encouraged compared to the home environment. At school, former homeschoolers must adapt to different learning styles immediately which life-long school children have already adapted to. Because this adaption can feel like trying to fit a square peg in a round hole, some homeschoolers prefer home to an ill-adapted environment.

'Homeschooling mothers are generally overprotective and possessive of their children, making them fearful and dependent. This at times borders on child abuse.'

Compared to other mothers, homeschooling mums *are* more protective – but not possessive – of their children. While homeschool mothers are not possessive of their children, they love spending time with them and regret giving time up. Homeschool mothers are protective because they don't want their children bullied at school. These parents see homeschooling as a great way to protect their children. Therefore, caring parents like these shouldn't be needlessly accused without evidence of wrongdoing.

Another homeschooling critic says homeschoolers are prone to abuse, as teachers won't notice abuse if children are at home. If this argument is to hold any water, we must be consistent and expect every homeschooling family to report to a police station every two days to discern possible abuse. School children must also report to police stations in their school holidays. We know this is ridiculous. We know abuse doesn't happen because children are homeschooled. Abuse occurs when people are immoral. So, abuse can occur irrespective of educational method.

Are School Teachers Favourable Towards Homeschoolers?

A 2012 study by researchers, Malone and Cecil, showed the views of student and new graduate teachers toward [ex-]homeschool students in their care. Their study showed teachers positive or negative views hinged on whether the teachers themselves were homeschooled or had a friend who homeschooled. Teachers who had positive views tended to know one or more homeschoolers, while those with negative views didn't (personally) know any homeschoolers.

The study made an interesting discovery when it found female student teachers who planned to teach high school had a significantly more negative view towards homeschoolers compared to their male counterparts. An implication of the study was that college programs should teach pre-service teachers to be more accepting of students from different educational backgrounds.[301]

In any case, abusive families are more likely to send children to public school as they would be less concerned with their children's educational improvement. These parents may be unwilling to spend any more money on their children than is necessary.

'It has always been a mystery to me, how a parent can possibly take on the job of several professional teachers, as well as the complex school administration, - and succeed at it.'

While most teachers deserve respect in spades (and a high percentage of them choose to homeschool themselves), some teachers or schools feel threatened by homeschooling because they feel their job is devalued 'if any parent can do my job'. Karen Hurlbutt, a homeschooling researcher, recorded some responses from Special Education teachers on this issue, saying:

> *Teachers felt school staff would feel offended if the parents pulled the child [out of school]. One teacher felt there may be some 'animosity or hurt feelings that parents feel that we would not do our best to serve the children in our care,' if they removed their child from school. She added it is 'sometimes hurtful when a parent does not trust or believe in your professional judgment and experience to attempt an intervention or support.' One teacher stated 'it's hard to not feel offended. It's like a slap in the face.'*

You Can Fail High School and Still Be a Great Homeschool Teacher

Although more highly educated parents are more likely to homeschool, parents with no college education can still homeschool and produce impressive academic results.

In a study looking at 15 independent studies, drawing from 12,789 homeschooled students in all 50 American states, researchers found a significant difference in the academic achievement of homeschoolers who had parents with more advanced educations. However, parents with no college education could produce impressive results.

Researchers found if neither parent had a college degree, their children scored in the 83rd percentile, well above the national average. If one parent had a college degree, children scored in the 86th percentile. If both parents had a college degree, children scored in the 90th percentile.

So, it seems teacher-educated homeschooling parents are not necessary for homeschooling success. Indeed, parents who never achieved a teaching degree (but, had some other sort of degree) had the same results as parents with education degrees. If neither parent was a certified teacher, their children scored in the 88th percentile. If one or both parents were certified teachers, children scored in the 87th percentile.

Parents don't need to be teachers to homeschool. They just need to be caring and committed educators.[302]

> *[Another] teacher elaborated by stating she felt schools view parents as a threat because 'if parents collect enough data about the effectiveness of a program, the school might be forced to implement it.' About half of the*

> teachers did feel parents who pulled their child [out of school] would be treated more negatively than when a child had never been enrolled. One teacher said, 'the district can just pretend they don't exist and don't have to acknowledge' the children who had been homeschooled from the start, and, 'if they remove their student, the district will feel that they have been [belittled].³⁰³

If every parent felt confident enough and inclined enough to homeschool, we would need far fewer formally trained teachers – but, even so, that would not devalue a teacher's job. We *know* Christian parents have every reason to be confident as Christian homeschooling parents do an even better educational job compared a host of school staff *just by virtue of being a parent*. Parents automatically command the respect due to them.[vi] This respect enables the homeschooling parent to confidently take on the role of coach, tutor, teacher, counsellor, librarian and disciplinarian. (Most parents do these jobs outside school hours every day with success and confidence).

In short, schools are overcomplicated, and children do not need complex school hierarchies to learn. School administration is uncomplicated – unless you make school administration complicated. Heavily regulated environments are superfluous unless you're a large business. The small business of homeschooling needs only loving, supportive environments for children to flourish.

In short, bureaucracy doesn't equal better organisation.

'Inspections by the Board of Studies appear to be rather superficial, - or the students would be better prepared for life.'

Statistics show higher regulation among homeschoolers produces no better results among homeschoolers. American homeschoolers with government regulation inspections scored in the 87th percentile. States with no, or weak regulation scored the same mark.³⁰⁴

[vi] See Chapter 13 for evidence on academic achievement and the better mental health homeschoolers experience.

For families doing the right thing, regulation stifles the ability to plan education creatively and reduces curriculum flexibility. However, in families that claim to homeschool, but hardly even teach their children basic life skills, regulation can be beneficial. Because these somnolent families are in the minority, the case for less regulation is strong.

'Children's Rights.'

Children have human rights, and these are usually (and should be) protected by their guardian parents. Children don't have rights independent of parents because children make immature decisions – that's what makes them vulnerable. Children don't have these rights anywhere in society – including in school.

In Australia, the government recognises children are immature and in need of guardians who have children's best interests in mind. This guardianship has been embedded into the law through the *Education Act 1900* s 4(a).

In this Act, education is the responsibility of a parent, not the child or the government. But, even if the government changed guardianship rights, guardianship would still be a parent's responsibility according to the Bible (Deut 11:9).[305]

'School rings the alarm bells, before counsellors, DOCS, police, etc. become involved. I believe that our society has an obligation to keep children at school and away from possible dangers, like abusive situations.'

This writer's previous comment accuses homeschooling parents of being overprotective. A few paragraphs later, the writer is saying homeschooling parents are abusive. Which is it? Perhaps it doesn't matter to the writer, so long as everyone goes to school.

School might be able to ring alarm bells, but they can't keep children away from abusive environments, as most school children return home after school and spend their weekends and school holidays at home. Also, parents can abuse children at home, without school authorities getting wind of anything. One child talked about the brutal beatings his father hid from school, saying, 'He would beat me using a bar of soap in a sock, so there weren't bruises to be seen at school.'[306]

Sometimes school children themselves are instigators of abuse. A child below age ten cannot be a 'perpetrator' according to the law. Children under ten years of age go unpunished for many crimes they commit – not deemed crimes by the law. Simply, the law says those under ten years old are unindictable. In other words, if a nine-year-old boy is sexually abusing an eight-year-old girl, the younger student will not be defended by police because the law says children under age ten are innocent. Therefore, how are schools able to alert authorities, when the law fails to back them up?[307]

Only when prosecutors can prove the child can distinguish between right and wrong is a conviction (sometimes) recorded. But, Criminal prosecution is 'only part of the range of societal responses to youthful wrongdoing, and usually invoked only when misbehaviour is sufficiently serious or repetitive that responses within the family or educational environment are deemed inadequate.'[308]

As Andrew Vachss, a lawyer for youth and children says, 'We don't protect our young, and we tolerate predators of our own species.'

'I believe our society has an obligation to keep children at school and away from possible dangers, like… religious fundamentalism.'

In any debate, it's always useful to define terms. The term 'religious' means 'relating to or believing in a religion'. The term 'fundamental' means, 'a central or primary rule or principle on which something is based'.

As Christians, we ought to joyfully respond to this person's objection, saying, 'Guilty as charged. We are religious fundamentalists. We are people who base our principals on our religion'.[vii] Christians are happy to have others know they believe in a religion, a religion on which they base their principles.

[vii] Col 2:6-10.

Many Christian homeschoolers aim to be fundamentalists. With many schools failing to teach the Bible, fundamentalists revel in teaching its full content. All Christians should return to the fundamentals and read what Christ said because Christ taught the fundamentals. Such thinking gives children a strong foundation on which to build their morality. 'Religious fundamentalism' removes children from the weak humanist religion taught in many public and Christian schools today.

The writer's objection to religious fundamentalism shows the perspective that flavours the whole letter – namely a vicious attack on homeschooling - an education method they see as religious. This letter is aimed at intimidating and belittling the Christian faith and the resolve of every Christian parent who wishes to homeschool.

'Parent's need regular training, to justify them functioning as teachers.'

Training parents more would be useless. Studies by the *National Home Education Research Institute* show a parent's education level makes little or no difference to a child's educational progress, especially if parents are already university trained.[309]

Other Common Objections to Homeschooling

Will I Be Bored If I Homeschooling?

In *The Home Schooling Father*, Michael Farris wrote about his wife who complained she lacked intellectual stimulation before they began homeschooling. For Farris' wife, life before homeschooling seemed to consist of cleaning up after her children and changing nappies. But after Farris' wife began homeschooling, it seemed she was no longer bored. Homeschooling began satisfying her intellect and she became happy in her role as a homeschooling mother.[310]

It seems boredom is rarely an issue for homeschooling parents because many are *too busy* to be bored. If boredom is an issue, parents can easily make homeschooling more enjoyable by seeking to become lifelong learners alongside their children. This is a phenomenon that is common among homeschooling parents. As Antoinette Hesford said, 'Homeschooling was so much fun!'

Will My Children Be Bored If I Homeschool?

All children become bored – even homeschooled ones. Homeschooled children, however, are a lot less bored than school children because they're able to control more of their formal and informal learning. Although you won't be guaranteed a life filled with excitement, homeschooling is enjoyable.

Because formal education at home usually takes less time than school, homeschoolers have ridiculous amounts of spare time compared to school children. Homeschooling mother, Cafi Cohen, said homeschooling let her kids get so far ahead because her family did only an hour and a half of academics a day. In this time, they did what school took seven or eight hours to do. With the spare time, Cafi's kids didn't watch TV or play video games. Instead, her son got a private pilot's license and her daughter earned money to study abroad. Her children worked in paid employment and did volunteer work.[311]

Because of the plentiful spare time homeschooling affords (over and above the time they have to do formal education) homeschoolers can study what interests them.[312] When students are interested in a topic, homework is a pleasure and can be a fun learning experience for the children and parents alike. Indeed, all homeschoolers interviewed in this book who had earlier been to school reported homeschooling was 'more fun' and 'less boring' than school.[313] This report is partly due to homeschooling's flexibility with subjects. If homeschoolers don't like a subject, they can easily replace it with a more interesting subject – a feat almost impossible in school.

Melissa, who averaged high distinctions in her subjects, replaced the subjects she disliked. She commented on homeschooling's flexibility, saying, 'I loved studying what I was interested in. When I really struggled with one topic, my Mum said, 'That's ok. You don't need to study that. It's not crucial. Pick another one.'

Even though homeschoolers may become bored at home, homeschooling appears to be far more interesting than school, especially when parents are excited about learning alongside their children. To sum it up, Ben (who attended public and homeschool) said, 'For me, homeschooling was boring. But school was way more boring – you'd spend hours doing nothing at school. At home, at least you could do your own thing.'

'Your child won't learn how to socialise properly if he's homeschooled.'

See chapter 12 'What About Socialisation'.

I'm Too Scared to Homeschool

The fear of failure is the driving force that keeps many potential home educators away from homeschooling. They are openly dissatisfied with school, but peer pressure from parents and teachers around them often keeps parents from committing to home education. These parents fear other parents as well as their families and the wider community. Indeed, homeschooling is sometimes considered vaguely unpatriotic – like sitting in your bedroom when everyone else is partying outside.

Potential home educators also feel inadequate to teach compared to professionally educated teachers. After all, there must be some reason everyone is at school (for the answer to this objection, see earlier in this chapter).

Perhaps this objection is best answered by pointing out that parents already homeschool. They do it before and after school hours. They also teach and tutor their children through their homework projects (or find tutors when they're unable to do this). Parents should feel empowered when they realise they unconsciously homeschool all the time. All parents homeschool

> ### *Love and Courage*
> While Antoinette doesn't have an education degree, she has two necessary characteristics for a homeschool Mum. She is **courageous in the face of opposition,** and she **loves her children**. Courage is not just being confident you can do it. Courage is being scared, yet having enough bravery to do the deed despite your fear.

their children before any of them enter a classroom! Some parents even teach their children the alphabet before school starts.

In this way, home education is just an extension of what parents are already doing. Parents find materials to keep their children learning through the time they have them. One parent, Lisa Rivero, wrote of this continuity, saying that, as parents, we can't imagine how we'll parent an infant, but we do. We teach them how to do practical things and how to live morally. Sometimes we educate them like teachers in a school, teaching them their ABCs, or sharing our interests with them. We teach them how to develop their own hobbies and find information themselves. When they tell us what they've learned, we find we're learning from them and trying to keep up. Rivero says we do all these things without an education degree because we have a responsibility to our children.[314]

Despite this, homeschooling will probably remain a minority pathway. It's radical and unpopular. Those who choose homeschooling will

Q AND A WITH HOMESCHOOL PARENTS

Did you find teaching challenging?

At times. Mathematics and algebra required some skill and know how. But, books, tutors and friends can always help with teaching.

Did you ever panic when you hit a brick wall?

Not really. The only difficult area was mathematics. I think it was a bit more frustration, in that we might know how to do it ourselves, but we mightn't be able to explain it in a way that they would grasp the concept. To teach maths you have to know the subject well. Some homeschooled families really know it well. Our third daughter, Ali, seemed to know math really well and was able to do it with her eyes shut. She was more inclined to get hold of it and run with it. She'd also teach her sisters. She was naturally inclined to do math.

Steven and Barbara Fraser, Homeschool Parents. (Interview conducted May 2015.)

probably be criticised and shunned because of their choice. Although the stigma is great, parents ought to feel confident they *can* teach their children well. The statistics and testimonials affirm mothers of any educational standing are perfectly capable of teaching their children successfully. Ask any homeschooling parent. It's not rocket science!

Are Homeschoolers Prone to Abuse?

See Chapter 9, section: 'Does More Child Abuse Happen in School or Homeschooling Settings?'

Can Single Parents Homeschool Too?

Homeschooling can seem like an impossible feat for single parents and few single parents homeschool today.[315] Many of these brave parents choose to homeschool because they realise they will never see their child if they don't – so they make it work.[316] Making it work from home is easier today that it has been in decades past. Online businesses are now viable ways of making a living. As Penelope Trunk said:

> *For me, this meant years of living in poverty in New York City while I tried to figure out how to support the family from home. We were late on rent all the time. We ran out of food on occasion. But I told myself that there was no way I was going back to an office job because I'd never see my kids. I made a huge career change, going from $150,000 a year to $30,000 a year. Almost overnight. It was traumatic and hugely disappointing. But after five years of doing that, I make plenty of money from home.*

For divorced parents, the need for continuity in a child's life is why some single parents choose to homeschool. If homeschooling parents divorce, one parent may choose to continue homeschooling and thus reduce the impact of an already drastic life change. Andrea Rosa, from *Single Parent Homeschooler*, says these parents can be there for their children in a way other divorced parents can't. Homeschooling parents can reduce the damage from a broken relationship in this way.

But, I Have An Only Child...?

Is socialisation a more significant issue for only children? Many parents feel homeschooling is not an option with only children as boredom and restlessness will become too big an issue. Others feel an only child will not receive enough social interaction at home, and so school is a better option.

To answer these qualms, many experienced parents (with only children) have written books testifying about homeschooling an only child. Professor Lisa Rivero, author of *The Homeschooling Option*, is one of them. She homeschooled her only child and explained how her son had an opportunity to find 'surrogate siblings' in other homeschooled families. Rivero said her son became good friends with children of different ages. He wrote a book with a homeschooling friend. Rivero said she watched his relationships with younger children improve and grow as he got to know them better

An only child will attach themselves firmly to other children, as they have no siblings to divide their attention. A strong attachment with other Christian homeschoolers means an only child can retain their friends, sometimes for life.

I'm Not Qualified to Teach My Children...?

When Bill and Antoinette began considering homeschooling, they asked themselves if they would be qualified enough to homeschool. Antoinette had every right to ask as she didn't finish high school. To compound things, Antoinette was born in Egypt, and, due to her dyslexia, she never grasped the English language properly. She knew only basic history and mathematics and only claimed an excellent knowledge in one area - fashion.

Are Homeschoolers Their Own Teachers?

In her book, *The Homeschooling Option*, Lisa Rivero asks us to consider what actually happens in many high school classrooms. Rivero, an Education professor, said that while a teacher might go over reading, answer questions, intitiate discussions and mark homework, students do the homework themselves. Rivero concluded that much of what the teacher does could be handled by someone else – even the students themselves![317]

Parents like Antoinette don't need to worry because statistics show there is *little or no or relationship between student achievement and parental teaching certification level,* according to homeschooling researcher, Dr. Brian Ray. No matter if the child has special needs or typical needs – a teaching certification isn't required.[318]

Dr. Donald Ericksen, Professor Emeritus of Education at the University of California Los Angeles, also knows certification makes no difference. He said, 'Some of the worst teachers I've seen are highly certified. Look at our public schools. They're full of certified teachers. What kind of magic is that accomplishing? But I can take you to the best teachers I've ever seen, and most of them are uncertified.'[319] In saying this, Ericksen makes an excellent point. He recognises no degree is needed to be a good teacher.

Even so, parents who have struggled academically will ask themselves this question. But, asking yourself whether you have the necessary ability to be a science, geography or four unit maths teacher is asking yourself the wrong question. Instead, you should inquire if you can direct your children's study. As a homeschooling parent, you need not teach every subject yourself. In fact, you will find you end up teaching them very little because children teach themselves – they do this even in school.

John Holt affirms this view in his book, *How Children Fail,* when he says, 'It is not the teacher's proper task to be constantly testing and checking the understanding of the learner. That's the learner's task, and only the learner can do it. The teacher's job is to answer questions when learners ask them, or to try to help learners understand better when they ask for that help.'

When you think about teaching Holt's way, the idea of being a homeschool Mum or Dad sounds easier.

What to do if you don't know how to teach a subject:
- Learn the subject yourself.
- Find someone who knows the subject.
- Buy a pre-made curriculum (perhaps with backup phone tutors) to teach the subject.
- Enrol your child in distance education like OTEN or Open Universities from 12 years-old.

I Want My Child to Be a Light to the School World

[Evangelising in] kindergarten is a big ask for a child who has only lived a few years. Some children can deal with school wonderfully, and I've seen this in schools (where little ones speak up matter of a factly for God or the reality of God), but it's not so common that you hear that. So I don't know that it's a realistic expectation for parents to have.

Sue, Kindergarten Teacher and Homeschool Mother.

Most parents put their children in school at age five, hoping their children will naturally evangelise to other children. Perhaps their expectations are a little high as evangelising to other five-year-olds after you've just learned to talk (and perhaps not even learned the gospel) is a bit much to expect from young children.

Due to time and cognitive restraints, most school children haven't been well-equipped for evangelising before they're sent into the world. Sending five-year-olds to school is like sending soldiers into the battlefield without training. Many will suffer and be killed fighting the spiritual battle. This is evident in statistics. We see more than 70%

Christian children walk away from the faith in high school.[320] High school sees apostasy at its greatest, with the average age of most apostates being 14.7 years.[321] schools draw many Christians away from their parents'

Christian values and religion. These teenagers are often converted to the humanism taught in their classrooms.

Christian homeschoolers, on the other hand, are often immersed in Christianity which they learn from their parent's. Homeschoolers become disciples of their parents. These families often remain close and encourage one another in faith. Unlike many schools, homeschooling doesn't cut young children off from the body of spiritual believers for seven hours a day.

In school, perseverance in the faith is hard when you don't have encouragement. While a single Christian child might be saying, 'Jesus is God!', many peers, teachers and parents are saying, 'God doesn't exist.' With only little scriptural basis to rely on, children start synthesising these conflicting messages and become confused.

With little armour, children are unable to filter out the bad ideas and absorb good ideas. Sending unprepared soldiers into a hostile environment without training likely means slaughter in any battle situation. Indeed, if mature missionaries train themselves up for years before entering unknown countries, how much more should we be training our children?

Missionaries need to learn different languages, develop practical skills and prepare their families for overseas service before they start evangelising. Most missionaries have Bible

> **Q: How would you respond to another parent who said, I want my children to go to school to evangelise:**
>
> A: It is much more likely a child will be pulled down to the other child's level when it comes to attitudes and behaviour. Small plants need nurturing to grow well in a safe environment before they're expected to blossom and produce fruit in a harsh environment.
>
> *Jenny Allan, Homeschool Mother. (Questionnaire, March 2014).*

degrees before they are sent out.[322] Even so, many Christian parents leave their children at school, untrained, unarmed, expecting them to fight the good fight without a helmet and sword (Eph 6:13-17).

Steven, a Baptist minister and homeschool father of four, commented on this topic, saying:

> *Primary school children are not missionaries. It's a bit unfair to put the responsibility of evangelising on such little shoulders. It's more important to grow their character so they can then enter the world properly equipped. It's not until they become adults that they can really become missionaries. They must learn and grown in their character and have strength before they're able to do that.*

Maturity is important as mature evangelists strike more blows and receive fewer wounds than immature evangelists.

This is not to say children can't evangelise. Rather, evangelical guidance from parents is a wiser move when children are young and impressionable. With practice, children become mature and learn effective evangelism and godly living under the leadership of mature homeschooling parents. At home, children can learn in a spiritually safe environment. This is important because mature evangelists are made, not born.

Conclusion

When looking through the arguments against homeschooling, we can easily see many of the issues are bred from misunderstanding or misinformation. Many studies show homeschooling is a safe and effective way to educate one's child. Although Christian homeschooling is not a panacea, in comparison to school, it is a good option.

17. Gifted, Disabled and Special Needs Students

MANY SPECIAL EDUCATION (SE) TEACHERS BELIEVE parents of children with autism are not up to the job of homeschooling their special needs children. Some of these teachers, surveyed in the US by Karen Hurlbutt, believe homeschool parents have made an 'incorrect judgement on what is right for their child'.[323]

One SE teacher even said many schools and teachers feel they are 'the most qualified to meet the needs of all students, and feel parents are second rate.' Another SE teacher, said schools might view parents 'with disdain because they don't feel parents are capable of homeschooling their child'. Many of these teachers thought homeschooling parents were not up to the job because they assumed parents had insufficient educational knowledge. About a third of SE teachers felt homeschooling parents had only an American high school diploma. Many felt homeschooling parents, no matter their education, were under-qualified to teach if parents didn't have a teaching degree. Only three out of the fifty-two SE teachers surveyed admitted parents of children with autism are quite knowledgeable in the field of autism.

Given most SE teachers are persuaded that parents of children with autism are unready, unqualified and unprepared to homeschool, we must ask ourselves a question: do the facts about Disabled and Special Needs (DSN) homeschooling support these teachers negative assumptions? This chapter will address these negative assumptions and look at:

- resources,

- life skill preparation,
- insufficient school teacher training,
- flexibility in the homeschool environment compared to school,
- academic progress of DSN children in the homeschool environment,
- opportunities to rest from constant and draining school socialisation and
- the success of gifted children and children with autism in the homeschooling environment.

What The Research Says

Research on homeschooling special needs children is overwhelmingly positive. Children with special needs flourish socially and academically in most homeschooling environments. One study by Lucy Reilly et al. asserts the individualised attention disabled students receive from homeschooling parents effectively meets the needs of students in a superior way to schools.[324] Other studies clearly show parents excel in teaching their special needs children at home.[325]

Gifted, Disabled and Autistic Homeschooling Students

Gifted Students

Many parents of gifted children turn to homeschooling when they realise the needs of their children are not being met to their full potential in school. Gifted school children find excelling in their studies difficult as their peers are slower and the class can only progress at the pace of the slowest learner. School teachers must slow gifted students down by giving them boring filler work to keep them needlessly occupied until the class catches up.[326] In school, some of these parents notice their children stagnating or regressing compared to parent's expectations or the child's giftedness. Therefore, they decide to homeschool.

Homeschooling lets gifted students work at the pace they desire or at a more challenging pace. The success of gifted homeschoolers has not been well studied. The best study to date is by researchers, Jolly, Matthews and Nester, who interviewed 13 parents of gifted homeschoolers.[327]

Jolly et al. found a few themes running through the data, some of which include:

- Parents know best when deciding whether to homeschool or not and
- Gifted children and their parents sometimes feel isolated when homeschooling.

Compared to school, parents of gifted children were better able to decide if school or homeschool was best given parents' interpretation of the child's giftedness. The decision was centred on their child's interests and needs. The families in Jolly's study only decided to homeschool after working with the public or private schools and failing to work things out satisfactorily on multiple occasions for several years.

Parents said they decided to homeschool after witnessing little or no academic improvement in their children when in the school environment and gifted programs. Parents were also finding their child's social and academic needs were not being met. One parent said her child found sitting and writing wasn't interesting because her child was so far advanced. It became painful for the mother to watch as the boy would end up writing far below his ability level because the work was boring to him.[328]

Another talked about the gifted program in her child's school, saying it was more interesting for the children because they got to leave the regular classroom, in which they were terribly bored. But the program failed to help the children's education because it was too short. The parent talked about the gifted program, saying the program gave their children a small taste of what they wanted all the time. So when they had to return to the slow classroom, things seemed even more tedious.

Homeschooling gifted children had its difficulties too. Many gifted children and their parents reported feeling isolated. At school, many gifted children felt alone, but their feeling of isolation didn't always abate with homeschooling. Failure to abate was due to asynchronous development, where gifted children were ahead of other children socially or academically. Because of different interests, this advancement made fitting in difficult for gifted children who were socially or academically older. One parent said, her daughter found it hard enough to find friends who could keep up with her and mentally challenge her, let alone share her passions. This parent said she found it hard to find older friends for her daughter as these friends were not always as nice due to age and social differences.

Another parent said their son didn't have the opportunity he might have had to build social networks if he had been of average intelligence. Another parent echoed this experience as they talked about how their children didn't want to play the same way other children of similar ages did because they were more mature and didn't see the point in [apparently] silly play.

Parents of gifted children also felt isolated. They felt that, while it was fine to discuss your child's sporting prowess or artistic abilities, talking about their children's giftedness was not acceptable: talking about your child's giftedness was viewed as bragging.

Despite these challenges and isolation, parents of gifted children still opt for homeschooling in increasing numbers due to the ability to choose an interesting and personalised curriculum, better learning opportunities and stronger one-on-one support.[i]

Disabled Students

Disabled [ii] students also benefit tremendously from a home education. American researchers, Duvall, Ward, Delquadri and Greenwood, studied the effect of home education's instructional environment on disabled students. While these researchers only studied four disabled homeschooling students with four controls, researchers confidently

---

[i] Jolly's study included many secular parents. It may be that Christian parents with gifted children would find more fellowship in Christian groups than secular parents might, given the nature and purpose of a Christian church. In the author's homeschool group, this seemed to be the case.

[ii] Disabled is defined in this book as referring to a mental or physical impairment that significantly limits one or more major life activities.

suggested disabled students see greater academic success at home compared to public school.[329]

For this reason (and many others), parents of disabled children choose to homeschool more often than parents with non-disabled children. The rationales given for homeschooling include:

- parents can tailor programs to the educational needs of their children,
- parents can gain control of their child's health and education,
- there is little satisfactory support for disability in school,
- homeschooling is consistent with the family dynamic,
- parents desire children will follow religious beliefs and
- improved academic results.[330]

Academic engagement time was found to be 2.6 times higher in disabled homeschooling students compared to disabled school peers. [331] Homeschoolers generally made greater progress compared to public school students in reading and writing; mathematic progress was

Curriculum Choices of Special Needs Parents
Duffey, J. (2002). Home Schooling Children with Special Needs: A Descriptive Study.

Curriculum Choice	Percentage
Other	1.2
School Program	6
Packed Curriculum	23
Design Their Own	58

equivalent. Duvall et al. clearly found *homeschooling parents could engage students more than SE teachers.*

Jane Duffey confirmed findings from Duvall et al. In her study looking at the families of 121 members of a special needs homeschooling support group, Duffey found most formal education at home was one-on-one instruction. Flexibility was increased as most of these parents made their own curriculum based on the child's abilities and interests (see graph).[332]

Homeschooling benefited their disabled children, with 96% of parents seeing academic progress. 89% saw average or improved social progress since homeschooling. Most special education children were attending four regular extracurricular activities.[333]

Autistic Students

Autism Spectrum Disorder, including Asperger's disorder, is one of the most challenging conditions to manage as diagnosis and treatment protocols fluctuate constantly. Many teachers admit a lot of schools and educators are unprepared to deal with children who have autism. Therefore, more families with these children are turning to homeschooling.[334]

The incidence of autism in Australia is around 1% and is four times more common among males compared to females. [335] [iii] Many children with autism have a difficult time at

Cage Used to Restrain Autistic Boy in Canberra School

A two by two meter cage made of blue metal pool fencing was used to restrain a 10-year-old autistic schoolboy in one of Canberra's public schools. Built by an external contractor for just over $5,000, the restraining cage was constructed as the child was physically abusive to staff and other children in the school.

The cage was used for two weeks before being dismantled by Education Authorities. The principal, who had approved the cage, was fired as investigators found him to be the sole instigator of the incidence.

[iii] Sources differ on prevalence, with some saying 0.5%, 1.0% and 2.0%.

school, with the incidence of issues such as bullying being increased four times compared to neurotypicals.[336] Dr. Karen Hurlbutt, who collected questionnaires from 52 SE teachers, found that, despite the high incidence of bullying, almost no SE teachers addressed issues that could be troubling for ASD school children like motor skills, sensory issues, different teaching styles or concrete versus abstract learning and understanding.[337]

Also, only four of the 52 teachers admitted school was a difficult place for children with autism because of the stress and constant pressure to socialise.[338] Indeed, all-day-socialisation is exhausting for most people; for children with autism, school is a killer because these introverted children have no opportunity to spend time alone, so often go into sensory overload.

The irony is that most teachers are worried about the lack of socialisation *homeschoolers* receive. In this case, we have less reason to worry about the lack of socialisation in homeschooling than we do the flood of over-socialisation in school.

Five Special Needs Problems Parents Can Remedy by Homeschooling

1. Too Much Socialisation

Most people need that hour or two alone everyday to build up their energy to be themselves again. The successful internet entrepreneur and confessing introvert, Sam Yagan, echoed many people's thoughts when he said he found it exhausting being around groups of strangers. Add an introverted, special needs child to the mix, and things are even harder.[339] Because the social and academic environment at school is angled towards non-Disabled, Special Needs (DSN) extroverts, introverted DSN students will likely experience more teasing, rejection and bullying.

Consequently, these children can experience enormous stress, taking their attention away from their studies.[340] Richdae and Prior confirmed children with autism went through considerable stress at school in their 1992 study.[341] These researchers measured the stress hormone cortisol to determine stress levels and found cortisol was hyper-secreted in children with autism. This high level of cortisol dropped to normal levels when children returned home. These results show children with autism have higher levels of stress at school compared to students at home.

Yes, Some Teachers Feel Rejected When You Pull Your Kid out of School

Many teachers feel you have scorned their teaching ability when you pull your children out of school. Many take your decision to homeschool personally and become negatively disposed towards you. Here are some comments from SE teachers on how they feel when parents pull their children out of school:
- There may be some 'animosity or hurt feelings [as] parents feel that we would not do our best to serve the children in our care.'
- It is 'sometimes hurtful when a parent does not trust or believe in your professional judgment and experience to attempt an intervention or support.'
- 'It's hard to not feel offended. It's like a slap in the face.'
- One teacher felt school sees parents as a threat because 'if the parents collect enough data about the effectiveness of a program, the school might be forced to implement it.'

Many teachers feel parents get negatively treated when they take their children out of school because teachers feel parents are making a mistake and are not qualified to teach their children.

What you can do to help?
- Affirm their teaching ability, if appropriate.
- Explain your decision to homeschool is not personal.
- If appropriate, explain the school structure is the problem, not the teacher's ability to teach.
- Educate them about the benefits of homeschooling as you see them.[342]

High stress from cortisol hypersecretion is usually useful in an occasional stressful incident. In the long term, however, stress is harmful in the long-term as too much pressure causes hypersensitivity. According to Professor Paul Gilbert, hypersensitivity is detrimental because our attention and thinking becomes narrowed and focuses too much on the negatives, causing children to perform with less cognitive function.[343]

Because DSN children wrestle with difficult social challenges, school life can be a harrowing time. One writer, Lenore Hayes, observed, 'It is a daily struggle for children to get an education when classrooms are overcrowded, learning materials are outdated and overworked teachers have been reduced to college-educated child care providers. For children who are different from 'normal', it is almost impossible to learn in such a chaotic environment.'[344]

Social difficulties can be alleviated by placing DSN children in peaceful home settings. In these environments, DSN children are under less stress and are unaware of their ability or disability. At home, children with ADHD can run around during the day and follow their interests, without disrupting 30 otherchildren. This makes children happier because they're not restrained, and parents more comfortable because their children are happy. Home is an environment where active boys can be facilitated as Professor Lisa Rivero knows. Rivero says that just like our diets and sleep differ, children's need for physical activity differs. Homeschooling lets children (especially young boys) engage in the movement they seem to crave without requiring children to glue themselves to a seat all day or line up quietly waiting for long periods of time.

A child with excess energy and heightened sensory inputs often has a wonderful education at home as parents can control the child's environment. DSN children can adapt to personalised and individualised environments far more easily than school environments with little individualised attention.

At school, children with autism sometimes shut down in busy or loud environments. Because children with autism are highly sensitive to sensory input, disruptive noises (that most children adapt to easily) stress these children out. Children with autism try blocking out disruptive input using (usually) socially unacceptable calming methods such as rocking or singing to themselves. These methods are also disruptive to the class and the teacher's schedule.

These children are sometimes disruptive in other ways as well; many are apathetic or misbehave. Both are due to sensory overload and can be remedied by slowing the social and sensory environment of children with autism.

2. **Slow Academic Progress at School**

Homeschooling DSN children produces impressive results. American studies by Dr. Steven Duvall showed homeschooled special needs students sat side-by-side with their teacher 43% of the time, whereas special needs, public school students only spent 6% of the time side-by-side with their teacher. Duvall's results also showed special needs homeschoolers *were academically engaged about two-and-a-half times* longer than special needs public school students. Duvall discovered public school special education classrooms spent about a quarter of their time with an academic response, while homeschoolers spent 60% of their time with an academic response. So, Duvall concluded homeschoolers were at a tremendous advantage academically.[345]

Homeschoolers were judged to have academically advanced faster than public school DSN students. While public school DNS children advanced the equivalent of two weeks in written language skills, homeschooled DSN students were judged to have advanced six months![346] Duvall summarised his findings by saying the results of the study clearly indicated homeschool parents (with no teaching certification) can create good instructional environments at home that greatly benefit children with learning disabilities so they can improve their academic skills.[347]

Because homeschooling academically engages DSN children for twice as long, homeschoolers complete their regular homework in half the time – usually around three hours per day.

Gifted students can also benefit from the self-paced academic environment that home provides. One gifted homeschooler who completed his homework quickly, Timothy, explained how ineffective school was for him:

> *'I'm what they called 'gifted'. I have a high work ethic and pick up new concepts easily. I was finding mainstream school very frustrating because the class often didn't learn as fast as I did. Once I understood something, I had my work done very quickly,*

> *but I had to wait for everyone else to catch up. On the other hand, my social and emotional skills were not well developed, and the other kids at school knew they could get a reaction by picking on me, so I ended up in trouble a few times over that.'*

Although Timothy could have skipped a grade and increased his academic engagement, moving into an older classroom would have been ineffective as Timothy was unprepared for a senior class in other ways. Timothy began homeschooling and found so many of these issues improved in the homeschool environment.

3. Inflexible Environment

Academic flexibility is useful for gifted and DSN students as these students can set the academic pace to their needs. Gifted students can increase the pace, while disabled and other special needs children can decrease the pace. Both options allow these students to study at a comfortable pace without feeling like a show-off or a failure.

Gifted students show high levels of imagination, curiosity and intelligence. They often find school frustrating and slow. Many prefer to learn and discover things on their own at home. Personalised home curriculums are a good option for gifted students as they allow for higher student engagement. These curriculums are less time restrictive compared to school's curriculum. At home, creative writing projects can be studied for hours. The project doesn't need to be confined to, for example, an english lesson time slot between 10 and 11am in classroom 3B.

Other DSN students need to learn at their own pace because of mental or physical limitations. These limitations often mean DSN children have more medical appointments. Homeschooling allows flexibility around these appointments and other unforeseen circumstances. Lessons can be rescheduled rather than missed. If needed, learning can also be reset to a slower or faster pace. This variable pace means parents can ensure children receive a thorough grounding in life skills.[348]

4. Inadequate School Resources

Most SE teachers in Karen Hurlbutt's study believe schools are better equipped to handle children with special needs.[349] Research by the *Australian Education Union*, however, showed four out of five principals in Australia admit their schools have insufficient resources to ensure the quality of the school program.[350] The Union estimated 100,000 students with disabilities got no extra funding, despite needing extra help to cope with their disabilities in class. Eighty percent of principals say they don't have enough funding for their special needs students. Furthermore, 84% of principals complained they had to spend funds dedicated elsewhere on disabled children.

Dyslexic Child: 'School Was a Waste of Time.'

Even though a child can give the right answer to a test, it doesn't guarantee they'll retain much after the test concludes. Children can give correct answers but may learn little or nothing.

Before homeschooling, Ben went to school, and got all the right answers, but could learn very little because of his dyslexia. Even though Ben had a photographic memory, he was unable to read or write (or understand what he read or wrote). Amazingly, Ben always managed to score at the top of his class by copying the photographic memory he had of different questions in his head. He reproduced these answers like a stencilled picture. But, Ben learned little and was barely able to write his name a few years later when his parents pulled him out of school. Ben recounted the following about his school experiences:

> *Due to being dyslexic, I needed hands-on education. The teacher would write something on the board and then I'd have to answer the question on paper. If I couldn't read the question, I couldn't answer it. So, I sat there twiddling my thumbs for a good few hours. Because I would pick up the concept from what I heard, not what I read, if the questions were phrased wrong, I couldn't seem to pick it up.*
>
> *At home, I was taught visually. When learning fractions, for instance, Mum would get a pizza box, and I'd learn my fractions that way. I needed another way to learn [besides writing]. Having one and four on a chalkboard doesn't help me. I needed something physical to pick up and say, 'That's*

> *a circle, and that's a quarter of that.' The teachers didn't have enough time in the day to assist me in that. So, I ended up being the class clown. I had nothing else to do for – well – hours. I'd make fun of everything that happened. I wasn't rude; I'd just have everyone else laughing and distracted because I was horribly bored.*
>
> I asked Ben if he still remembered the things he'd learned at school, but he said he'd forgotten the information and added that he considered his school years to be 'a waste of time'. Instead, he learned to do carpentry after *his parents had decided the school had inadequate resources to teach Ben.* Carpentry was a much better option for Ben because the trade called for little academic study and hands-on work.
>
> Benjamin Buckley, Homeschool Graduate. (Interviewed May 2014.)

Despite the dire need for SE funding, the government says schools have more money than they've ever had at their fingertips. This plethora of funding hasn't stopped the flood of calls from angry parents of disabled children who are frustrated about the poor educational experiences their children are having. These children are having trouble accessing support resources and experience. Funding is so bad that, in some cases, parents have been told to only bring their children to school for a few hours as the schools don't have enough funding to educate the student through the whole day.[351]

Kevin Meadow, the principal of Meadow Heights Primary School, said that in terms of funding for children with Autism, Attention Deficit Disorder, and sight and speech difficulties, schools were chronically under-resourced.[352]

School Greed: When Private School Fees Come Before Pupils

A story written by an anonymous primary school teacher to *The Guardian* newspaper told the story of an autistic girl, Sara, who went to a greedy private school. After several weeks of 'misbehaviours' Sara's teacher approached the school's principal and implored her to recommend sending Sara to a special needs school. The principal responded to the teacher saying Sara couldn't leave because the numbers were too low.

The writer continued her article saying she should have argued with the principal, but she didn't. Soon she had to watch the confidence of the little girl fade as Sara was faced with reprimand after reprimand by other school teachers who expected Sara to 'act her age'. Her speech and writing was far behind that of the class and difficult to understand at times.

Sadly, such institutional greed in private schools isn't as rare as you might think. This same teacher had worked at another school with clear rules: if you're teaching an intelligent child, tell the child's parents their children are average, so they don't leave for a better school. While not every private school principle is this deceptive (and we hope the vast majority are not), it's certainly important to realise private schools are businesses – and they aim to make a profit. The more profit, the happier the shareholders.[353]

5. Lack of Teacher Training

Lack of funding leads to lack of properly DSN-trained teachers. 74% of principals say their schools don't have the funding to train teachers about autism and special needs.[354] Fifty percent of principals said that if they got extra funding for special needs, the funding would be spent on professional development in these areas.[355]

But, SE funding is so tight, parents are routinely turned away from schools because of their child's disability. Federal Senator Sue Lines, who chaired the cross-party *Education and Employment Reference Committee* said parents were told (when they wanted to enroll their child with disabilities) that the school just didn't have the funding. This made enrolment difficult and meant that if parents wanted to get their children enroled in a local school, they had to go to government minsters and the Equal Opportunity Commissioner.[356]

Even if parents managed to enrol their disabled children without an issue, the committee found schools failed parents as schools didn't teach their children effectively, partly because of the lack of teacher training. This lack of training left parents dissatisfied with the education schools provided.

Conclusion

Even though principals and some teachers admit teachers are significantly under-prepared and under-resourced to deal with DSN children, many teachers still further the view that schools are the best places for DSN students. Many SE teachers believe they are better at teaching DSN students despite the research which suggests many are woefully unprepared for DSN children, especially children with autism who have behaviour problems.[357] Though schools and teachers are relieved when children with autism who have 'behaviour problems' are homeschooled (because 'someone else gets the job'), teachers still insist they are the best educators for DSN children.[358] Even though the evidence shows DSN homeschoolers have much better outcomes compared to their peers in school, teachers still think schools are the best places for DSN education.[359]

18. What About Secondary and Tertiary Education?

THE PURPOSE OF CHRISTIAN HOMESCHOOLING is to ground and equip a child in the gospel. When they are equipped, we send them out into the world so they can be arrows for God's glory (Psalm 127:4). We want them to put on the armour of God so they are equipped to stand firm in the faith regardless of what the world throws at them. But, are homeschoolers ever equipped enough to go to high school?

Many homeschooling parents send their teenagers to school when children reach their later high school years. This seemed to be the case with around half the homeschooling families in my homeschool group. Among other reasons, many parents believe they can no longer teach their children at home as tutoring has become too difficult. Other parents respond to their children's desire to go to school for high school, reasoning teenagers are now old enough to make wise moral decisions for themselves.

Even my own parents thought they had little choice in the matter and were going to send us to school after we finished primary education at home. They only decided to keep homeschooling us when we strongly (and tearfully) objected to school. This decision made, my parents found appropriate information and resources that allowed us to continue homeschooling and doing distance education easily throughout high school.

I think this was the right decision as, in my experience, homeschoolers (just like Christian children who have been to school) are rarely equipped to deal with the worldy opinions and behaviours seen in high school.

Elizabeth Smith, the wife of Home School Legal Defense Association (HSLDA) President, J. Michael Smith, says parents should homeschool during their whole education including their latter high school years. She gives the following reasons parents should persevere through homeschooling, saying homeschooling through the high school years is better because:

1. It cements teenagers' relationships within the family, so they last a lifetime. Smith says homeschooling is as useful in high school as in junior school. The same reasons to homeschool apply to older teens as they do to younger children.
2. It helps stop teenagers from becoming confused as they must serve 'two masters' when at school: parents and the school/peers.
3. One-on-one teaching is the most efficient way to learn. This education is only provided at home.
4. It means teenagers can choose what interests them with a personalised curriculum. Personalised curriculums make learning easier.
5. It means teenagers can skip high school and continue to tertiary education through higher education institutes (discussed below).
6. It means parents can influence peer relationships more and oversee the amount of time spent inside and outside the family.
7. It means parents can protect children from the need to conform, by keeping them in an environment where they're free to think about things without having to accept a bloated and politically correct agenda (i.e. safe schools).
8. It allows more flexibility than school.
9. It keeps children in a safe environment, away from potential places with high volumes of drugs or violence.[360]

Secondary Education

After homeschooling through primary school, parents may become anxious about their homeschoolers ability to enter further education. This chapter will list the three ways Australian homeschoolers can enter university. All pathways to university are valid ways to tertiary education.

We will look at how homeschoolers enter university or other tertiary education facilities without an end of school certificate, such as the High School Certificate (HSC) or an Australian Tertiary Admission Rank (ATAR). We'll look at three ways to get to tertiary education, namely through Technical And Further Education (TAFE), Open Universities and the Open Training and Education Network. (These are the pathways my family took to tertiary education).

Open Training and Education Network (OTEN)

My older brother, Joshua, completed an Architecture degree through the Open Training and Education Network (OTEN). OTEN is correspondence education for Year 10-12 students. It runs through all the fundamentals public school students study. Students study elective and mandatory units like school students. After completing Year 10, OTEN grants a Year 10 certificate students can use to enter TAFE or other tertiary institutes.

How Melissa Did It

'I went from homeschool to university. I applied for Open Universities Australia, which is open to everyone. They mark like a traditional university. And after I did ten units (which is equivalent to over a year's study), I applied for a university in Sydney and got credit for all my study and finished my degree. I worked at the same time and paid off the units I did. Not having a massive debt hanging over your head is important. I was able to get workplace experience while studying part-time.'

Melissa, Homeschool Graduate. (Interview conducted, November 2014.)

Alternatively, after completing Year 12 with OTEN, homeschoolers can earn a HSC score. This score is used to enter university or other higher education facilities. If an ATAR score is too low, a bridging course can be completed, allowing entry into many desired degrees. (A student can enter a course with a lower ATAR score and then swap into the course they want after a semester of work, providing their marks are sufficient).

University Bridging Course – (UC-Connect)

One such bridging course is *UC-Connect*. The University of Canberra has an excellent bridging program called UC-Connect. This bridging program allows students with inadequate high school marks (or unrecognised education backgrounds like homeschooling) indirect entry into many courses if they satisfactorily complete two relevant units of the desired degree (often an easy feat for a homeschooler).

When these two units are completed successfully, students have already made a start on their course and upon completion of the bridging course, homeschoolers will have made a two-unit start into their desired course. Usually, the bridging course takes around six months.

Other university bridging courses similar to UC-Connect are available in most Australian universities today.

Open Universities

My younger brother, Neville, completed a Law degree through Open Universities (OU), an Australian correspondence university. OU offers correspondence courses through different universities around Australia under its umbrella name, Open Universities. Courses or units can be done online, or partly online, allowing students to attend campus for part of the unit if they wish. Universities credit the units and courses undertaken, that then count toward future university courses.

Anybody can do a unit at OU. Many students start at a young age and do OU rather than the high school curriculum. *In this way they skip two years of HSC preparation, and directly study units that interest them.* They need not go through the frustration of completing subjects which are irrelivant to their chosen course of study simply for the sake of an HSC or ATAR mark.

Technical and Further Education (TAFE)

For those less academically inclined, TAFE offers homeschoolers an excellent opportunity to learn a trade or non-university/blue collar course. TAFE is Australia's largest provider of job training and education. Most TAFE courses can be entered with a Year 10 certificate (obtainable through OTEN). From there, students can start their chosen trade. The TAFE option is often ideal for teenagers who can't sit still and prefer 'hands-on' learning. This was my chosen pathway to higher education and university.

Tertiary Education (University, College, TAFE, Entrepreneurial Ventures)

As homeschoolers grow older, parents start thinking of tertiary education. They wonder if their child is prepared enough to enter the secular world. They wonder if homeschoolers can cope with lifestyle rigours that accompany further education. But, parents need not be anxious. University preparedness studies in America found homeschoolers often outperform their peers in many areas in testing done by the American College Testing (ACT).[361]

Homeschoolers are now far from disadvantaged when applying for universities. Some colleges actively favour homeschoolers over school children. Colleges favour homeschoolers because of their demonstrated critical thinking and impressive life skills portrayed in their portfolios. These portfolios are often impressive as homeschoolers usually have creative educational backgrounds with plenty of socialisation and extra-curricular activities.

Surviving in an unfamiliar environment – will my child fit in?

What about unfamiliar tertiary settings? If homeschoolers never expose themselves to secular culture, how do they cope when launched into such environments? In a study examining over 180 students, two-thirds of which were homeschooled, homeschool graduates were found to have lower depression scores compared to other students in university. They also received higher academic scores and rated their time at university more favourably than the school graduates.[362] Researchers, Bolle-Brummond and Wessel, said:

> We found that [homeschoolers] experienced college in many of the same ways that other, non-homeschooled students, did. In most regards, their undergraduate experiences were unidentifiable from the overall student population: they were normal college students.[363]

Homeschooling also nurtures other pro-tertiary skills. According to studies, excellence in leadership is standard among homeschooled graduates, with many participating in church activities and community events regularly.[364]

While at university (or other tertiary facilities), homeschoolers hold more appointed leadership roles, especially, spiritual leadership positions compared to public and private school graduate peers.[365] Their additional skills have set them up to help other students.

Because of the experience gained in the wider community before university, homeschooling university graduates usually find jobs quickly after university. Because homeschoolers learned plenty of life skills before they started tertiary education, they slip into the 'real world' easily.[366]

Entrepreneurial Ventures

While most homeschoolers aim for university, a handful start entrepreneurial ventures. Gary Knowles, an Education Professor at the University of Michigan, found many homeschoolers involve themselves in entrepreneurial professions that encourage independence.[367] A high proportion of homeschoolers like doing things themselves – just like they did when they were homeschooled.

Having grown up teaching themselves different types of skills, many homeschoolers find entrepreneurial ventures are a natural step into working life. Nathanael van der Kolk is a homeschooling entrepreneur. He talked about his experience in his submission to the 2014 Parliamentary Inquiry. The submission was later used in the final report:

> *Mr. Nathanael van der Kolk outlined that his experience with homeschooling enabled him to have a 'tailor-made education, to build my skills...and to be able to jump into being an entrepreneur at a young age'. He informed the committee that from 16 to 22 years old he could grow his abilities and learning about search engine optimisation and web design, enabling him to become a young entrepreneur and Director of the Australian Institute of Internet Marketing at age 24.*[368]

Evidence given to the Inquiry showed many homeschoolers are also involved in family businesses. Some homeschoolers continue to work in these businesses after they finish formal education. Perhaps we should be encouraging some of our teens to think creatively and consider starting their own business instead of going through the traditional routes of TAFE or University.

Jessica Robertson's Story

Overcoming Illness & Fostering Creativity

I MET JESSICA AT A CHURCH WE VISITED while on holidays. Her quiet and gentle spirit was evident to everyone she met. Jessica is passionate about homeschooling! The story of how Jessica came to be homeschooled is unique, and her story is an interesting one I hope you will enjoy!

Rebbecca Devitt: What influenced your parents to homeschool?

Jessica Robertson: I was probably their primary reason for homeschooling. I went to a Christian school for Kindergarten and then Year 1. Because I was anxious, I was often sick at school and used to throw up a lot. Most days I remember throwing up in front of (and over) all the kids in the classroom, and on the carpet. The vomit went on my clothes and down my front. One of my friends always used to take me to the bathroom, and she would say, 'Jess, look at you!' because it was all down my front and on my sleeve. Then we would wash off the vomit. I remember my teacher getting cranky at the situation – at having to clean the vomit off the carpet. Another reason was that I had bad health problems – the doctors didn't know what it was until they found out later that I had bad tonsillitis.

Going to school and throwing up every day caused me a lot of stress. I used to say to Mum, 'Mum, I just want to be at home with you!' and I used to cry.

She felt awful because she used to naturally think, 'I've got to send my kids to school – that's what you do.' But because I was sick all the time she decided to take me out at times…so, I would be at home more than I was at school. And then, when I went to school, I just wanted to be at home with Mum all the time. I think I was throwing up because I was sick and the anxiety of being sick didn't much aid my concentration.

RD: Did you find you were learning a lot at school?

JR: I struggled a lot academically. I'm naturally more creative. I need to work at my pace to get things done (and do it well). If I have to go by certain time frames, I'm not that great. School tends to force you to work at a certain pace and keep up with everyone. It wasn't that I was dumb, it was just that that wasn't how I learned, and school wasn't catering to my needs.

Eventually, Mum started considering homeschooling because I was at home more than I was going to school. They began researching, reading books, going to seminars, talking to people and then she took me out after Year 1.

RD: So they started reading homeschooling books and researching it?

JR: Yes, one of my relatives started homeschooling and talked to my Mum about homeschooling, and she asked her, 'Would you ever homeschool your girls?' My Mum replied, 'Oh, no, no, I wouldn't do that,' – because homeschooling is this thing which you just don't do. Therefore, my Mum's first response was interesting. But, because I didn't get better she started looking into it.

RD: Jess, I know that you're keen on homeschooling…probably more than anybody I've met. Why are you so keen on homeschooling?

JR: Well, I've had a taste of both worlds. I did school for a year, homeschooled for a year, then went back to school for two years, then I homeschooled again from about Year 4 onwards until the end. I've had a taste. I've not been a person who has *just* homeschooled or *just* been to school – I've had that taste. And, being able to compare the two for me makes me able to say what I prefer…and that would be homeschooling for sure. That's because I've felt the benefits of being able to grow in different ways – grow academically. Feeling like I could learn at my own pace made me feel like I was excelling. *I was in a relaxed environment where I felt loved and cared for – not being put under pressure to compete with everyone else's learning.* I could also pursue subjects I cared about – not just do the subjects the school said I had to. I could pursue my creativity.

RD: So, at school, you were studying a curriculum. How was that different when you homeschooled?

JR: My parents always encouraged me in my creativity. *There were weeks we would spend just on creativity alone* (then we would do our academics again). Homeschooling has the flexibility you don't get in a structured school system. You can structure things how you want to. That's the great thing about homeschooling – you can do things differently. *My parents saw that I had a gift in my creativity with art, so they encouraged it.*

RD: What sort of gift was it, specifically?

JR: It's interesting, because while I was still at school and struggling, Mum took me to get tested to see…because they said I was not very good at school. Mum had been to a parent-teacher interview at the end of Year 3. And my teacher said, 'Jessica's work is good, but I'm worried about her in high school – that she won't be able to keep up.' And so, they took me out of school again (besides, I was always saying I was desperate to do homeschooling again because I'd had a taste of it).

In the test, they took me to see a specialist lady who focused on children and learning development. She held up pictures and told me to tell her what the opposites of different things are and to draw this or that. There were certain areas I was below my age in (on the academic side of things), but she said with art, spatial awareness and hand-and-eye coordination, I was double my age. I was about 7 when I got tested, and she said I had the rating of a 13-year-old. That was exciting and encouraging for my parents. Because when you hear negatives from school it can be discouraging. *I might not have been an academic, but I was strong in other areas.*

RD: Do you still use that artistic ability now?

JR: Definitely. I believe things that interest and motivate you as a child are the things you should think about doing as an adult. Ever since I was little, I always loved drawing, putting on shows and plays and that sort of thing – and I still love these things now. Sometimes it's sad when you see children doing these amazing, creative things and then they lose their creativity when they get older and work in a field or area where they don't use it at all. What I'm doing now is writing and illustrating. One day I am hoping to publish and illustrate some children's stories. And I'm working on a puppet theatre which I hope to use to get work someday.

RD: Do you work, Jess?

JR: Yes, I'm working as a dental nurse and a childcare worker which is great…I'm able to use my creativity with the kids and encourage their creativity, something I like doing. I'm also a nanny on occasion. I love spending time with children.

RD: Did you notice a difference as you changed from school to homeschool and back again?

JR: As you know, I was sick and had plenty of anxiety. When I homeschooled, I was able to improve my reading and writing…and my health improved a lot. At home, my health didn't take a long time to improve because I was immediately relaxed. But this is particularly interesting because, when I went back to school a second time, *my Mum said she noticed a difference in me and my sister and our relationship. She said we were best friends when we homeschooled. When we went back to school, we fought a lot.* And then, when we returned to homeschooling, we were best friends again. And holiday time at school we became close again. Then when we went back to school, we went to our peer groups…they were our friends, and that's who we hung out with. You weren't allowed to socialise with your big sister because she wasn't in your age group.

RD: So there was a bit of a forbidden age thing happening?

JR: Yes, I remember getting into trouble at school socialising with some children younger than me.

RD: Who got you into trouble?

JR: A teacher.

RD: A teacher got you in trouble for socialising?

JR: Yes, she told me to stay with my age group. I used to like playing with kids a bit younger than myself. That was a bit sad.

RD: You mentioned before that you think parents should train up their child in the Lord's way. Do you think parents can do that and still send their kids to school?

JR: Yes, of course. I don't doubt that. But I think education is a big part of children's lives. Going to school is a big part of their lives. And if their parents are involved in their lives more than the norm then I think that's better.

RD: So you wouldn't say homeschooling is the only way to be a good parent?

JR: No, of course not. *But just having that increased involvement with their children's learning is better.* I find it sad that parents miss that. It's a great way of bonding between parents and children. School separates children from parents. *Homeschooling causes children to respect their parents more.* I'm not saying kids who go to school don't respect their parents…but I think it does do something.

Because parents have invested that time in your life, as a kid you look at that as, 'They have spent time with me…and they care enough about me to spend that time with me.' *I now look at my parents and think, 'Oh, wow, they took that time with me. They could have sent me to school and had it easy.' It does make you look at them differently. I like hanging out with my parents. I like doing things with my parents.* We so often hear about some kids who go to school saying negative things about their parents, like, 'I don't want to hang out with them. I want to spend time with my friends.' Even as adults this happens – and it's *so* sad. Your parents are the ones that have given you life. They deserve more respect than that. They're my friends too.

Conclusion

CHRISTIAN HOMESCHOOLING IS NOT JUST GOOD because it is homeschooling. Rather, Christian homeschooling is good because it allows a parent to transmit their beliefs and values to the next generation effectively. All other benefits that come with homeschooling – better academics, family bonding and maturity – are a bonus.

Christian homeschooling, when lovingly done, has the power to bring about change in the youth of our day. This book has given you answers to the most important questions parents ask about homeschooling such as:

- Can school have a detrimental effect on my child?
- Will homeschooling harm my child socially? and
- Can I afford to homeschool?

We've seen socialisation among homeschooling families is the most effective type of socialisation, especially when compared to peer socialisation at school. Homeschooling allows socialisation among children and parents of different age groups and allows children to avoid detrimental peer influence in favour of good, Christian family influence. Of course, this depends on a parent's commitment to holiness – homeschooling isn't a panacea. However, it does prevent unintended bad influences. Maturity is developed in the homeschooling environment through the modelling of the parents' good examples and opportunities to socialise and work in the community – in real life.

These real-life opportunities to mature give homeschoolers added social and practical skills. Socially, homeschoolers tend to have healthy relationships with those in authority, such as their professors. These good relationships are possible because their teacher/parent has always been someone who had time to show they cared about the child's life and their success. Practically, homeschoolers learn by directing their study. This self-direction tends to make more creative and hands-on individuals.

The success of Christian homeschooling families is largely because children are away from environments where there is peer pressure to conform and do things the group way (what we call group-think). This pressure stifles individuality. School also rushes students and creates a frustrating environment in which it is difficult to learn effectively. By contrast, homeschoolers usually spend half the time on regular homework tasks and have an (almost) unlimited amount of time to spend on activities or practical tasks they enjoy.

Even if school children could get their work done quickly and spend time directing study as they liked, school might still be distracting because of the bullying some children experience. (Australian primary schools are among the worst in the world for bullying). Bullying, thankfully, is uncommon in Christian homeschools as relationships are often closely monitored by Christian parents and corrected when bullying occurs. This monitoring can prevent many years of hardship and make for a more comfortable and enjoyable childhood.

Pressure to engage in risky behaviours such as alcohol and drug use and premarital sexual relationships are also rarer among Christian homeschoolers. Homeschooling protects children from unnecessary temptation and teaches children how to avoid risky behaviours. Children learn to avoid these things as they watch their godly parental role models. In contrast, alcohol and drug use and premarital sexual relationships are all more common among school children. The consequences of engaging in these risky behaviours mean many school children will be more distracted from their study and a relationship with God. (Perhaps this is unsurprising given many schools were created with the aim of distracting their students from God).

Although public schools seem to be bigger promoters of some of these behaviours (see Safe Schools), the issues of bad behaviour are not always resolved when Christian parents place their children in Christian schools. Many of these temptations still exist and affect students in Christian schools. Indeed, when a family's preexisting religiosity is considered (controlled for), the environment in Christian schools seem to do very little to increase a student's desire to follow God. In contrast, Christian homeschool environments provide fertile ground for parents to teach their children, without distraction, in the way of the Lord.

Armed with these facts and statistics, I hope you will be confident to start your own homeschooling journey in the knowledge homeschooling is an effective educational pathway for caring Christian parents. It is possible to feel confident stepping into a homeschooling role in your own family!

Christian homeschooling has the power to change Christian families from families that are doing damage control after kids return from school to families that are progressively teaching their children in the way of the Lord. Perceptive Christians can use homeschooling to give their children spiritual meat while teaching them much more than a school can teach – minus all the garbage!

Through homeschooling, we know how to be proactive, not reactive. Share the secret by telling your Christian friends about homeschooling!

From the Author

I'd love to hear your story and why you are considering homeschooling. Readers with questions or comments can write directly to me at rebbeccadevitt@gmail.com or 321 Old Coowong Farm, Tugalong Rd, Canyonleigh, NSW, Australia.

Please visit my website at **www.whyonearthhomeschool.com**. You will find lots of extra resources and tips for the whole family. Also, review the book on Goodreads, Amazon or another website and **get this book as a FREE eBook**. Notify the author of your review through the website or at rebbeccadevitt@gmail.com and I'll send you your free copy. You can also opt to send this free eBook to a friend.

If you need a Christian homeschooling mentor, I can connect you with a personal homeschooling guide. The aim of this service is to help interested and new homeschooling parents remove potential mental hurdles and/or seemingly insurmountable difficulties. There is usually a way to solve or minimise problems, and experienced mentors can contribute fresh perspectives and previously undiscovered solutions.

God bless you and keep you.

www.whyonearthhomeschool.com

why_homeschool

Why on Earth Homeschool (group)

rebbeccadevitt@gmail.com

Why on Earth Homeschool

Appendix 1: Legal Requirements and Registration

Each Australian state and territory has laws about homeschooling. Some are more specific than others. Below is an overview of the relevant laws taken from the Australian Education Acts in each state and territory.

Australian Capital Territory

Chapter 5 of the Education Act (2004) ACT outlines the legal requirements for homeschooling in the ACT. The philosophy that underpins this legislation says parents have a right to hold diverse religious and educational philosophies on educational choices. Under s130, parents must register children with the authorities. Once the application has been received the child is provisionally registered for six months until their application is approved. Under s131, the application is made in writing to the Director-General. Then the application may be approved for up to two years if the authorities are satisfied.

The decision of whether to approve a homeschooling application is made when a homeschooling inspector inspects the homeschooling property and the homeschooling materials being proposed for use. Under s132, parents must provide high-quality education and must document educational 'opportunities' offered to children and the strategies they use to encourage their child to learn. The educational programs, materials and other records used for home education must be available for review by the home education inspector. When the application is made and approved, the Director-General will award the parents with a certificate of registration for their child. Application for renewal must be given before the expiry of the previous certificate. The Director-General keeps the child's name on a register of homeschoolers.

Every year parents must give the Director-General a report on the progress of their child's education. Registration may be cancelled by the Director-General if they think the parent has contravened the condition on which they were approved to homeschool. Before the registration is cancelled, however, the Director-General must give parents with a written notice outlining why registration is to be cancelled. The parents then have an opportunity to respond to the allegationS. Then the Director-General must consider this response before cancelling registration. If the parents have rectified the contravention and say they'll comply with regulations, registration may be reinstated.

New South Wales

Under Part 7 of the Education Act 1990 (NSW) parents must apply in writing to the Minister of Education. The Minister will check there are no obstacles to registration (such as previous records of unfit homeschooling) before refusing registration, or registering the child on a state Register of Homeschoolers. They may register more than one child of a parent simultaneously. Upon approval of the application, the Minister produces a certificate and writes to parents telling them of his or her approval. Children are registered for two years. The child must be instructed so they meet 'the relevant requirements of Part 3 [of the Education Act 1990 (NSW)] about the minimum curriculum for schools.' These are outlined below:

Key Learning Areas for Primary Education (Years K-6): English, Mathematics, Science and Technology, Human Society and its Environment, Creative and Practical Arts, Personal Development, Health and Physical Education. Study of Australian History and Culture is to be done in Human Society and its Environment. Art and music are to be in Creative and Practical Arts.

Courses of study in a key learning area are to be based on and taught in accord with a syllabus developed or endorsed by the Board and approved by the Minister.

Key Learning Areas of Secondary Education (Years 7-10): English, Mathematics, Science and Technology, Human Society and its Environment, Languages (besides English), Technological and Applied Studies, Creative Arts, Personal Development, Health and Physical Education. 'Six out of eight' key learning areas are to be provided for each child according to s10. English, Mathematics, Science and Human Society and its Environment must be studied each year.

A parent can apply to the Board to modify the syllabus so long as the Board considers the syllabus incompatible with the educational philosophy or religious outlook of the homeschool.

Key Learning Areas of High School Certificate candidates (Years 11-12): Students must study English and a broad range of study. See s12 for more information.

Registration may be cancelled if parents fail to instruct children according to the law, refuse entry to homeschooling inspectors or breach any condition of their registration. A registration certificate must be given in writing, at which time the parent can make an application to the Tribunal within 30 days for a review.

Under s75, a parent can tell the Minister they don't want to be registered as they are a conscientious objector to registration on religious grounds. The Minister will then decide if he will accept this objection and notify parents in writing. Again, an appeal can be made to the Tribunal to have the decision overturned. If accepted, the Minister must write a certificate of exemption which expires after two years.

Victoria

Under s4.3.9 of the Education and Training Reform Act (2006) VIC parents must register their children for homeschooling in Victoria. Registration may be cancelled if parents refuse inspectors access to review their children's educational program, material or other records or if parents fail to comply with the rules of registration. Children must be registered by age six. Failing to give children adequate educational instruction is an offence, which carries a fine (2.1.2A).

Queensland

Parents must make an application for registration as a homeschooler under Part 5 of the Education (General Provisions) Act 2006 (QLD). The child will be provisionally registered after the application is received. This ends after 60 days. Each application applies to only one child.

The application must include, 'a summary of the educational program to be used, or learning philosophy to be followed, for the home education; and any other documents, identified in the approved form, the Chief Executive reasonably requires to decide the application.' This information must be verified by statutory declaration. If the Chief Executive finds parents do not comply with a requirement, they must give 28 days where parents can try to rectify the requirement and tell them thereof. This period may be extended if the Chief Executive is agreeable. An example of a failed requirement is insufficient information provided or statutory declaration not provided.

Registration may be cancelled if false or misleading information is given, if conditions are not adhered to, or if the Chief Executive is not satisfied with a child's educational progress. If the Chief Executive believes grounds exist for registration cancellation, they must give notice in writing which states the reasons (s222). The parent has 30 days to respond to the allegations. The chief must consider these in their response. If registration is cancelled, parents must return the certificate of registration to authorities within two weeks of cancellation. A parent is obliged to surrender registration if they stop homeschooling and must make an application to a school for the child's schooling. Simultaneous enrolment in homeschool and another school is prohibited.

If the Chief Executive is satisfied, they'll approve the application and notify parents in writing. A certificate will also be issued stating as much. If the application is not decided within 90 days of receiving the application (or within 90 days of receiving further information), the application is taken to be refused.

According to s127, parents must ensure children receive a high-quality education and give the Chief Executive a written report of educational progress. This report must be given at least two months, but not more than three months, before each anniversary of registration. If moving, parents must tell authorities of their new address. The Chief Executive can impose conditions as they sees fit.

South Australia

The Education Act 1972 (SA) does not explicitly reference homeschooling like the other states. The SA Education Department was consulted for clarification. A departmental spokesman had the following to say:

While South Australia's Education Act does not specifically reference homeschooling, Section 81A allows for exemptions from compulsory attendance to be granted.

Parents can apply for an exemption to educate their children at home. For this exemption to be granted, parents need to demonstrate they will provide:

- An appropriate learning program
- Resources to support the learning program
- A suitable learning environment
- Opportunities for social interaction.

If an application is successful, an exemption from attendance at school is usually granted for 12 months. The exemption can be renewed annually by participation in a review of the home education program.

Northern Territory

Parents must apply to the Chief Executive Officer before homeschooling with details of the proposed home education under s20E of the Education Act (NT). Approval is for one year only, and inspections are compulsory.

Western Australia

Legislation concerning home education in WA is found in ss46-54 of the School Education Act 1999 (WA). Parents must apply to the Chief Executive for permission to homeschool. Information supplied may have to be backed up by documentary evidence. An application can relate to more than one child. Once the Chief Executive is satisfied with an application, they must issue the family registration and a certificate. Registration is for an indefinite period, meaning annual or biannual registration is not necessary. Inspectors are allowed to inspect educational programs of children for sufficiency. The first inspection comes within three months of being first registered and, after that, annually. An appointment time is to be made between the parent and the inspector at the child's home. After the inspection, the inspector will make out a report, a copy of which will go to the parents.

Registration may be cancelled if conditions have not been followed or if parents have hindered the inspectors. Before deciding a child's educational program is not satisfactory, the Chief Executive must take account of the School Curriculum and Standards Authority Act 1997 (WA) and the learning environment's effect on a child's educational progress and anything else of relevance. Parents can write to the Minister to review the Chief Executive's decision to cancel registration within 14 days of receiving notice.

Tasmania

Children must be registered for homeschooling from ages 5-16 years. Division 3 of the Tasmanian Education Act 1994 (TAS) says parents must make an application to the Minister for registration. Registration is valid for two years.

Cancellation can occur if the Minister deems the child's best interests are served best with cancellation.

Endnotes

[1] See Book V in Cornford, F. *The Republic of Plato*. (1945). 1st ed. London: Oxford University Press.
[2] Wiggins, G. *The 31 most influential classic books in education – a crowd-sourced list*. (2012). Granted And... Retrieved 8 December 2016, from https://grantwiggins.wordpress.com/2012/12/01/the-31-most-influential-classic-books-in-education-a-crowd-sourced-list/.
[3] Ibid.
[4] See *Republic* and Rousseau, J. (1948). *Emile*. 1st ed. London: Dent.
[5] Campbell, K. *Those ugly emotions*. (1996).1st ed. Fearn: Christian Focus.
[6] Reinsberg, K. *Behaviour Due to an Emotional Need*. (2015). Ability Path. Retrieved 8 December 2017, from http://abilitypath.org/2014/01/17/behaviour-due-to-an-emotional-need/; Dr. T. Berry Brazelton and Dr. Stanley I. Greenspan cited in LaMeaux, E. (2014). *5 Needs Your Child Must Have Met at Home*. Gaiam Life. Retrieved 8 December 2014 from http://life.gaiam.com/article/5-needs-your-child-must-have-met-home.
[7] See the *Humanist Manifesto I, II* and *III* at American Humanist Association. *Humanist Manifesto I*. (2016). American Humanist Association. Retrieved 10 December 2016, from https://americanhumanist.org/what-is-humanism/manifesto1/.
[8] Ibid.
[9] Encyclopedia Britannica. *tabula rasa | philosophy*. (2016). Retrieved 10 December 2016 from, https://www.britannica.com/topic/tabula-rasa.
[10] Careersinpsychology.org. *How to Become A Child Psychologist*. (2016). Retrieved 10 December 2016, from http://careersinpsychology.org/becoming-a-child-psychologist/.
[11] Rousseau, J. *A Discourse on Political Economy*. (1755). Public Domain.
[12] Ibid.
[13] Markson, S and Hansen, N. *Class's Asylum Farce*. Retrieved 16 December 2016, from The Daily Telegraph, p. 1, 9.
[14] Neufeld, G and Maté, G. *Hold on to your kids*. (2005). 1st ed. New York: Ballantine Books.
[15] Ibid.
[16] Proverbs 22:15 (NLT).
[17] Simons-Morton, B and Farhat, T. *Recent Findings on Peer Group Influences on Adolescent Substance Use*. (2010). Journal of Primary Prevention. 31 (4), 191–208.
[18] Moore, R and Moore, D. (1994). *The successful homeschool family handbook*. 1st ed. Nashville: T. Nelson Publishers, p. 49. Bronfenbrenner, U and Condry, J. *Two worlds of childhood*. (1970). 1st ed. New York: Russell Sage Foundation.
[19] Neufeld, G. and Maté, G. *Hold on to your kids*. (2005). 1st ed. New York: Ballantine Books.
[20] Australian Bureau of Statistics. *Risk Taking By Young People*. (2016). Canberra: Australian Bureau of Statistics.
[21] Australian Institute of Health and Welfare. *Policy and Attitudes*. (2013). Retrieved 24 January 2017, from http://www.aihw.gov.au/alcohol-and-other-drugs/ndshs-2013/ch9/.
[22] Also see McEntire, TW. *Religious Outcomes in Conventionally Schooled and Home Schooled Youth*. (2005). Home School Researcher. 16 (2) pp. 13-18.
[23] *Alcohol and Health in Australia*. National Health and Medical Research Council. Retrieved 13 June 2016, from http://www.nhmrc.gov.au.
[24] *Statistical trends - Drug Prevention and Alcohol Facts*. (2017). DrugInfo. Retrieved 20 January 2017, from http://www.druginfo.adf.org.au/topics/statistics-trends#illicit.
[25] Ibid.
[26] Also see McEntire, TW. *Religious Outcomes in Conventionally Schooled and Home Schooled Youth*. (2005). Home School Researcher. 16 (2) pp. 13-18.
[27] Szalavitz, M. *The Link Between Marijuana and Schizophrenia*. (2010). Time. Retrieved 20 January 2017, from http://content.time.com/time/health/article/0,8599,2005559,00.html.

[28] *Australian secondary school students use of tobacco, alcohol, and over-the-counter and illicit substances in 2011.* (2011). Australian Government Department of Health and Ageing, p. 48. Retrieved 24 January 2017, from http://www.nationaldrugstrategy.gov.au/internet/drugstrategy/Publishing.nsf/content/BCBF6B2C638E1202CA257ACD0020E35C/$File/National%20Report_FINAL_ASSAD_7.12.pdf.

[29] Benns, M and Banks, L. *Pupil Pill Poppers Running Rampant in Ritalin.* (2016). The Daily Telegraph. 13 February 2016.

[30] *Baby One More Time.* Wikipedia. Retrieved 30 May 2017, from https://en.wikipedia.org/wiki/...Baby_One_More_Time_(song).

[31] Fife-Yeomans, J. *Domestic Violence Crisis: Mums and Dads Live in Fear of Their Kids.* (2016). The Daily Telegraph.

[32] Papisova, V. *20 Girls in Their 20s Open Up About How They Were Bullied – And How They Overcame It.* (2017). Teen Vogue. Retrieved 20 January 2017, from http://www.teenvogue.com/story/20-personal-bullying-stories.

[33] Fife-Yeomans, J. *Domestic Violence Crisis: Mums and Dads Live in Fear of Their Kids.* (2016, April 16). Daily Telegraph.

[34] *11 Facts About Teen Dating Violence.* DoSomething.Org. Retrieved 10/6/2016 https://www.dosomething.org/us/facts/11-facts-about-teen-dating-violence.

[35] Hastings, K. *Teenager commits suicide after 'sexting' a nude photo to her boyfriend made her life a misery.* (2009). Daily Mail Australia. http://www.dailymail.co.uk/tvshowbiz/article-1161112/Teenager-commits-suicide-sexting-nude-photo-boyfriend-life-misery.html.

[36] See movies *Easy A, Mean Girls* and *John Tucker Must Die.*

[37] French, BH, Tilghman, JD and Malebranche, DA. *Sexual Coercion Context and Psychosocial Correlates Among Diverse Males.* (2014). University of Missouri. Psychology of Men and Masculinity.

[38] Ibid

[39] LW Fink, J. *Talking to Boys about Sexually Aggressive Girls.* (2017). LinkedIn. Retrieved 20 January 2017, from https://www.linkedin.com/pulse/20141117161322-24843451-talking-to-boys-about-sexually-aggressive-girls.

[40] Bui, S. *Homeschooling is a bad idea.* (2009). Retrieved 8 October 2013, from http://www.examiner.com/article/homeschooling-is-a-bad-idea.

[41] See Devitt, R. *You Can Fail High School and Still be a Great Home Educator.* (2017). Retrieved 16 June 2017, from http://whyonearthhomeschool.com/you-can-fail-high-school-and-still-be-a-great-home-educator.html.

[42] Biddle, B and Berliner, D. *Synopsis of Class Size Literature: Small Class Size and Its Effects. Weston Public Schools.* (2017). Retrieved 20 January 2017, from http://www.westonps.org/uploaded/documents/Central_Office/Educational_Services/Synopsis_of_Class_Size_Literature.pdf.

[43] See Robinson, K. *Do Schools Kill Creativity?* TED Talks. Retrieved 25/8/2016, from https://www.youtube.com/watch?v=iG9CE55wbtY .

[44] Ibid.

[45] Ibid.

[46] *Effective Study Environments.* (2017). Advising and Learning Assistance Center. Retrieved 6 June 2016, from http://alac.rpi.edu/update.do?artcenterkey=9. Also see Willingham, D. *Are Decorated Classroom Walls Too Distracting?* (2017). Latest News. Retrieved17 June 2017, from http://www.cdl.org/articles/are-decorated-classroom-walls-too-distracting/.

[47] Strauss, D. *A therapist goes to middle school and tries to sit still and focus. She can't. Neither can the kids.* (2014). Washington Post. Retrieved 16 June 2017, from http://ostrc.org/newsletter/documents/Atherapistgoestomiddleschoolandtriestositstill.pdf.

[48] Charles, CM. *Building Classroom Discipline.* (2011). 10th ed. Pearson 41.

[49] Strauss, D. *A therapist goes to middle school and tries to sit still and focus. She can't. Neither can the kids.* (2014). Washington Post. Retrieved 16 June 2017, from http://ostrc.org/newsletter/documents/Atherapistgoestomiddleschoolandtriestositstill.pdf. 2003 had 7.8%, 2007 had 9.5% and 2011 had 11% of ADHD kids to school.

[50] Strauss, V. *Why so Many Kids Can't Sit Still in School Today*. (2014). The Washington Post. Retrieved 20 January 2017, from http://www.washingtonpost.com/blogs/answer-sheet/wp/2014/07/08/why-so-many-kids-cant-sit-still-in-school-today/.
[51] Kuo, F and Taylor, A. *A Potential Natural Treatment for Attention-Deficit/Hyperactivity Disorder: Evidence From a National Study*. (2004). American Journal of Public Health. 94 (9), pp. 1580–1586.
[52] Duvall, S, Delquadri, J and Ward, L. *Preliminary Investigation of the Effectiveness of Homeschool Instructional Environments for Students With Attention-Deficit/Hyperactivity Disorder*. (2004). School Psychology Review. pp. 140–158. Increased attention by their parents, in the role of the teacher will allow ADHD students to focus their attention on tasks and avoid getting lost in the distracting mêlée around them.
[53] Media Watch. 26 March 2007. [Television Series Episode 5]. http://www.abc.net.au/mediawatch/transcripts/s1882075.htm.
[54] Media Watch. 26 March 2007. [Television Series Episode 5]. http://www.abc.net.au/mediawatch/transcripts/s1882075.htm.
[54] Diamond, MR. *Encountering Faith in the Classrooms*. (2008). Stylus Publishing. pp. 7-9.
[55] Ibid, pp. 13-14.
[56] *Religious Education*. (2010). Western Australia Department of Education. Retrieved 25 February 2015, from http://www.det.wa.edu.au/curriculumsupport/religiouseducation/detcms/navigation/about/. See also Haynes, CA. *Teacher's Guide to Religion in the Public Schools*. (2008). First Amendment Centre. Retrieved 20 January 2017, from http://www.firstamendmentcenter.org/madison/wp-content/uploads/2011/03/teachersguide.pdf.
[57] Ibid, 24.
[58] 1 Samuel 15:3.
[59] Diamond, MR. (2008). *Encountering Faith in the Classrooms*. Stylus Publishing. p. 68.
[60] Ibid.
[61] Neill, R. (2016). Schools in many parts of Australia are study in self-segregation. *The Australian*.
[62] Ibid.
[63] Katz, L. *The Benefits of Mixed-Age Grouping*. (1995). ERIC Digest. Retrieved 20 January, from http://www.ericdigests.org/1996-1/mixed.htm.
[64] Gray, P. *Why We Should Stop Segregating Children by Age: Part I*. (2017). Psychology Today. Retrieved 21 January 2017, from https://www.psychologytoday.com/blog/freedom-learn/200809/why-we-should-stop-segregating-children-age-part-i.
[65] Ibid. Also see Moore, R and Moore, D. *The successful homeschool family handbook*. (1994). (1st ed.). Nashville: T. Nelson Publishers.
[66] Coulson, J. *Why my kids won't do the NAPLAN*. (2016). Kidspot.com.au. Retrieved 21 January 2017, from http://www.kidspot.com.au/school/primary/testing/why-my-kids-wont-do-the-naplan.
[67] *Say No to NAPLAN*. (2017) (1st ed.). Retrieved 16 June 2017, from http://sydney.edu.au/education_social_work/news_events/resources/No_NAPLAN.pdf.
[68] Patty, A. *NAPLAN-style testing has 'failed' US Schools*. (2011). Sydney Morning Herald. Retrieved, from http://www.smh.com.au/national/education/naplanstyle-testing-has-failed-us-schools-20110501-1e395.html.
[69] *Say No to NAPLAN*. (2017). (1st ed.). Retrieved 16 June 2017, from http://sydney.edu.au/education_social_work/news_events/resources/No_NAPLAN.pdf.
[70] Wyn, J. *NAPLAN testing does more harm than good*. (2014). The Conversation. Retrieved 21 January 2017, from http://theconversation.com/naplan-testing-does-more-harm-than-good-26923
[71] Ibid.
[72]*Fatigue*. (2012). Canadian Centre for Occupational Health and Safety. Retrieved 21 January 2017, from https://www.ccohs.ca/oshanswers/psychosocial/fatigue.html.

[73] Rubin, CM. *The Global Search for Education: A Look at Finnish Schools*. (2011). Huffington Post. Retrieved 21 January 2017, from http://www.huffingtonpost.com/c-m-rubin/the-global-search-for-edu_17_b_1066527.html.
[74] Ibid.
[75] Hull, J. *Time in school: How does the U.S. Compare?* (2011). Center for Public Education.
[76] *School phobia - what you need to know*. Retrieved January 22, 2017, from http://www.drugs.com/cg/school-phobia.html
[77] *School Refusal*. Anxiety and Depression Association of America. Retrieved 26 December 2015, from http://www.adaa.org/living-with-anxiety/children/school-refusal.
[78] Ibid.
[79] Milburn, C. *Homework Horrors*. Sydney Morning Herald. (2009). Retrieved 25 January 2017, from http://www.smh.com.au/national/education/homework-horrors-20090821-et5j.html.
[80] *Homework Policy: Research Scan*. Education and Communities Department: Public Schools NSW. Retrieved 3 July 2015, from https://www.det.nsw.edu.au/policies/curriculum/schools/homework/Hwk_Res%20scan.pdf.
[81] Ibid, p. 8.
[82] Ibid, p. 8.
[83] Ibid, p. 8.
[84] Ibid, p. 8.
[85] Ibid, p. 11.
[86] Mitchell, A, Patrick, K, Heywood, W, Blackman, P and Pitt, M. *National Survey of Australian Secondary Students and Sexual Health 2013*. (2014). La Trobe University. p. v. Retrieved 23 January 2017, from http://www.redaware.org.au/wp-content/uploads/2014/10/31631-ARCSHS_NSASSSH_FINAL-A-3.pdf.
[87] *Sexting among young people: Perceptions and practices*. (2015). Australian Institute of Criminology. Retrieved 25 January 2017, from http://www.aic.gov.au/publications/current%20series/tandi/501-520/tandi508.html.
[88] Ibid.
[89] Kendrick, K. *'Sexting' amongst schoolchildren seen as normal behavior*. (2015). MSN Lifestyle. Retrieved 23 January 2017, from http://www.msn.com/en-au/lifestyle/smart-living/sexting-amongst-schoolchildren-seen-as-normal-behaviour/ar-BBf1nra?ocid=mailsignout.
[90] Ibid.
[91] *Teenage sexual health snapshots La Trobe University*. (2009). La Trobe University. Retrieved 11 September 2016, from https://www.latrobe.edu.au/news/articles/2009/article/teenage-sexual-health-snapshots.
[92] *Teenage sexual health snapshots La Trobe University*. (2009). La Trobe University. Retrieved 11 September 2016, from https://www.latrobe.edu.au/news/articles/2009/article/teenage-sexual-health-snapshots.
[93] *Abortion Risks: A list of major psychological complications related to abortion*. Elliot Institute. Retrieved 31 May 2017, from <http://afterabortion.org/2011/abortion-risks-a-list-of-major-psychological-complications-related-to-abortion/>.
[94] *Abortion Facts*. Emily's Voice. Retrieved 10 October 2016, from https://www.emilysvoice.com/get-informed/abortion- October facts/.
[95] Ibid.
[96] Ibid.
[97] O'Brien, S. *Toddlers to be taught about cross-dressing in controversial sex ed program*. (2016). The Herald Sun.
[98] Bita, N. *Safe Schools Coalition: Sexual Politics in the Classroom*. (2013). The Australian. Retrieved 16 June 2017, from http://www.theaustralian.com.au/news/inquirer/safe-schools-coalition-sexual-politics-in-the-classroom/news-story/bf58ff141ba0b08bf165e3d53cc8a055 .
[99] Anderson, K. *Richard Dawkins: There's nothing wrong with a little 'mild pedophilia'*. (2013). Retrieved 23 January 2017, from https://www.lifesitenews.com/news/richard-dawkins-

theres-nothing-wrong-with-a-little-mild-pedophilia. Also see Limbaugh, R (writer). (2013). The Rush Limbaugh Show [Radio Program]. *Don't Pooh-Pooh the Left's Push to Normalize Pedophilia*. Transcript retrieved 23 January 2017, from https://www.rushlimbaugh.com/daily/2013/01/07/don_t_pooh_pooh_the_left_s_push_to_normalize_pedophilia/ for an interesting discussion on the normalisation of pedophilia. Handel, M. *Early Childhood Sex Education (Excerpts)*. Scribd. Retrieved 14 September 2017, from https://www.scribd.com/doc/37306501/Early-Childhood-Sex-Education-Excerpts.

[100] Godfrey, M. *Calls for NSW judge Garry Neilson to step down as he says incest and pedophilia may no longer be considered 'taboo' in society*. (2014). The Daily Telegraph. [print]. Also see Hall, L. *Judge compares incest and paedophilia to past attitudes towards homosexuality, claiming they might not be taboo anymore*. The Sydney Morning Herald. Retrieved 23 January 2017 from http://www.smh.com.au/nsw/judge-compares-incest-and-paedophilia-to-past-attitudes-towards-homosexuality-claiming-they-might-not-be-taboo-anymore-20140708-zt0v2.

[101] Henley, J. *Pedophilia Bringing Dark Desires to Light*. (2013). The Guardian. Retrieved 23 January 2017, from https://www.theguardian.com/society/2013/jan/03/paedophilia-bringing-dark-desires-light.

[102] See the Christian movie Scott, M, Wolfe, R and Zielinski, A (Producers), and Cronk, H. (Director). *God is Not Dead*. [Motion Picture]. (2014). United States: Pure Flix Entertainment.

[103] Brooks, C. *Prayer in Schools*. In Plain Sight. Retrieved 23 January 2017, from http://www.inplainsite.org/what_happened_when_the_praying.html.

[104] Knowles, L and Branley, A. *Data Reveals Allegations of Children Sexually Abusing Peers at School, Experts Call for Action*. (2014). ABC News. Retrieved 3 June 2014, from http://www.abc.net.au/news/2014-06-03/calls-for-action-to-halt-child-on-child-sex-abuse/5497196.

[105] Imbesi, R. *Sexual Assault Prevention Program for Secondary Schools: (SAPPSS) Report*. Center Against Sexual Assault. [PDF]. Retrieved 23 January 2017, from http://www.partnersinprevention.org.au/wp-content/uploads/CASA-House-Sexual-Assault-Prevention-Program-for-Secondary-Schools-SAPPSS-Report-.pdf. Also see Gordon, C. *Exclusive: 23 school districts face sexual assault investigations*. (2014). Aljazeera America. Retrieved 23 January 2017 from http://america.aljazeera.com/watch/shows/america-tonight/articles/2014/11/11/map-title-ix-schooldistricts.html.

[106] Knowles, L and Branley, A. *Data Reveals Allegations of Children Sexually Abusing Peers at School, Experts Call for Action*. (2014). ABC News. Retrieved 3 June 2014, from http://www.abc.net.au/news/2014-06-03/calls-for-action-to-halt-child-on-child-sex-abuse/5497196.

[107] Ibid.

[108] Ibid.

[109] Understanding Juvenile Sex Offenders. *Children's Services Practice Notes*. (2002). pp. 7, 2. Retrieved 23 January 2017, from http://www.practicenotes.org/vol7_no2/understand_jso.htm.

[110] M. Glasser, I. Kolvin, D. Campbell, A. Glasser, I Leitch and S Farrelly. *Cycle of child sexual abuse: links between being a victim and becoming a perpetrator*. (2001). The British Journal of Psychology. 179, 6. Retrieved 23 January 2017, from http://bjp.rcpsych.org/content/179/6/482.

[111] Ibid.

[112] Australian Government. Australian Institute of Family Studies. *Children Who Bully at school: Understanding School Bullying*. (2014). Paper No. 27. Retrieved 23 January 2017, from https://aifs.gov.au/cfca/publications/children-who-bully-school/understanding-school-bullying.

[113] Queensland Government. *Bullying and Cyberbullying Facts*. Retrieved 23 January 2017, from http://www.qld.gov.au/disability/children-young-people/bullying/facts.html. Taylor, A. *School, not online, most likely place for bullying, study finds*. (2017). The Sydney Morning Herald.

[114] Australian Institute of Family Studies: Child Family Community Australia. *Understanding school bullying*. (2014). CFCA Paper No. 27. Retrieved 31 May 2017, from https://aifs.gov.au/cfca/publications/children-who-bully-school/understanding-school-bullying.
[115] Gordon, S. *What Is Bullying? 3 Key Components About Health*. (2014). Retrieved 23 January 2017, from http://bullying.about.com/od/Basics/a/What-Is-Bullying-3-Key-Components.htm.
[116] Grohol, J. *Bullies More Likely to have Mental Disorders*. (2016). PsychCentral. Retrieved 23 January 2017, from http://psychcentral.com/blog/archives/2012/10/22/bullies-more-likely-to-have-mental-disorder/.
[117] Juvonen, J and Graham, S. *Peer Harassment in School*. (2001). The Guilford Press. p. 267. [PDF].
[118] **Jesse Rose, Graduate Homeschooler. (Interview conducted May 2015.)**
[119] Ibid, pp. 38-39.
[120] Do Something.Org. *11 Facts About Bullying*. Retrieved 23 January 2017, from https://www.dosomething.org/facts/11-facts-about-bullying.
[121] Wandler, K. *Bullying and Body Image*. (2016). Eating Disorder Hope. Retrieved 23 January 2017, from http://www.eatingdisorderhope.com/information/eating-disorder/bullying-and-body-image.
[122] Ibid.
[123] Prisk, T and Koziol, M. *Orange school principal calls students with mental health issues 'morons' and 'village idiots'*. (2014). The Sydney Morning Herald. Retrieved 23 January 2017, from http://www.smh.com.au/.
[124] Isaiah 64:6.
[125] Highfield, R. *Newton beats Einstein in scientist poll*. (2005). The Telegraph UK. Retrieved 1 June 2017, from http://www.telegraph.co.uk/news/uknews/1503801/Newton-beats-Einstein-in-scientist-poll.html.
[126] Charles, CM. *Building Classroom Discipline*. (2011). *Pearson*, 10th ed. p. 31.
[127] Friel, T (Host) and Burning Bush Communications (Producer). *What Hath Darwin Wrought?* [DVD].
[128] Kaelber, L. Eugenics. *Compulsory Sterilization in 50 American States*. (2012). University of Vermont. Retrieved 23 January 2017, from http://www.uvm.edu/~lkaelber/eugenics/.
[129] Cohen, E and Bonifield, J. *California's dark legacy of forced sterilizations*. (2012). CNN. Retrieved 23 January 2017, from http://edition.cnn.com/2012/03/15/health/california-forced-sterilizations/index.html.
[130] *German Eugenics Program*. Children in History. Retrieved 23 January 2017, from http://histclo.com/essay/war/ww2/cou/ger/w2g-eug.html.
[131] McDougal, B et al. *Burwood Girls High School: Anger over gay parenting documentary 'Gayby Baby'*. (2015). The Daily Telegraph. Retrieved 23 January 2017, from http://www.dailytelegraph.com.au/news/nsw/burwood-girls-high-school-anger-over-gay-parenting-documentary-gayby-baby/story-fni0cx12-1227498780623.
[132] McKenna, M. *Transgender Toilet Suite Sparks Review*. (2013). The Australian. Retrieved 23 January 2017, from http://www.theaustralian.com.au/national-affairs/state-politics/special-needs-will-be-taken-into-account/story-e6frgczx-1226721285147.
[133] *German Eugenics Program*. Children in History. Retrieved 23 January 2017, from http://histclo.com/essay/war/ww2/cou/ger/w2g-eug.html.
[134] *Self Actualization Psychology*. (2014). Self Actualizing. Retrieved 23 January 2017, from http://self-actualizing.org/maslow.html.
[135] Wiki Ehow page now removed. Also see Campbell, DE. *The Work of Abraham Maslow*. (2014). Education.com. Retrieved 23 January 2017, from http://www.education.com/reference/article/work-Abraham-Maslow/>.
[136] James 1:2-4.
[137] Urban, R. *Federal election 2016: Labor commits $6m for Safe Schools*. (2016). The Australian. http://www.theaustralian.com.au/federal-election-2016/federal-election-2016-labor-commits-6m-for-safe-schools/news-story/3fb6e9433848413a4caf92cecca24a8a.

[138] Jacks, T. *Christian Lobby Boycotts Gay Student Lobby*. (2014). The Age. Retrieved 23 January 2017, from http://www.theage.com.au/victoria/christian-lobby-boycotts-gay-student-program-20141218-12a0xf.html.
[139] Ibid.
[140] Tomazin, F. *Victorian ALP plan to support gay students that "come out"*. (2014). The Age Victoria. Retrieved 23 January 2017, from http://www.theage.com.au/victoria/victorian-alp-plan-to-support-gay-students-that-come-out-20140201-31u56.html.
[141] Ibid.
[142] Hitchins, C. *God is Not Great*. (2007). Atlantic Books. p. 75.
[143] Mitchell, D. *Growing Up Godless*. (2014). Sterling Ethos.
[144] Ibid.
[145] Ibid.
[146] Thomas, K and Gunnell, D. *Suicide in England and Wales 1861-2007*. (2010). International Journal of Epidemiology. Retrieved 23 January 2017, from http://ije.oxfordjournals.org/content/39/6/1464/F1.expansion.html.
[147] Dervic, K, Oquendo, M, Grunebaum, M, Ellis, S, Burke, A, and Mann, J. *Religious affiliation and suicide* attempt. (2017). Am J Psychiatry, 161(12).
[148] Deborah Mitchell (2014). *Growing Up Godless*. Sterling Ethos. pp. 2-9.
[149] Deborah Mitchell (2014). *Growing Up Godless*. Sterling Ethos.
[150] Critchley, C. *A Parent's Dilemma: Should Your Four-Year-Old Start Prep?* (2016). The Herald Sun. Retrieved 23 January 2017, from http://www.heraldsun.com.au/news/victoria/a-parents-dilemma-should-your-fouryearold-start-prep/news-story/c7c8d86f6811b08fc5eb9d0187e16bfb.
[151] Aus Gov Dept Social Serv. *Number 40: Child care and early education in Australia - The Longitudinal Study of Australian Children*. (2012). Retrieved 23 January 2017, from https://www.dss.gov.au/about-the-department/publications-articles/research-publications/social-policy-research-paper-series/number-40-child-care-and-early-education-in-australia-the-longitudinal-study-of-australian-children?HTML#exe.
[152] See research evidence in Whitebread, D. *The Importance of Play*. (2012). University of Cambridge. Retrieved 23 January 2017, from http://www.importanceofplay.eu/IMG/pdf/dr_david_whitebread_-_the_importance_of_play.pdf. [PDF]. Also see *Hard Evidence: at what age are children ready for school?* (2014). The Conversation. Retrieved 23 January 2017, from http://theconversation.com/hard-evidence-at-what-age-are-children-ready-for-school-29005.
[153] Smith, M. Preschool Loosens Parent-Child Bond. (2005). *The Washington Times*. Retrieved 23 January 2017, from http://www.washingtontimes.com/news/2005/jun/12/20050612-103145-2475r/. Southwest Policy Institute report cited in Smith, M. (2005).
[154] Ibid.
[155] See McDougall, B. *Families avoid huge childcare fees by sending kids to school early*. (2014). The Daily Telegraph. Retrieved 23 January 2017, from http://www.dailytelegraph.com.au/news/nsw/families-avoid-huge-childcare-fees-by-sending-kids-to-school-early/story-fni0cx12-1227057128469.
[156] Bates, G. *Engineered for duty*. (2017). Creation.com. Retrieved 20 January 2017, from http://creation.com/engineered-for-duty.
[157] Australian Bureau of Statistics. *Median Age of Parents*. (2010).; *The Return of the Stay-At-Home Mother*. (2014). The Economist.
[158] Titus 2:3-4, and Proverbs 31.
[159] Tin, J. *Treasurer Joe Hockey's message to Aussie Mums: 'We need you to work'*. (2014). *The Courier Mail*. Retrieved 23 January 2017, from http://www.couriermail.com.au/news/queensland/treasurer-joe-hockeys-message-to-aussie-mums-we-need-you-to-go-to-work/story-fnihsrf2-1226920501924?nk=06df141843157a31a05231a08cff52ac.
[160] Australian Government. *Mother's Day 2012: More mums heading to work*. (2012). Australian Bureau of Statistics.

[161] Angela Shanahan. *Stay-home Mums Productive Too*. (2014). The Australian. Retrieved 23 January 2017, from http://www.theaustralian.com.au/opinion/columnists/stayhome-mums-productive-too/story-fn562txd-1226834136139.

[162] Dotterweich, D, McKinney, M and Michael, LA. *Economic Impact of Home and Private Schooling on the Public Education System: Iowa as a Case Study*. (2013). 29 (3), pp. 1-11.

[163] United States Census Bureau. *Public Elementary–Secondary Education Finance Data*. (2012). Retrieved 23 January 2017, from http://www.census.gov/govs/school/.

[164] Tebbutt, G. *Answers to Questions on Notice and additional information: Mr Guy Tebbutt NSW Parliamentary Enquiry into Homeschooling*. (2014). Retrieved 23 January 2017, from http://www.parliament.nsw.gov.au/prod/parlment/committee.nsf/0/502eccac289c2a56ca257d7200083379/$FILE/140908%20Answers%20to%20QoNs%20and%20additional%20information%20Mr%20Guy%20Tebbutt.pdf.

[165] Ibid.

[166] Ibid.

[167] Lyman, I quoted in Seago, J. *A Third Reason to Home School: Leadership Development*. (2012). Home School Researcher. 28 (1), pp. 1-7.

[168] Evans, C and Gaze, B. *Discrimination by Religious Schools: Views from the Coal Face*. (2010). Melbourne University Law Review, pp. 392-424 http://www.law.unimelb.edu.au/files/dmfile/34_2_2.pdf. Also see the Gen2 survey by Ray, B. *Gen2 Survey Results. Generations with Vision*. (2015). Retrieved 23 January 2017, from https://generationswithvision.com/gen2-survey-results/.

[169] McConnell, S. (2007). *LifeWay Research Finds Reasons 18- to 22-Year-Olds Drop Out of Church*. Retrieved 23 January 2017, from http://www.lifeway.com/ArticleView?storeId=10054&catalogId=10001&langId=-1&article=LifeWay-Research-finds-reasons-18-to-22-year-olds-drop-out-of-church.

[170] Kunzman, R. *Write These Laws on Your Children: Inside the World of Conservative Christian Homeschooling*. (2009). Beacon Press.

[171] Dr. Harding cited in NSW Government. *Parliamentary Inquiry into Homeschooling*. (2014). p. 20 (2.87).

[172] *Submission 145 by the Home Education Association to the Parliamentary Inquiry*. p. 51. Retrieved 23 January 2017 from http://23.101.218.132/prod/parlment/committee.nsf/0/787be59c8ed775ebca257d39001c3a12/$FILE/0145%20Home%20Education%20Association%20(HEA).pdf. [PDF].

[173] Ray, B. *Homeschooling Across America: Academic Achievement and Demographic Characteristics*. (2009). National Home Education Research Institute. Retrieved 23 January 2017, from http://www.nheri.org/research/nheri-news/homeschooling-across-america-academic-achievement-and-demographic-characteristics.html.

[174] Branley, A. *No place like home for home-schooled Hunter kids*. (2009). The Herald.

[175] McCrindle, M. *A Snapshot of Schools in Australia 2013*. (2013). McCrindle Research. Retrieved 23 January 2017, from http://mccrindle.com.au/resources/Snapshot-of-Schools-in-Australia-2013_McCrindle-Research.pdf. p. 1. [PDF].

[176] Ibid.

[177] Smith, A. *Rise in home schooling spurs parliamentary inquiry*. (2014). The Sydney Morning Herald. Retrieved 23 January 2017, from http://www.smh.com.au/national/education/rise-in-home-schooling-spurs-parliamentary-inquiry-20140531-39b0a.html. Also see the Parliamentary Inquiry into Homeschooling.

[178] Ibid.

[179] Ray, B. *Worldwide Guide to Homeschooling*. (2003). Broadman and Holman Publishers. p. 107.

[180] Ibid.

[181] Education Act 1900, s4 (NSW).

[182] NSW Government. *Parliamentary Inquiry into Homeschooling*. (2014). p. 76.

[183] Ibid. pp. 76-78.

[184] Kriz, G. *"We're everywhere"*. (2014). Honi Soit. Retrieved 23 January 2017, from http://honisoit.com/2014/10/were-everywhere/.

[185] Ray, B. *Homeschooling and Child Abuse, Child Neglect, and Child Fatalities.* (2016). National Home Education Research Institute.
[186] *Some Preliminary Data on Homeschool Child Fatalities.* Homeschooling's Invisible Children. Retrieved 16 June 217, from http://hsinvisiblechildren.org/commentary/some-preliminary-data-on-homeschool-child-fatalities/.
[187] NSW Government. *Parliamentary Inquiry into Homeschooling.* (2014). p. 42. Grossman, R. *Home is Where the School Is.* (2001). p. 60. Retrieved 23 January 2017, from http://www.freerepublic.com/focus/fr/578270/posts.
[188] Carl, J, Baker, S, Robards, B, Scott, J, Hillman, W and Lawrence G. *Think Sociology.* (2003). Pearson. p. 140.
[189] Montes, G. *Parental Reasons by Grade Level.* (2006). Home School Researcher. 16 (4), pp. 11-17.
[190] Ibid.
[191] Gray and Resetar cited in Kingston, S and Medlin, R. *Empathy, Altruism and Moral Development.* (2006). Home School Researcher. 16 (4), pp. 1-10.
[192] Cubberley, E. *Public Education in the United States.* (1919). p. 167.
[193] Monsma, S and Soper, C. *The Challenge of Pluralism: Church and State in Five Democracies.* (2008). Rowman and Littlefield Publishers. pp. 18-22.
[194] Gorman, L. *Sex, Drugs and Catholic Schools.* (2015). The National Bureau of Economic Research. Retrieved 23 January 2017, from http://www.nber.org/digest/may01/w7990.html.
[195] Pennings, R. *Do Christian Schools Produce Good Citizens? The Evidence Says Yes.* (2014). Christianity Today. Retrieved 23 January 2017, from http://www.christianitytoday.com/ct/2014/september-web-only/do-christian-schools-produce-good-citizens-evidence-yes.html.
[196] Ibid.
[197] Smithwick, D. *Home Page.* The Nehemiah Institute. Retrieved 23 January 2017, from http://www.nehemiahinstitute.com/index.php.
[198] *The 'Peers Worldview' Grid.* The Nehemiah Institute. Retrieved 23 January 2017, from http://www.nehemiahinstitute.com/PEERS-Worldview.pdf.
[199] Kingston, S and Medlin, R. *Empathy, Altruism and Moral Development.* (2006). Home School Researcher. 16 (4), pp. 1-10.
[200] Hunsberger, B. *Apostasy: A Social Learning Perspective. Religious Research Association.* (1983). p.21.
[201] Ibid.
[202] Ibid.
[203] Ibid.
[204] Ibid.
[205] Ibid, pp. 6-9.
[206] Romm, T. *Home Schooling and the Transmission of Civic Culture.* (1993). Clark Atlanta University.
[207] McEntire, TW. *Religious Outcomes in Conventionally Schooled and Home Schooled Youth.* (2005). Home School Researcher. 16(2) pp. 13-18.
[208] Ray, B. *Gen2 Survey.* (2015). Generations with Vision and National Home Education Research Institute. p. 2.
[209] Ibid, pp. 12-13.
[210] Romm, T. *Home Schooling and the Transmission of Civic Culture.* (1993). Clark Atlanta University.
[211] McEntire, TW. *Religious Outcomes in Conventionally Schooled and Home Schooled Youth.* (2005). Home School Researcher. 16(2) p. 13-18.
[212] Ibid.
[213] Ibid.
[214] Ibid.
[215] Ibid.
[216] Ray, B. *Worldwide Guide to Homeschooling.* (2003). Broadman and Holman Publishers.

[217] McEntire, TW. *Religious Outcomes in Conventionally Schooled and Home Schooled Youth*. (2005). Home School Researcher. 16(2) p. 13-18.
[218] Duffey, JG. *Home Schooling Children with Special Needs: A Descriptive Study*. (2002). Home School Researcher Journal. 15 (2), pp. 1-13.
[219] See *F-10 Overview*. Australian Curriculum. Retrieved 23 January 2017, from www.australiancurriculum.edu.au/overview/f-2.
[220] *Australia Private School Fees and Costs*. (2014). The Australian Expatriate's Gateway. Retrieved 23 January 2017, from http://www.exfin.com/private-school-costs.
[221] Morrow, M. *What is the Financial Cost of Homeschooling?* Retrieved 24 April 2014, from http://www.homeschoolingdownunder.com/homeschool_curriculum/cost_of_homeschooling.html.
[222] Ibid.
[223] Garris, Z. Is Homeschool Affordable? *Teach Diligently*. Retrieved 22/10/2016, from http://teachdiligently.com/articles/is-homeschool-affordable.
[224] *Submission 145 by the Home Education Association to the Parliamentary Inquiry*. p. 51. Retrieved 23 January 2017, from http://23.101.218.132/prod/parlment/committee.nsf/0/787be59c8ed775ebca257d39001c3a12/$FILE/0145%20Home%20Education%20Association%20(HEA).pdf. [PDF].
[225] Allen, J. *The 10 Most Expensive Schools to Attend in Australia*. (2016). Retrieved 23 January 2017, from https://www.stayathomemum.com.au/my-kids/schooling/the-10-most-expensive-schools-to-attend-in-australia/
[226] *Australia: Private School Fees and Costs*. (2014). Exfin. Retrieved 23 January 2017, from http://www.exfin.com/private-school-costs.
[227] Bagshaw, E. *Government funding for private schools to outstrip average public schools by 2020*. (2015). The Sydney Morning Herald. Retrieved 23 January 2017, from http://www.smh.com.au/national/education/government-funding-for-private-schools-to-outstrip-average-public-schools-by-2020-20150714-gicdjt.html.
[228] Smedley, T. *Socialization of Home Schooled Children: A Communication Approach*. (1992). Radford University, pp. 4-6.
[229] Socialization. *In The Collins Dictionary Online*. (2017). Retrieved 11 June 2017, from https://www.collinsdictionary.com/dictionary/english/socialization. Harper Collins Publishers Limited.
[230] *Socialization*. (2017). In Dictionary.Com Online. Retrieved 11 June 2017, from http://www.dictionary.com/browse/socialization.
[231] Haverluck, M. *Socialization: Homeschooling vs. Schools*. (2007). CBN News. Retrieved 23 January 2017, from http://www.cbn.com/cbnnews/us/2007/may/socialization-homeschooling-vs-schools/?mobile=false.
[232] Smedley, T. *Socialization of Home Schooled Children: A Communication Approach*. (1992). Radford University. Virginia.
[233] Kelley, S. *Socialization of Homeschooled children: A Self-Concept Study*. (1991). Home School Researcher. 7, pp. 1-12; Medlin, R. *Predictors of Academic Achievement in Home Educated Children: Aptitude, Self-Concept and Pedagogical Practices*. (1994). Home School Researcher. 10, p. 1-7. For other references see Ray, B. *Worldwide Guide to Homeschooling*. (2003). Broadman and Holman Publishers. p. 57-59. Study References 17-23.
[234] McFarland, H. *Quivering Daughters*. (2010). [Self-published.]
[235] Haverluck, M. *Socialization: Homeschooling vs. Schools*. (2007). CBN News. Retrieved 23 January 2017, from http://www.cbn.com/cbnnews/us/2007/may/socialization-homeschooling-vs-schools/?mobile=false.
[236] Ray, B. *Research Facts on Homeschooling*. (2016). National Home Education Research Institute. Retrieved 23 January 2017, from https://www.nheri.org/research/research-facts-on-homeschooling.html.
[237] Grossman, R. *Home is Where the School Is*. (2001). p. 62. Retrieved 23 January 2017, from http://www.freerepublic.com/focus/fr/578270/posts.
[238] Jackson, G. *Home education transitions with formal schooling: student perspectives*. (2007). Issues in Educational Research 17, p 1.

[239] Kelley, S. *Socialization of Homeschooled children: A Self-Concept Study*. (1991). Home School Researcher 7, 1-12; Medlin, R. *Predictors of Academic Achievement in Home Educated Children: Aptitude, Self-Concept and Pedagogical Practices*. (1994). Home School Researcher. 10, p. 1-7.
[240] Ibid.
[241] Ibid.
[242] Levine, B. How Teenage Rebellion Has Become a Mental Illness. (2008). Retrieved June 12, 2017, from alternet.org: http://www.alternet.org/healthwellness/75081/?page=entire.
[243] Smedley, T. *Socialization of Home Schooled Children: A Communication Approach*. (1992). Radford University.
[244] Ibid.
[245] Meighan cited in Seago, J. *A Third Reason to Home School: Leadership Development*. (2012). Home School Researcher. 28 (1), p. 1-7.
[246] Neufeld, G and Maté, G. *Hold on to your kids: Why parents need to matter more than peers*. (2004). New York: Ballantine Books.
[247] Ibid.
[248] Jolly, J. Mathews, M and Nester, J. *Homeschooling the Gifted: A Parent's Perspective. Gifted Child Quarterly*. (2012). 57 (2), pp. 121, 122.
[249] Duvall, S, Bannink-Misiwicz, J and Bareman, S. *A Comparison of the Fundamental Motor Skill Abilities of Home School and Conventional Schoolchildren*. (1992). Home School Researcher. 8, p. 1-8.
[250] Jackson, G. *Home education transitions with formal schooling: student perspectives*. (2007). Issues in Educational Research. 17, p. 1.
[251] Ray, B. *Worldwide Guide to Homeschooling*. (2003). Broadman and Holman Publishers. p. 9.
[252] See the *BOSTES report on the Academic Outcomes of Homeschooling*. (2014).
[253] *Select Committee on Homeschooling in New South Wales*. (2015). NSW Government Legislative Council. p. 37. Retrieved 16 June 2017, from http://www.parliament.nsw.gov.au/prod/parlment/committee.nsf/0/3a5b892ff6c728b6ca257da50019b2d0/$FILE/141203%20Final%20Report.pdf.
[254] Ray, B. *Worldwide Guide to Homeschooling*. (2003). Broadman and Holman Publishers. p. 11.
[255] West, R. *The Harms of Homeschooling*. (2009). Philosophy and Public Policy Quarterly. 29 (3) p. 7, 9.
[256] Aiken, W. *The Story of the Eight Year Study With Conclusions and Recommendations*. (1942). Harper and Brothers. Retrieved 24 January 2017, from http://www.archive.org/stream/storyoftheeighty009637mbp/storyoftheeighty009637mbp_djvu.txt.
[257] Moore, R. *School Can Wait*. (1979). Brigham Young University Press.
[258] Rowher cited in Moore, R and Moore, D. *The Successful Homeschool Family Handbook*. (1994). Thomas Nelson Publishers. p. 43.
[259] Rubin, CM. *The Global Search for Education: A Look at Finnish Schools*. (2011). Huffington Post. Retrieved 23 January 2017, from http://www.huffingtonpost.com/c-m-rubin/the-global-search-for-edu_17_b_1066527.html .
[260] Evans, M. *Do We Spend Too Much Time in School?* (2014). Australian Institute for Teaching and School Leadership. Retrieved 23 January 2017, from http://www.ceo.aitsl.edu.au/blog/do-we-spend-too-much-time-school. Also see *How Much Time Do Primary and Lower Secondary Students Spend in the Classroom?* (2014). OECDiLibrary. Retrieved 24 January 2017, from http://www.oecd-ilibrary.org/education/how-much-time-do-primary-and-lower-secondary-students-spend-in-the-classroom_5jz44fnl1t6k-en.
[261] Evans, M. *Do We Spend Too Much Time in School?* (2014). Australian Institute for Teaching and School Leadership. Retrieved 23 January 2017, from http://www.ceo.aitsl.edu.au/blog/do-we-spend-too-much-time-school. Extracted from the AITSL CEO Blog of 18 August 2014 with the permission of the copyright holder, AITSL.
[262] Illich, I. *Deschooling Society*. (1971). Harper and Row. Retrieved 24 January 2017, from http://www.davidtinapple.com/illich/1970_deschooling.html.
[263] Medlin, R. *Learning Style and Academic Achievement in Homeschooled Children*. (2010).
[264] Seago, J. *A Third Reason to Home School: Leadership Development*. (2012). Home School Researcher. 28 (1), p. 1-7.

[265] Harding, K and Harding, ML. *The Brainy Bunch: The Harding Family's Method to College Ready by Age 12*. (2014). Gallery Books.
[266] Moore, R and Moore, D. *The successful homeschool family handbook*. (1994). 1st ed. Nashville: T. Nelson Publishers, p. 52, 57-58. Also see Taylor V, JW. *Self-Concept in Home-Schooling Children*. The Moore Foundation. Retrieved 24 January 2017, from http://www.moorefoundation.com/article/49/faqs/self-concept-in-home-schooling-children.
[267] Moore, R and Moore, D. *The successful homeschool family handbook*. (1994). 1st ed. Nashville: T. Nelson Publishers, p. 52, 57-58.
[268] Goodlad, JI. *A study of schooling: Some findings and hypotheses*. (1983). Phi Delta Kappan. 64 (7) p. 465. Also see Moore, R and Moore, D. *The successful homeschool family handbook*. (1994). 1st ed. Nashville: T. Nelson Publishers, p. 45.
[269] McEntire, TW. *Religious Outcomes in Conventionally Schooled and Home Schooled Youth*. (2005). Home School Researcher. 16 (2) p. 13-18.
[270] Metlzer, L. quoted in Ray, B. *A Brief Review of 'Study: Homeschool Students Sleep Better.'* (2013). Home School Researcher. 29 (1) p. 15.
[271] Also see Ray, B. *A Brief Review of 'Study: Homeschool Students Sleep Better.'* (2013). Home School Researcher. 29 (1) p. 15.
[272] Seago, J. *A Third Reason to Home School: Leadership Development*. (2012). Home School Researcher. 28 (1) p. 1-7.
[273] Moreau, K. *Specific Differences in the Education Outcomes of Those Students who are Homeschooled vs. Traditionally Schooled*. (2012). [Master of Education Paper]. Northern Michigan University. Retrieved 24 January 2017, from https://www.nmu.edu/education/sites/DrupalEducation/files/UserFiles/Moreau_Kathi_MP.pdf. [PDF].
[274] Ibid.
[275] Grossman, R. *Home is Where the School Is*. (2001). Retrieved 23 January 2017, from http://www.freerepublic.com/focus/fr/578270/posts. Also see Smedley, T. (1992). *Socialization of Home Schooled Children: A Communication Approach*. Radford University. Virginia.
[276] NSW Government. *Parliamentary Inquiry into Homeschooling*. (2014). 3.16, p. 37.
[277] Society of Human Resource Management. HR Magazine Publisher.
[278] Ray, B. *Worldwide Guide to Homeschooling*. (2003). Broadman and Holman Publishers. p. 114.
[279] McDowell, SA. *Home Schooling as a Key Factor in a Political Election: A Case Study*. (2002). Home School Researcher. 15 (2) p. 15-21.
[280] Seago, J. *A Third Reason to Home School: Leadership Development*. (2012). Home School Researcher. 28 (1), p. 1-7.
[281] Bolle-Brummond, MB and Wessel, R. *Homeschooled students in college: Background influences, college integration and environmental pull factors*. (2012). Journal of Research in Education 22 (1), p. 236.
[282] Ibid, p. 223.
[283] Ray, B. *Gen2 Survey*. (2015). National Home Education Research Institute. p. 7.
[284] Cappello et al. cited in Seago, J. *A Third Reason to Home School: Leadership Development*. (2012). Home School Researcher. 28 (1) p. 1-7.
[285] 2 Timothy 3:1-5.
[286] Sharick, HM and Medlin, R. *Compliance in Homeschooled Children*. (2012). Home School Researcher. 26 (3), p. 1-10.
[287] Grusec and Davidov cited in Sharick, HM and Medlin, R. *Compliance in Homeschooled Children*. (2012). Home School Researcher. 26 (3) p. 1-10.
[288] Sharick, HM and Medlin, R. *Compliance in Homeschooled Children*. (2012). Home School Researcher. 26 (3), p. 1-10.
[289] Wenner, M. *Study: Religion is Good for Kids*. (2008). LiveScience Website. Retrieved 24 January 2017, from http://www.livescience.com/1465-study-religion-good-kids.html.
[290] Ibid.

[291] James 1:27.
[292] West, R. *The Harms of Homeschooling*. (2009). Philosophy and Public Policy Quarterly. 29 (3/4) p. 7-12.
[293] Kingston, S and Medlin, R. *Empathy, Altruism and Moral Development*. (2006). Home School Researcher. 16 (4), pp. 1-10.
[294] Brunner, K. *Undoing The Harms of Homeschooling From Reaction to Prevention*. (2010). Retrieved 23 July 2015, from http://homeedmag.com/HEM/272/undoing-harms.php.
[295] Apple, M. *Away With All Teachers: The Cultural Politics of Homeschooling*. (2000). International Studies in Sociology of Education. 10 (1) 3-8.
[296] Ibid, p. 8-9.
[297] Ibid.
[298] Ibid.
[299] Name Suppressed. *Submission #1: Submissions to Homeschooling*. (2014). NSW Government Parliamentary Enquiry into Homeschooling. Retrieved 24 January 2017, from http://www.parliament.nsw.gov.au/.
[300] Board of Studies Teaching and Educational Standards. *Academic Outcomes of Homeschooling*. (2014). NSW Government. pp. 4-5.
[301] Malone, LY and Cecil, MJ. *An Exploratory Study of U. S. Pre-Service Teachers' Beliefs About Homeschooling Outcomes*. (2012). 26 (2), p. 1-10.
[302] National Centre for Education Statistics, Digest of Education Statistics. (2012). Table 206.10; Slatter, I. *New Nationwide Study Confirms Homeschool Academic Achievement*. (2009). Home School Legal Defense Organisation.
[303] Hurlbutt, K. *Special Education Teachers' Perceptions and Beliefs Regarding Homeschooling Children with Autism Spectrum Disorders*. (2012). Minnesota State University.
[304] Slatter cited in Seago, J. *A Third Reason to Home School: Leadership Development*. (2012). Home School Researcher. 28 (1), p. 1-7.
[305] Deuteronomy 11:9.
[306] O'Reilly, CO. *What is it like to be a son or daughter of a psychopath*. (2016). Quora. Retrieved 24 January 2017, from https://www.quora.com/What-is-it-like-to-be-a-child-of-a-psychopath.
[307] Urbas, G. *The Age of Criminal Responsibility*. (2000). Australian Institute of Criminology. Retrieved 24 January 2017, from http://www.aic.gov.au/media_library/publications/tandi_pdf/tandi181.pdf.
[308] Ibid.
[309] National Centre for Education Statistics, Digest of Education Statistics. (2012). Table 206.10. Retrieved 24 January 2017, from https://nces.ed.gov/programs/digest/d13/tables/dt13_206.10.asp?current=yes>. Ian Slatter. (2009). *New Nationwide Study Confirms Homeschool Academic Achievement*. Home School Legal Defense Organization. Retrieved 24 January 2017, from http://www.hslda.org/docs/news/200908100.asp.
[310] Farris, M. *The Home Schooling Father*. (2001). Broadman and Holman Publishers. p. 67.
[311] Grossman, R. (2001) *Home is Where the School Is*. p. 62. Retrieved 23 January 2017, from http://www.freerepublic.com/focus/fr/578270/posts.
[312] Ibid.
[313] Unpublished survey by author.
[314] Rivero, L. *The Homeschooling Option: How to Decide When It's Right for Your Family*. (2008). 1st ed. New York: Palgrave Macmillan. pp. 141-142.
[315] *NSW Parliamentary Inquiry into Homeschooling*. (2014). Tabled document. The what, whys and wherefores of home education and its regulation in Australia. p 64.
[316] Trunk, P. *How to homeschool as a single parent*. (2013). Penelope Trunk. Retrieved 23 January 2017, from http://education.penelopetrunk.com/2013/11/05/how-to-homeschool-as-a-single-parent/.
[317] Rivero, L. *The Homeschooling Option: How to Decide When It's Right for Your Family*. (2008). Palgrave Macmillan.
[318] Ray, B. *Home schooling: The ameliorator of negative influences on learning?* (2000). Peabody Journal of Education. 75 (1 and 2), p. 71-106.

[319] Ericksen, D quoted in Submission 266 to the Parliamentary Inquiry into Homeschooling. (2014). NSW Government. Retrieved 23 January 2017, from https://www.parliament.nsw.gov.au/committees/DBAssets/InquirySubmission/Body/37826/0266%20Mrs%20Lyndell%20Williamson.pdf.

[320] Stetzer, E. *Church Dropouts and Disciples: How many students are really leaving the church?* (2014). Christianity Today. Retrieved 23 January 2017, from http://www.christianitytoday.com/edstetzer/2014/may/dropouts-and-disciples-how-many-students-are-really-leaving.html

[321] Hunsberger, B. Apostasy: *A Social Learning Perspective*. (1983). Religious Research Association. 25 (1), p.32.

[322] Peach, D. *How to Become a Christian Missionary: Following God's Call*. (2013). What Christians Want to Know. Retrieved 23 January 2017, from http://www.whatchristianswanttoknow.com/how-to-become-a-christian-missionary-following-god%E2%80%99s-call/.

[323] Hurlbutt, K. *Special Education Teachers' Perceptions and Beliefs Regarding Homeschooling Children with Autism Spectrum Disorders*. (2012). Minnesota State University.

[324] Reilly, L, Chapman, A and O' Donoghue, T. *Home schooling of children with disabilities*. (2002). Queensland Journal of Educational Research. 18. Retrieved 24 January 2017, from http://www.iier.org.au/qjer/qjer18/reilly.html.

[325] Duvall, SF, Ward, DL, Delquadri, JC and Greenwood, CR. *An exploratory study of home school instructional environments and their effects on basic skill of students with learning disabilities*. (1997). Education and Treatment of Children, 20 150-172.

[326] Jolly, J, Mathews, M and Nester, J. *Homeschooling the Gifted: A Parent's Perspective*. (2012). Gifted Child Quarterly. 57 (2), p. 126.

[327] Ibid.

[328] Ibid.

[329] Duvall, SF, Ward, DL, Delquadri, JC and Greenwood, CR. *An exploratory study of home school instructional environments and their effects on basic skill of students with learning disabilities*. (1997). Education and Treatment of Children, 20, 150-172.

[330] Duffey, JG. *Home Schooling Children with Special Needs: A Descriptive Study*. (2002). Home School Researcher Journal. 15 (2), pp. 1-13.

[331] Duvall, SF, Ward, DL, Delquadri, JC and Greenwood, CR. *An exploratory study of home school instructional environments and their effects on basic skill of students with learning disabilities*. (1997). Education and Treatment of Children, 20, 150-172.

[332] Duffey, JG. *Home Schooling Children with Special Needs: A Descriptive Study*. (2002). Home School Researcher Journal. 15 (2), pp. 1-13.

[333] Ibid.

[334] Gaither, M. *Homeschooling and Autism*. (2012). Homeschooling Research Notes: WordPress. Retrieved 24 January 2017, from https://gaither.wordpress.com/2012/04/23/homeschooling-and-autism/.

[335] *Autism Prevalence in Australia 2015*. [Media Release]. Autism Aspergers Advocacy Australia. Retrieved 24 January 2017, from http://www.a4.org.au/prevalence2015. *Autism in Australia*. (2012). Australian Bureau of Statistics. Retrieved 24 January 2017, from http://www.abs.gov.au/AUSSTATS/abs@.nsf/Latestproducts/4428.0Main%20Features32012.

[336] Attwood, Simpson and Myles cited in Hurlbutt, K. *Special Education Teachers' Perceptions and Beliefs Regarding Homeschooling Children with Autism Spectrum Disorders*. (2012). Minnesota State University.

[337] Hurlbutt, K. *Special Education Teachers' Perceptions and Beliefs Regarding Homeschooling Children with Autism Spectrum Disorders*. (2012). Minnesota State University.

[338] Ibid.

[339] *The Stigma of Introversion and Why It's Wrong*. (2013). PIT Journal. Retrieved 24 January 2017, from http://pitjournal.unc.edu/fall2013/proposal/stigma-introversion-and-why-its-wrong.

[340] Wight, S. *Home Education and Special Needs Research*. Home Education Network Otherways Magazine. Retrieved 24 January 2017, from https://home-ed.vic.edu.au/home-education-and-special-needs-children/.

[341] Richdale, P, and Prior, M. *Urinary cortisol circadian rhythm in a group of high-functioning children with autism.* (1992). Journal of Autism and Developmental Disorders. 22 (3), p. 1.
[342] Hurlbutt, K (2012). *Special Education Teachers' Perceptions and Beliefs Regarding Homeschooling Children with Autism Spectrum Disorders.* Minnesota State University.
[343] Gilbert, P. *Psychotherapy and Counselling for Depression.* (2007). Sage Journal. Retrieved 24 January 2017, from https://au.sagepub.com/en-gb/oce/psychotherapy-and-counselling-for-depression/book227024.
[344] Hayes, L. *Homeschooling the Child with ADD (or Other Special Needs).* (2002). Prima Publishing. [Book].
[345] Duvall, S. (1994). *The Impact of Home Education on Learning Disabled Children: A Look at New Research.* Presented to the Home School Legal Defense Association, Purcellville, VA.
[346] Ibid.
[347] Ibid.
[348] Reilly quoted in Wight, S. *Home Education and Special Needs Research.* Home Education Network Otherways Magazine. Retrieved 24 January 2017, from https://home-ed.vic.edu.au/home-education-and-special-needs-children/.
[349] Hurlbutt, K. *Special Education Teachers' Perceptions and Beliefs Regarding Homeschooling Children with Autism Spectrum Disorders.* (2012). Minnesota State University.
[350] *State of Our Schools Survey.* (2015). Australian Education Union Victorian Branch, p. 1, 8. Retrieved 24 January 2017, from https://docs.education.gov.au/system/files/doc/other/australianeducationunion.pdf. [PDF].
[351] *New AEU report shows most principals can't meet needs of students with a disability.* (2015). Retrieved 8 May 2015, from http://www.news.com.au/.
[352] Ibid.
[353] The Secret Teacher. *Secret Teacher: I was told to ignore a child's autism to keep fees coming in.* (2014). The Guardian. Retrieved 14 June 2017, from https://www.theguardian.com/teacher-network/teacher-blog/2014/aug/02/secret-teacher-autism-fees-private-school-teaching.
[354] *State of Our Schools Survey.* (2015). Australian Education Union Victorian Branch, p. 2. Retrieved 24 January 2017, from https://docs.education.gov.au/system/files/doc/other/australianeducationunion.pdf. [PDF].
[355] Ibid.
[356] Milligan, L and Holland, D. *Children With Disabilities Failed By Education System: Senate Committee.* (2016). ABC News. Retrieved 24 January 2017, from http://www.abc.net.au/news/2016-01-15/children-with-disabilities-failed-by-education-system-senate/7092144.
[357] Hurlbutt, K. *Special Education Teachers' Perceptions and Beliefs Regarding Homeschooling Children with Autism Spectrum Disorders.* (2012). Minnesota State University.
[358] Ibid.
[359] Ibid.
[360] Smith, E. *Why Homeschool Teens?* Homeschool Legal Defense Association. Retrieved 24 January 2017, from http://www.hslda.org/highschool/docs/TenReasonsHTHS.asp.
[361] Galloway, R. *Homeschooled Adults: Are They Ready for College?* (1995). Paper presented at the annual meeting of the American Educational Research Association, San Francisco, CA, p. 18.
[362] Ray, B. *A Brief Review of 'The Impact of Homeschooling on the Adjustment of College Students' by Drenovsky and Cohen.* (2012). Home School Researcher. 28 (1), p. 8.
[363] Bolle-Brummond, MB and Wessel, R. (2012). *Homeschooled students in college: Background influences, college integration and environmental pull factors.* Journal of Research in Education. 22 (1), p. 223-249.
[364] Galloway, R and Sutton, J. *College Success of Students from Three High School Settings: Christian School, Home School and Public School.* (1997). Paper presented at the National Home Educators Leadership Conference, Boston, MA.
[365] Ibid.
[366] Ibid.

[367] Ray, B. *Worldwide Guide to Homeschooling.* (2003). Broadman and Holman Publishers. p. 71. Also see Swanbrow, D. *Study: Home-educated children not disadvantaged.* (1993). University of Michigan.
[368] NSW Government. *Parliamentary Inquiry into Homeschooling.* (2014). pp. 37-38.

www.ingramcontent.com/pod-product-compliance
Lightning Source LLC
Chambersburg PA
CBHW050530300426
44113CB00012B/2033